NIETZSCHE'S METAPHYSICS OF THE WILL TO POWER

Nietzsche's controversial will to power thesis is convincingly rehabilitated in this compelling book. Tsarina Doyle presents a fresh interpretation of his account of nature and value, which sees him defy the dominant conception of nature in the Enlightenment and overturn Hume's distinction between facts and values. Doyle argues that Nietzsche challenges Hume indirectly through critical engagement with Kant's idealism and that, in so doing and despite some wrong turns, he establishes the possibility of objective value in response to nihilism and the causal efficacy of consciousness as a necessary condition of human autonomy. Her book will be important for scholars of Nietzsche's metaphysics and of the history of philosophy and science more generally.

TSARINA DOYLE is Lecturer in Philosophy at the National University of Ireland, Galway. She is the author of *Nietzsche on Epistemology and Metaphysics: The World in View* (2009) and numerous journal articles.

T0381540

NIETZSCHE'S METAPHYSICS OF THE WILL TO POWER

The Possibility of Value

TSARINA DOYLE

CAMBRIDGE
UNIVERSITY PRESS

CAMBRIDGE
UNIVERSITY PRESS

University Printing House, Cambridge CB2 8BS, United Kingdom

One Liberty Plaza, 20th Floor, New York, NY 10006, USA

477 Williamstown Road, Port Melbourne, VIC 3207, Australia

314-321, 3rd Floor, Plot 3, Splendor Forum, Jasola District Centre, New Delhi - 110025, India

79 Anson Road, #06-04/06, Singapore 079906

Cambridge University Press is part of the University of Cambridge.

It furthers the University's mission by disseminating knowledge in the pursuit of education, learning and research at the highest international levels of excellence.

www.cambridge.org
Information on this title: www.cambridge.org/9781108404860
DOI: 10.1017/9781108265447

First published 2018
First paperback edition 2019

A catalogue record for this publication is available from the British Library

ISBN 978-1-108-41728-0 Hardback
ISBN 978-1-108-40486-0 Paperback

Cambridge University Press has no responsibility for the persistence or accuracy of URLs for external or third-party internet websites referred to in this publication, and does not guarantee that any content on such websites is, or will remain, accurate or appropriate.

For John

Contents

Acknowledgements

Chapter 2 is derived, in part, from an article, 'Nietzsche, Value and Objectivity', published in *International Journal of Philosophical Studies,* Volume 21, Issue 1, 2013, pp. 41–63. The first two sections of Chapter 3 appeared in 'The Kantian Roots to the Will to Power' in Marco Brusotti and Herman Siemens (eds.), *Nietzsche's Engagements with Kant and the Kantian Legacy, Volume I: Nietzsche, Kant and the Problem of Metaphysics* (London: Continuum, 2017), pp. 205–232 and are included in revised form here. An earlier version of Chapter 5 was published as 'Nietzsche, Consciousness and Human Agency', *Idealistic Studies,* Volume 41, Issue 1/2, 2011, pp. 11–30 and has been revised and expanded for inclusion in the present volume.

I thank Hilary Gaskin and two anonymous reviewers at Cambridge University Press for their helpful comments and suggestions. My deepest personal thanks go to John O' Reilly, to my young friends Ibrahim, Maryam and Adam Dahmani, to Tom Doyle and to my mother, Marie J. Doyle, whose memory is a reminder that value is possible.

Abbreviations

KSA   *Sämtliche Werke. Kritische Studienausgabe,* 15 volumes, Giorgio
       Colli and Mazzino Montinari (eds.) (Berlin and New York,
       NY: Walter de Gruyter, 1967–1977). Cited by volume and note
       number. If a section is particularly long, citation will be by
       volume and page number (pp.).

KGW   *Werke. Kritische Gesamtausgabe,* ca 40 volumes. Founded by
       Giorgi Colli and Mazzino Montinari. Volker Gerhardt,
       Norbert Miller, Wolfgang Müller-Lauter and Karl Pestalozzi
       (eds.) (Berlin and New York: Walter de Gruyter, 1967–). Cited
       by volume, part and page number.

English translations have been used where available. They are cited by
section number. If sections are particularly long, page numbers will be
provided (pp.).

AC   *The Anti-Christ,* included in *Twilight of the Idols/The Anti-Christ,*
       trans. R. J. Hollingdale (London: Penguin, 1990).

BGE   *Beyond Good and Evil,* trans. Marion Faber (Oxford: Oxford
       University Press, 1998).

BT   *The Birth of Tragedy and Other Writings,* trans. Ronald Speirs
       (Cambridge: Cambridge University Press, 2000).

CW   Friedrich Nietzsche, 'The Case of Wagner' in Keith Ansell
       Pearson and Duncan Large (eds.), *The Nietzsche Reader*
       (Oxford: Blackwell Publishing, 2006), pp. 451–455.

D   *Daybreak,* trans. R. J. Hollingdale (Cambridge: Cambridge
       University Press, 1993).

DWW   Friedrich Nietzsche, 'The Dionysiac World View' in *The Birth
       of Tragedy and Other Writings,* trans. Ronald Speirs
       (Cambridge: Cambridge University Press, 2000), pp. 117–138.

EH   *Ecce Homo*, trans. R. J. Hollingdale (London: Penguin, 1992). Cited by part and section number.

GM   *On the Genealogy of Morality,* trans. Maudemarie Clark and Alan J. Swensen (Indianapolis: Hackett Publishing Company, 1998).

GS   *The Gay Science,* trans. Walter Kaufmann (New York, NY: Vintage Books, 1974).

HC   'Homer's Contest' in Keith Ansell Pearson and Duncan Large (eds.), *The Nietzsche Reader* (Oxford: Blackwell Publishing, 2006), pp. 95–100.

HAH   *Human, All Too Human,* trans. R. J. Hollingdale (Cambridge: Cambridge University Press, 1996).

PPP   *The Pre-Platonic Philosophers,* trans. Greg Whitlock (Urbana, IL, and Chicago, IL: University of Illinois Press, 2001).

PTG   *Philosophy in the Tragic Age of the Greeks,* trans. Marianne Cowan (Washington, DC: Regnery Publishing, 1998). Cited by page number.

SE   'Schopenhauer as Educator' in *Untimely Meditations,* trans. R. J. Hollingdale (Cambridge: Cambridge University Press, 1994).

TI   *Twilight of the Idols,* trans. Duncan Large (Oxford: Oxford University Press, 1998). Cited by part and section number.

TL   'On Truth and Lies in a Nonmoral Sense' in *Philosophy and Truth: Selections from Nietzsche's Notebooks of the Early 1870's,* Daniel Breazeale (ed.) (London: Humanities Press International, 1991).

WP   *The Will to Power,* trans. R. J. Hollingdale and Walter Kaufmann (New York, NY: Vintage Books, 1968). Dual references to WP and KSA will be given.

Z   *Thus Spoke Zarathustra,* trans. R. J. Hollingdale (London: Penguin, 1969).

Introduction

This book is motivated by a desire to make sense of Nietzsche's much maligned metaphysics of the will to power. Since Heidegger and perhaps because of him, it has become unpopular to interpret Nietzsche as a metaphysician. To interpret him thus carries connotations of philosophical failure, in particular, of having perpetuated rather than overcome the history of Western thought and the nihilistic logic that, according to Heidegger, informs this history. Nietzsche's conception of Being as will to power is, for Heidegger, an anthropomorphic treatment of the issue that ultimately does away with the question of Being by reducing it to value. In so doing, rather than overcoming the metaphysics of the West and its nihilistic forgetfulness of the question of Being, Nietzsche, he argues, represents its culmination. Abstracting from the particularities and aims of Heidegger's interpretation of Nietzsche, his claim that Nietzsche anthropomorphizes metaphysics is an objection that has stuck and has served to seriously discredit the will to power as a metaphysical thesis.

Although the book is not about Heidegger or his interpretation of Nietzsche, it nevertheless shares some things in common with Heidegger. First, Nietzsche is interpreted metaphysically, and the will to power is taken as central to his metaphysics. Second, Nietzsche's proposal of the metaphysics of the will to power is explored in the context of his critical engagement with central figures in the history of Western philosophy. Third, the connection between the metaphysics of the will to power and his account of value is examined.[1] However, unlike Heidegger, I do not take Nietzsche's

---

[1] According to Heidegger, the 'Will to Power is the "principle of a new valuation", and vice versa: the principle of the new valuation to be grounded is the will to power.' Heidegger, *Nietzsche*, Volume 3, trans. Joan Stambaugh, David F. Krell and Frank A. Capuzzi (New York: HarperCollins, 1991), p. 15. Although Eugene Fink agrees with Heidegger that the will to power ontology is an anthropomorphic projection of our values, unlike Heidegger, he denies that Being is reducible to the will to power. Rather, he appeals to the notion of cosmic play as a non-anthropomorphic artistic vision into reality that is beyond all value and which gives birth to the Apollonian illusions of the will to power. However, Fink's interpretation, it seems to me, commits Nietzsche to the possibility of extra-perspectival

metaphysics to be a complete failure and instead focus on its potential viability as a response to nihilism and as a metaphysical thesis more generally. Although I do not aim to offer a defence of Nietzsche on the issues of metaphysics and value *per se*, I nevertheless aim to interpret and reconstruct his arguments charitably in order to make the most sense of them. In particular, I try to make sense of the will to power as a thesis about the character of the world and the human being's place in it that avoids the reduction of either one to the other. I execute this argument, specifically, by examining how the will to power thesis provides him with the necessary conceptual and metaphysical resources to address the problem of nihilism as he rather than Heidegger understood the problem.

Nihilism, according to Nietzsche, entails the willing of nothingness (GM, III, 28). It has its roots in the appeal to and ultimate demise of the traditional Platonic and Judeo-Christian view that our highest values are grounded and realizable in a metaphysical world beyond the empirical one that we bodily inhabit. Platonism and Judeo-Christianity are nihilistic in the sense that they will nothingness by appealing to a metaphysical support for our highest values that does not actually exist. The nihilism of this view comes into focus when the will to truth that informs the appeal to a metaphysical basis to our values in the first place reveals that this metaphysical basis is in fact an empty notion (WP, 5 KSA 12: 5 [71]). It is when this revelation comes to pass, when the will to truth becomes conscious of itself (GM, III, 27) and reveals that our highest values are without metaphysical foundation and our highest values devaluate themselves as a result (WP, 2 KSA 12: 9 [35]), that nihilism becomes a particularly acute evaluative and existential crisis. The crisis is acute because these devaluated values form the basis of Western European culture. Nihilism, then, for Nietzsche, incorporates many questions, including questions of a metaphysical, existential, psychological and cultural nature. But the first question is of primary importance and grounds all of the others. This is because nihilism emerges in the context of a metaphysical realist presupposition about the status of our values, that they are objective and hence meaningful by virtue

knowledge and hence to the very dogmatism and unconstrained speculation that, I will argue throughout, he cautions us against (Eugene Fink, *Nietzsche's Philosophy*, trans. Goetz Richter (London: Continuum, 2003), pp. 170–172). Gilles Deleuze's interpretation of Nietzsche also aligns value with the will to power. Although I have a lot of sympathy with this claim, my interpretation offers a more robustly metaphysical interpretation of the will to power as an account, on Nietzsche's part, not just of human value but of the true character of the world itself. Deleuze's reduction of truth to a symptomology of value (activity/nobility and reactivity/baseness) falls short of my stronger metaphysical claims. See Gilles Deleuze, *Nietzsche and Philosophy*, trans. Hugh Tomlinson (London: Athlone Press, 1992), pp. 89–94.

of corresponding to value properties instantiated in a mind-independent and non-empirical world, and the subsequent revelation that this presupposition is an error, which, in turn, subjects to challenge our capacity to act in accordance with values that are now revealed to be metaphysically groundless. The appeal to and the ultimate unjustifiability of the traditional realist presupposition of a metaphysical support to our values is thus the root cause of nihilism.[2] Nietzsche writes that 'the faith in the categories of reason is the cause of nihilism. We have measured the value of the world according to categories that *refer to a purely fictitious world*' (WP, 12 KSA 13: 11 [99]). The willing of nothingness and the belief in and ultimate demise of the appeal to a realist metaphysical basis to our values are intimately intertwined. Accordingly, nihilism culminates in 'disbelief in any metaphysical world and forbids itself any belief in a *true* world' (WP, 12 KSA 13: 11 [99]). However, the problem of nihilism and the metaphysical homelessness of our values following the demise of the non-empirical metaphysical support offered by the 'true' world is compounded by the fact that our values cannot find a metaphysical home in the empirical world, the only world that is left, and seem destined to float free of that world into oblivion.

I will argue that despite the metaphysical challenges posed by nihilism, Nietzsche's response must not be the reactionary one of throwing the baby

---

[2] Ken Gemes has argued, contrary to my claim here, that nihilism for Nietzsche is primarily an affective disorder rather than a cognitive issue. Affective nihilism, according to Gemes, is evident in the Christian and ascetic practice of denying the drives. However, Gemes concedes that there is a tension in Nietzsche's philosophy between its affective roots in Christianity and its more cognitive expression in the secular world that ensues from the death of God. The tension resides in the fact that the Christian, by virtue of their belief that value is housed in another metaphysical world, does not consider themselves to be nihilistic and that secular nihilism arises from the demise of the metaphysical basis of the Christian belief. Christian nihilism is affective whereas secular nihilism is cognitive. Gemes suggests that Nietzsche moves from the affective to the secular view as two stages in the coming to consciousness of nihilism. However, whereas Gemes thinks that affective nihilism is the most profound form of nihilism, for Nietzsche, viewing secular nihilism as just a cognitive expression of the Christian practice of suppressing the drives, it seems to me that emphasis should be placed on the cognitive expression of nihilism as the root cause rather than just symptom of nihilism. That is, the cognitive issue is evident in the Christian's affective nihilism. This is because it is the belief that our values are grounded in another metaphysical world that leads the Christian to deny the drives. Equally, it is the disbelief in such a metaphysical world that leads to secular nihilism. Moreover, the seeds of secular nihilism are grounded in Christian nihilism because, for Nietzsche, the demise of the traditional metaphysical basis of our values results from the Christian will to truth turning on itself and revealing that the idea of a metaphysical other world is an elaborate fiction (WP, 1 KSA 12: 2 [127]), in addition to the influence of growing scientific caution and knowledge of naturalistic facts (AC, 48, 49). See Ken Gemes, 'Nietzsche and the Affirmation of Life: A Review and Dialogue with Bernard Reginster', *European Journal of Philosophy*, 16.3, December 2008, pp. 459–466, pp. 461–462. For a recent study of the varied meanings of nihilism in Nietzsche, see Jeffrey Metzger (ed.), *Nietzsche, Nihilism and the Philosophy of the Future* (London: Bloomsbury, 2013).

out with the bathwater. That is, if we are to be motivated to act according to values that do not correspond to value properties mind-independently instantiated in either a non-existent 'true' world or the actual empirical world then they must be deemed to be objective in some other way that connects and subjects them to constraint by the empirical world. This alternative account of the objectivity of our values must, therefore, be a metaphysically laden one and must reflect the fundamental relationship between mind and the empirical world. Else, Nietzsche is guilty of perpetuating the will to nothingness that informs nihilism rather than adequately responding to it. However, although the argument of the book is framed against the backdrop of the problem concerning the metaphysical status of our values bequeathed to us by nihilism, the book is about the metaphysical issue rather than about nihilism *per se*.[3] As a result, the issue of nihilism will be used to frame the metaphysical problem of value rather than the other way around and Nietzsche's response to the root metaphysical cause of nihilism will be prioritized over its broader existential, psychological and cultural dimensions.

I argue that Nietzsche's views with regard to the status of values stems from his reflection on the character of the relation between mind and world, which ultimately, in his view, must be understood to be metaphysically continuous and naturalistic by virtue of appealing to explanations that are confined within the spatio-temporal boundaries of nature and that

---

[3] It has been argued that Nietzsche is a theoretical rather than a practical nihilist (Nadeem J. Z. Hussain, 'Honest Illusion: Valuing for Nietzsche's Free Spirits' in Brian Leiter and Neil Sinhababu (eds.), *Nietzsche and Morality* (Oxford: Oxford University Press, 2007), pp. 157–191, p. 161). Hussain takes the distinction between two forms of nihilism from Nietzsche (WP, 4 KSA 12: 5 [71]) where theoretical nihilism entails the demise of the traditional Platonic-Christian metaphysical basis of our values and the consequent valuelessness that follows from the denial that our values can be mind-independently and non-naturalistically instantiated in reality. Practical nihilism entails the psychological responses of disorientation and despair to theoretical nihilism (see Bernard Reginster, *The Affirmation of Life: Nietzsche on Overcoming Nihilism* (Cambridge, MA: Harvard University Press, 2006), pp. 26–28). In this study, however, I will refrain from addressing the question of whether Nietzsche is a nihilist despite the fact that he sometimes describes himself as one (WP, 25 KSA 12: 9 [123]). This is because it seems to me that Nietzsche's response to nihilism is to alter rather than accept the terms and conditions of the theoretical nihilist's world view by allowing, for example, that our values can be considered objective without being mind-independently and non-naturalistically instantiated in the 'true' world. Nietzsche's response to nihilism, as I interpret it, entails reworking from within some of its oppositional presuppositions. Moreover, theoretical nihilism, for Nietzsche, does not just entail the demise of Platonic and Judeo-Christian metaphysics, it also entails the belief in such metaphysics, which amounts to willing nothingness. I argue that Nietzsche responds to nihilism in this broader sense also by showing that our values can be objective in an alternative sense to the Platonic and Judeo-Christian nihilist. See Simon May, 'Nietzsche and the Free Self' in Ken Gemes and Simon May (eds.), *Nietzsche on Freedom and Autonomy* (Oxford: Oxford University Press, 2009), pp. 89–106, pp. 100–103 for how Christianity is nihilistic on account of willing nothingness.

eschew explanations of the supernatural variety. By metaphysical continuity, then, I mean that the mind, for Nietzsche, is immersed in nature by virtue of sharing certain metaphysical features in common with nature but that it is also irreducible to it. Metaphysical continuity entails not mere correlations of events observed from the outside but rather a shared metaphysical character, which emanates from within, that is, from the essential nature of a thing. The irreducibility of the mind to nature is evident in the manner in which Nietzsche, throughout his writings, understands the mind to be immersed in but differentiated from nature by virtue of its capacity to engage in certain evaluative practices, aesthetic practices involving invention and imagination, epistemic practices involving the giving of justifications and reasons, in addition to conscious reflective practices more generally. Since to be differentiated from nature does not entail that the human mind is divorced from it, the issue of a value's objective standing, for Nietzsche, is intrinsically connected to its metaphysical continuity with the character of mind-independent, empirical, reality.

The preceding interpretation of Nietzsche is not intended to provide an exhaustive overview of his philosophy as a whole. Rather, the aim is to identify a problem, that of the metaphysical status of our values in the wake of nihilism, and to trace one thread in his writings to its logical conclusion. Accordingly, I do not claim in the manner of Heidegger, for example, that the will to power is Nietzsche's central thought, but rather, more in the manner of Karl Jaspers, my interpretation of Nietzsche is a constructive one that assembles his many perspectives in relation to value under one guiding interpretive thread.[4] But, it will surely be argued, there are problems with my attempt to follow only one thread in his writings. That is, it will be argued that even if I can make a case for the feasibility of a metaphysically laden account of the objectivity of our values as a response to nihilism, we cannot simply ignore the fact that Nietzsche himself sometimes denies that our values are objective. That is, it may be argued that despite the fact that Nietzsche often articulates value judgements about, for example, the inferiority of some value systems over others, he nonetheless, at times, holds that all our values are, metaphysically speaking, fictions. My aim is not to deny that a fictionalist interpretation of Nietzsche poses problems for my particular account of the objectivity of our values. Rather, my strategy is to address the issue head-on by conceding that Nietzsche sometimes presents himself as a fictionalist but that to the extent that he does so he must fail to offer an adequate response to the problem of nihilism. Moreover, I will contend that although there is evidence of alternative views in Nietzsche, the metaphysically laden one that I highlight and follow to its logical conclusion is potentially feasible even if it is not necessarily Nietzsche's only possible response and, moreover, that the terms and conditions of what would constitute a feasible response emerges from reflection on why other possible responses such as fictionalism ultimately fail. For example, I will argue that if our values are fictions, then they are cut off from the metaphysical character of the natural world contrary to Nietzsche's aim to return the human being back to nature by way of rejecting the old metaphysical view that the human being is other than nature (BGE, 230), a view that is at the root of the problem of nihilism. Yet, if he is to avoid reducing the human being to the natural world in the manner of those he describes as bungling naturalists (BGE, 12), he needs to allow that values fundamentally pertain to and reflect the concerns of human beings and do not merely mirror value properties independently instantiated in the world. Nietzsche, therefore, needs to provide an account of value that is neither metaphysically realist, on the one hand, nor subjectively idealist, on the other. That is, values do not correspond to value properties residing in the natural world independently of human beings, but neither are they simply reducible to the wishes and interests of human beings without further constraint.

Now, one might argue that this constraint can be of the purely inter-subjective and metaphysically neutral kind. This intersubjective constraint might be thought to stem from the rule-governed character of language[5] or from the character of shared human consciousness itself,[6] or indeed it might stem from mere pragmatic agreement.[7] But appealing to such intersubjective constraints situates Nietzsche's account of value in various and different ways in the idealist camp and fails to account for the manner in which our values are, for him, metaphysically continuous with nature by virtue of the human being's immersion in it. A possible rejoinder might claim such an explanation is not forthcoming on the basis that Nietzsche holds that whilst there are aspects of the human being that can be explained naturalistically we also have higher – 'unnatural' – cognitive capacities that

---

[5] See Simon Blackburn's arguments for 'quasi-realism' in Simon Blackburn, *Essays in Quasi-Realism* (Oxford: Oxford University Press, 1993).

[6] See J. N. Findlay, *Values and Intentions* (London: George Allen and Unwin Ltd. and New York: The Macmillan Company, 1961).

[7] See Richard Rorty, *Truth and Progress: Philosophical Papers, Volume 3* (Cambridge: Cambridge University Press, 1998), pp. 43–63, and Rorty's 'Response to Putnam' in Robert Brandom (ed.), *Rorty and His Critics* (Oxford: Blackwell, 2000), pp. 87–91.

are incapable of the same naturalistic explanation. However, such a response is simply a refusal to answer the question. Whilst it is true that Nietzsche appeals to such higher capacities, such as our capacity for self-awareness, for providing justifications for our beliefs and for forming value judgements, it is not correct to say that they must be *sui generis*.[8] Rather, what Nietzsche needs to argue is that our values reflect the interests and concerns of human beings but that they can be understood to be metaphysically continuous with the character of the mind-independent world such that our values reflect the manner in which the mind and world fundamentally interact. Such a focus also allows Nietzsche to distinguish between objective and non-objective values according to the extent to which those values reflect and are constrained by the character of the mind-independent empirical world. However, by virtue of being metaphysically continuous, the relation between our evaluative practices and the mind-independent world should not, for Nietzsche, be understood dualistically. Rather, the relationship is one of reciprocal metaphysical engagement that is made possible by the degree of the evaluating agent's activity in the world and the normative receptivity of the world to this activity.

Nietzsche's argument here is prescient and is of philosophical significance beyond the confines of historical scholarship. In particular, it is of interest to those concerned with the issue of how to reconcile naturalism and normativity. Specifically, Nietzsche can be seen to remedy a deficiency in some contemporary attempts to forge such a reconciliation. As Joseph Rouse notes, there is a general tendency, even amongst those who aim to treat normativity naturalistically in contemporary debates, to describe the natural and the normative as parallel rather than intra-acting domains. Despite his praise for the arguments of Robert Brandom and John Haugeland, for example, regarding questions of naturalism and normativity, Rouse argues that a broader conception of naturalism is needed to overcome the residual dualism and voluntarism that he detects in the arguments of his contemporaries. Rouse contends that this residual dualism and voluntarism is evident in their respective tendencies to view the constraint exerted by the world on our normative practices in terms of a constraint by a normatively inert and scientistically characterized world. According to Rouse, Brandom and Haugeland are correct to want to avoid reducing our normative commitments to mere desires on the part of

---

[8] See John McDowell, *Mind and World* (Cambridge, MA: Harvard University Press, 1996), pp. xxii, 67, 74, 89, 110.

human valuers by viewing those commitments as constrained by the world. However, Rouse contends that this claim can be properly secured only if we appreciate that the world does not exert a constraint by virtue of being dualistically separate and apart from our evaluative practices. Rouse writes that '[t]hey are right to see meaning and action as intelligible only as accountable to something not under the agent's own control'.[9] However, he contends that, as a result of the tendency to view the world as normatively inert, 'what Brandom and Haugeland have both shown is that commitments and desires could only be contentful and binding if they were accountably beholden to something outside of themselves. In the end, their own projects once again show how distinctions between meanings and things, norms and causes, subjects and objects can become dichotomies whose components cannot be intelligibly related to one another'.[10] Rouse also targets McDowell with the charge of dualism despite the latter's denial that the natural and the normative are mutually exclusive.[11] The sceptre of dualism raises its head, according to Rouse, in McDowell's presentation of what he calls the reason-giving sphere of second nature as operating parallel to the sphere of first nature whilst eschewing any account of how the two spheres are ultimately connected.[12] As we shall see, Nietzsche, in some respects, pre-empts Rouse's response to these contemporary accounts that what we mean by naturalism needs to be broadened to include the human evaluative point of view.

Whilst I will argue that Nietzsche ultimately has the conceptual resources to avoid the dualism of some contemporary approaches, it results from some wrong turns taken on his part but which he ultimately corrects. I argue that both these wrong turns and corrections come through a very particular historical route, specifically Nietzsche's engagement with Kant's epistemology and metaphysics and ultimately, and through Kant, with Hume's philosophy of value. It will be seen that Nietzsche's account of how values reflect the manner in which the human being is immersed in but irreducible to nature does not come metaphysically cheap but rather entails a commitment on his

---

[9] Joseph Rouse, *How Scientific Practices Matter: Reclaiming Philosophical Naturalism* (Chicago, IL: University of Chicago Press, 2002), p. 257.

[10] Ibid., pp. 257–258.   [11] McDowell, *Mind and World*, p. xix.

[12] McDowell writes that '[h]uman life, our natural way of being, is already shaped by meaning. We need not connect this natural history to the realm of law any more tightly than by simply affirming our right to the notion of second nature' (ibid., p. 95). Contrary to McDowell, Rouse contends that second nature permeates first nature (Rouse, *How Scientific Practices Matter*, p. 103). And, rather than view Wilfrid Sellars's realm of natural causes captured by science as an 'appendage to the meaningful human world', Rouse contends that what Sellars describes as the manifest image of human normativity and meaning permeates the scientific image (ibid., p. 98).

part to the metaphysics of the will to power. Since the status of this thesis is a controversial one in the Nietzsche literature, effort will be made to demonstrate the rationale informing the thesis and to put to bed concerns about it being a 'silly' and 'crackpot metaphysics'.[13]

The argument developed in the book will employ a combination of historical and rational reconstruction where the former ultimately serves the ends of the latter. Nietzsche himself alerts us to the fact that he employs various historical figures as representatives of views or philosophical positions that he endorses or rejects (EH, 'Why I Am So Wise', 7). The philosophical history gives us a sense of the historical roots to the philosophical problem that perplexes Nietzsche and frames his response to the problem. However, historical explanations alone cannot provide an assessment of the overall philosophical merits or demerits of Nietzsche's arguments. Rational reconstruction of his arguments will therefore be deployed to assess their general philosophical cogency. The principal historical lens employed in the book will be Nietzsche's engagement with Kant's epistemology and metaphysics, which, it will be argued, ultimately gives us insight into the reasons why Nietzsche sometimes sounds like a Humean fictionalist but ultimately isn't and shouldn't be. Nietzsche's account of the metaphysical status of human values reflects his engagement with Kant's idealism as a way of understanding the relation between mind and world. This engagement is ultimately a critical one that sees Nietzsche adopt a specifically non-Humean metaphysical account of the world and, in the end, a non-Humean account of value. However, these conclusions are drawn from implications that follow from Nietzsche's engagement with Kant's idealism rather than from Nietzsche's adoption of an explicitly non-Humean stance.

There is a generally held view amongst Nietzsche commentators that Nietzsche's epistemology and metaphysics of value are shaped by Hume rather than Kant. The rationale informing this view is that Nietzsche's naturalism aligns him with empiricism rather than with philosophical idealism. Consequently, it is generally thought that when Nietzsche engages with Kant, that engagement focuses on a rejection of the moral implications of Kant's appeal to the thing-in-itself and particular formalistic conceptions of agency.[14] The implications of Nietzsche's rejection of

---

[13] Brian Leiter, 'Nietzsche's Naturalism Reconsidered' in *The Oxford Handbook of Nietzsche*, Ken Gemes and John Richardson (eds.) (Oxford: Oxford University Press, 2013), pp. 576–598, p. 594.

[14] See, for example, Paul Katsafanas, *Agency and the Foundations of Ethics: Nietzschean Constitutivism* (Oxford: Oxford University Press, 2013); Garrath Williams, 'Nietzsche's Response to Kant's Morality', *The Philosophical Forum*, 30.3, 1999, pp. 201–216.

Kant on these issues, the dominant view goes, is his adoption of a Humean-inspired naturalism.[15] As a result, it is generally thought that when Nietzsche proposes views that suggest that values are metaphysical fictions, he does so because of the influence of Hume rather than Kant. I will contend that whilst there are certain philosophical overlaps between Nietzsche and Hume, Nietzsche's engagement with Hume is mediated by his critical reflections on Kant's epistemology and metaphysics. Thus, for example, when Nietzsche writes like a fictionalist about value, his fictionalism is not a straight-forward appropriation of Hume's argument but rather is complicated by his engagement with what he views as Kant's account of the aesthetic relation between mind and world. My aim is to focus on how Nietzsche's critical reflections on Kant's idealism draw our attention to a non-Humean account of metaphysics and value. This methodology is justified by the fact that there is no evidence that Nietzsche read Hume directly[16] and whilst the extent to which he read Kant directly is disputed,[17] it remains the case, as R. Kevin Hill notes, that

---

[15] See Maudemarie Clark, 'On Knowledge, Truth and Value: Nietzsche's Debt to Schopenhauer and the Development of His Empiricism' in Christopher Janaway (ed.), *Willing and Nothingness: Schopenhauer as Nietzsche's Educator* (Oxford: Clarendon Press, 1998), pp. 37–78. She writes that Nietzsche adopts Hume's fact-value distinction, which he interprets in terms of an error theory of value in HAH although in GS he interprets it as the claim that the world of value is a human creation but not necessarily an error (ibid., p. 68). Although Clark later revises her account of Nietzsche on value to adopt the Spirean distinction between causes and reasons, it is nonetheless clear that the general 'Humean' flavour to her account of Nietzsche persists despite her acknowledgement that 'we presently have little evidence that Nietzsche actually read Hume . . . ' (ibid., p. 68). The Humean flavour of her interpretation persists because she contends that Spir acts as a valuable resource for Nietzsche's knowledge of the British empiricist tradition and that to the extent that Spir provides Nietzsche with a critical insight into that tradition, the insight comes in the form of an awareness of the need to distinguish between physical causes, which simply are, and the normative reason-giving role of judgement (Maudemarie Clark and David Dudrick, 'The Naturalisms of *Beyond Good and Evil*' in Keith Ansell Pearson (ed.), *A Companion to Nietzsche* (Oxford: Blackwell, 2006), pp. 148–168, p. 161).

[16] Clark, 'On Knowledge, Truth and Value', p. 68.

[17] There is a divergence of opinion on this issue. For example, R. Kevin Hill argues that Nietzsche read Kant's texts directly. His evidence for this is the fact that Nietzsche cites all three of Kant's *Critiques* in addition to a pre-critical text, *Universal Natural History and Theory of the Heavens*, at various points throughout his writings (*Nietzsche's Critiques: The Kantian Foundations of His Thought* (Oxford: Clarendon Press, 2003), p. 20). Thomas Brobjer makes a similar claim in relation to Nietzsche's acquaintance with Kant's third *Critique* (*Nietzsche's Philosophical Context: An Intellectual Biography*, Urbana, IL: University of Illinois Press, 2008, pp. 36–39, 48, 195, 202, 226–227). Tom Bailey, however, pointing to the fact that Nietzsche seems never to have owned or borrowed a copy of any of Kant's texts, suggests that Nietzsche's acquaintance with Kant was mediated through secondary sources, such as Kuno Fischer's commentary on Kant, *Immanuel Kant und seine Lehre* (Tom Bailey, 'Nietzsche the Kantian' in Ken Gemes and John Richardson (eds.), *The Oxford Handbook of Nietzsche* (Oxford: Oxford University Press, 2013), pp. 134–159). Thus, the fact that Nietzsche quotes from Kant's texts does not support the view that Nietzsche actually read those texts directly. However, since my aim is to examine how Nietzsche's understanding of Kant influences his

Kant is the third most mentioned philosopher in Nietzsche's writings, after Plato and Schopenhauer.[18]

It will be argued that Nietzsche's ultimately critical engagement with Kant makes way for a distinctive dispositional account of the metaphysical status of our values. This dispositional account will lead us further into Nietzsche's account of the metaphysical character of the world as articulated in his will to power thesis and which, I will argue, stems, once again, from his critical engagement with Kant in relation to Hume. I will contend that Nietzsche allows for the objectivity of value by holding that values are metaphysically continuous with the dispositional fabric of reality. Values reflect the metaphysically continuous but non-reducible relation between mind and world to the extent that they are dispositional and normative properties of intentionally directed psychic drives. The evaluative perspective of these drives are normative, for Nietzsche, by virtue of their dominancy over the other drives that make up the self and which results from their ability to overcome internal resistance from these other drives. However, although our values do not mirror mind-independently instantiated value properties in the world, they are not ideal or dualistically separate from the world. Rather, Nietzsche argues that the character of the dominant drive of the evaluating agent as active or reactive, strong or weak, is determined by its degree of activity in the world. According to Nietzsche, reactivity is continuous with and, therefore, a degree of, activity (GM, I, 10). It follows that drives that react to the world and turn away from it can still dominate other drives that constitute a self even if its form of activity in the world is reactive. Nietzsche gives the example of the

---

own arguments, my interpretation does not rest on whether Nietzsche's acquaintance with Kant's texts is first-hand or second-hand.

[18] Hill, *Nietzsche's Critiques*, p. 20. It has been argued that Nietzsche arrives at Hume's fact-value distinction as a result of his critical engagement with Schopenhauer (Clark, 'On Knowledge, Truth and Value'). However, this interpretation relies on adopting a non-metaphysical interpretation of Nietzsche that sees him take the natural sciences at face value. Although Nietzsche's engagement with Schopenhauer is undoubtedly important, I argue that his naturalism arises from his critical engagement with philosophical idealism and that this critical reflection does not result in a metaphysically neutral conclusion but rather implies the distinctive metaphysics of the will to power. Schopenhauer certainly informs Nietzsche's interpretation of Kant, but I focus on Nietzsche's reflections on Kant's idealism rather than Schopenhauer's because, as I have argued elsewhere, Nietzsche sides with Kant, contrary to Schopenhauer, in his identification of force with efficient causality, indicating his approval of Kant's restriction of the objective applicability of the concept of causality to the empirical world, even though Nietzsche is ultimately critical of and attempts to rectify Kant's appeal to the thing-in-itself as the sphere of inner determinations ('The Kantian Background to Nietzsche's Views on Causality', *The Journal of Nietzsche Studies*, 43.1, 2012, pp. 44–56). In the current study, I develop the argument that Nietzsche's will to power thesis arises as a result of his critical engagement with Kant by focussing on the non-Humean implications for Nietzsche's account of the character of the natural world and human value.

religious Ascetic who turns away from the world but nonetheless displays a high degree of self-control (BGE, 51), albeit through the extirpation of its subordinate drives, which renders the will of the Ascetic weaker than one who wills by unifying rather than extirpating the drives (TI, 'Anti-Nature', 1). However, it is important to appreciate that, for Nietzsche, any distinction between inner and outer is made from within the evaluating agent's immersion in the world, such that its degree of activity in the world is constitutively normative and does not presuppose that the agent's evaluative viewpoint is external to the world. However, Nietzsche makes it clear that whilst all values are normatively structured, only some of those values are properly objective in an epistemic sense. The distinction between the epistemic subjectivity and objectivity of value-norms is drawn in terms of the powerful capacity, or lack thereof, of a psychological value disposition to manifest its nature by complementing or cooperating with what the dispositional fabric of reality affords. As a result, the objectivity of our values does not presuppose correspondence to and mind-independent instantiation in the world, but neither are they cut off from the world. Rather, our values are realistically constrained by the world. Moreover, rather than being reductively ideal or dualistically separate from the world, both the normative character of dominating drives and their epistemic objectivity, or not, reflect the manner in which the evaluating agent interacts with reality and reality resists, in the form of either facilitating or curtailing the manifestation of the powerful character of value dispositions. The argument will conclude with an examination of the non-reductive but metaphysically continuous account of the relation of mind and world in the context of Nietzsche's account of the causal efficacy of consciousness. It will be argued that to the extent that Nietzsche holds that mind and world are metaphysically continuous, contrary to Descartes and through partial endorsement and critical engagement with both Leibniz and Kant, he can cater for the causal efficacy of conscious thought and meaningful human action.

The preceding argument fits with much of the literature on Nietzsche to date in conceding that one of the central aspects of Nietzsche's response to the demise of the traditional – Platonic – metaphysical basis of our values is to acknowledge that values reflect human interests and concerns. My interpretation also confronts a similar challenge to much of the literature. The challenge is to ascertain whether such values can also be objective without corresponding to or mirroring mind-independently instantiated value properties in the world. Although the fictionalist interpretation of Nietzsche answers this question negatively, a range of non-fictionalist interpretations have been proposed. Yet, despite important points of intersection with the literature, my conclusions differ from the predominant but varied non-fictionalist interpretations of Nietzsche's response to the challenge in specific and significant ways. In particular, I argue that Nietzsche allows that our values can be objective and that whilst their objectivity does not entail correspondence and mind-independence, it does entail a metaphysically laden rather than metaphysically neutral account of value. Moreover, I contend that Nietzsche's metaphysically laden account steers a delicate course between the twin polarities of idealism and realism and that, in so doing, it must ultimately be understood along alternative lines to the predominant one that sees Nietzsche committed to the Humean-inspired fact-value distinction. That is, whilst values do not correspond to mind-independently instantiated value properties in the world, they are not cut off from the metaphysical character of the world itself. Unfortunately, much of the current literature on Nietzsche takes his view that values must reflect human beings to mean that our values are reductively ideal or dualistically separate and apart from the world. This idealism and dualism is evident even in the arguments of those interpreters that seek to overcome such separation and it results from their tendency to interpret Nietzsche within a broadly Humean frame of reference.

This Humean tendency is evident in the interpretation of Nietzsche's approach to value that goes by the name of 'normative subjectivism'.[19] According to this view, our values, which are grounded in contingent and affective perspectives informed by our needs and dominant ideologies, are normative because these perspectives are enabling conditions of experience and form the context in which evaluative claims are justified. Despite claiming that value perspectives are necessary conditions of experience, the value of our values, for the normative subjectivist, does not depend on their objective standing.[20] Similarly, a recent 'constitutivist' interpretation

---

[19] It is to be noted that Reginster maintains that there is evidence of two meta-ethical positions in Nietzsche's writings, which Reginster describes as normative subjectivism and normative fictionalism. Although Reginster claims that Nietzsche doesn't ultimately choose between the two (Reginster, *The Affirmation of Life*, p. 100), and although he argues that meta-ethics by itself has limited capacity to respond to the lack of an objective ground to our values that informs nihilism, it is nonetheless clear that he takes normative subjectivism to be the stronger of the two meta-ethical views. His reasoning is that subjectivism, unlike fictionalism, gives us an account of the nature of values (ibid., p. 98) and by virtue of its claim that evaluative judgements are interpretations of the world from the point of view of our desires (ibid., p. 75), subjectivism fits better with Nietzsche's substantive ethical aim to revalue suffering in light of the value of power (ibid., p. 181), where this revaluation is made possible by understanding the will to power as an insatiable desire to seek out and overcome resistance. In Chapter 4, I offer an alternative and more metaphysical account of the will to power and resistance than Reginster's predominantly psychological version, which, it will be seen, ultimately and despite some affinities with subjectivism, avoids reductive idealism in a metaphysical sense.

[20] Ibid., p. 69. Alan Thomas proposes subjective realism, a close cousin to Reginster's normative subjectivism. He argues that whilst all values stand in a constitutive relation to a mental subject, they

holds that every action has a constitutive aim, which generates normative reasons for acting. On this account, although values are existentially dependent on the human mind, they are nevertheless subject to a normative standard whereby power is taken as a 'standard of success for willing' such that 'Nietzsche denies that there are objective values, but treats power as the one standard of evaluation that readily meets challenges to its authority.'[21] Contrary to arguments such as these, I deny that questions of normativity must entirely swing free of questions about the objectivity of our values. Whilst there is evidence that Nietzsche thinks that normativity can be distinguished from objectivity, not all values that are norms must be non-objective. Such a conclusion follows only if we accept an – extra-perspectival – account of objectivity that Nietzsche thinks is ultimately incoherent. Rather, I argue that although value dispositions reflect human beings, they are characterized by their degree of power in interacting with the world and their capacity to manifest their natures in cooperation with it. Value dispositions that prove weak in relation to reality and are defined as weak on account of that relation are normative by virtue of being the dominant drive of the evaluating self. However, a drive that is characterized as strong in its relation to reality can also be objective by virtue of its capacity to manifest its nature in cooperation with the dispositional character of reality. This distinction between normativity and objectivity is made, however, without rendering values reductively ideal or dualistically apart from the world because the objectivity, or not, of our values is determined from within our immersion in and normative interaction with the world.

are irreducible to mental states of an agent (Alan Thomas, 'Nietzsche and Moral Fictionalism' in Christopher Janaway and Simon Robertson, *Nietzsche, Naturalism and Normativity* (Oxford: Oxford University Press, 2012), pp. 133–159). Distinguishing between value and evaluation, it is claimed that the evaluating agent's responsiveness to value is conditioned by their biological type, culture, history and context of choice. However, although Thomas is clear about the conditions of evaluations, he is less clear about what a value is, other than claiming that it is irreducible to our evaluative responses. Despite describing the distinction between value and evaluation as a 'property-response pair', what kind of property a value is, is left opaque. We might say that values are properties of propositions, in which case values are properties of language and, for Nietzsche, then, constituted intersubjectively and conventionally. Or we might say that values are response-dependent properties of mind-independent objects in a similar manner to the secondary qualities that Thomas discusses in his essay. Thomas's lack of clarity on the issue stems from his conceptual treatment of the reality of value, as evidenced in his reference to the 'provisoed biconditionals used to capture the relevant property-response pairs'. Understood as a conceptual argument, Thomas does not specify what a value property is in metaphysical terms, beyond saying that it is 'indexically tied' to our responses (ibid., pp. 149–150). In the absence of such specificity, we cannot say that our evaluations are meaningfully constrained by reality, which makes it difficult to appreciate in what sense values, as described by his subjective realism, are realist.

[21] Katsafanas, *Agency and the Foundations of Ethics*, pp. 162–163.

Still, proponents of the Humean interpretation of Nietzsche will, no doubt, object to my argument by claiming that it makes him vulnerable to violating Hume's distinction between the *is* and the *ought*. But this is precisely what I see Nietzsche as wanting to do. For him, the Nihilist is the man who judges of the world as it is that it ought not to be and of the world as it ought to be that it does not exist (WP, 585 KSA 12: 9 [60]). According to my interpretation of Nietzsche, what ought to be is grounded dispositionally in what is. However, the fact that the dispositional account of value that I offer does not render values reductively ideal does not entail that it reduces the human being and its evaluative activities to the world instead. This is because although values are dispositions, for Nietzsche, he nonetheless emphasizes the importance of articulating reasons in justifying our evaluative stance. Moreover, despite its irreducibility to the world, the process of articulating reasons, which ultimately entails conscious awareness and language, is metaphysically continuous with the causal-dispositional fabric of reality itself. This claim is a contentious one in its own right as a result of its running counter to the popular view that holds that normativity entails the giving of reasons and that the normative giving of reasons must be demarcated in kind from natural causes.[22] However, I will argue, that the spheres of causes and justificatory reasons are metaphysically continuous, for Nietzsche, by virtue of operating according to the same dispositional modality. I contend that Nietzsche's account of continuity entails capturing the essence of some phenomena from the inside such that our capacity for giving reasons differs from natural causes only in degree rather than kind and, consequently, that there is, for Nietzsche, only one – causal – order, which contains the normative within it. And, as I will argue, it is from within our normative immersion in the world that we not only can give reasons but can

---

[22] See McDowell, drawing on Sellars, in *Mind and World*, p. xv. Strictly speaking, McDowell distinguishes between the logical space of reasons and the logical space of law rather than causes, on the grounds that the space of law is the space of scientific description, which, more accurately, speaks of law governed processes. Additionally, he claims that justifiable talk about causes takes place within the space of reasons (ibid., p. 71n2). However, it is to be noted that this qualification on McDowell's part is not significant for our use of the distinction in a Nietzschean context. This is because Nietzsche does not appeal to laws of nature (BGE, 22), as McDowell does, or the causal relation to objects merely as a condition of knowledge, and instead appeals to causal powers in a metaphysical sense with which our capacity to give reasons is metaphysically continuous. The root to McDowell's discussion is Wilfrid Sellars, 'Empiricism and the Philosophy of Mind' in Herbert Feigl and Michael Scriven (eds.), *Minnesota Studies in the Philosophy of Science* (Minneapolis, MN: University of Minnesota Press, 1956), pp. 253–329, pp. 298–299. Clark and Dudrick deny that the application of the distinction between causes and reasons to Nietzsche is anachronistic on the grounds that Nietzsche was familiar with a distinction of this type from his knowledge of Afrikan Spir (Maudemarie Clark and David Dudrick, *The Soul of Nietzsche's Beyond Good and Evil* (Cambridge: Cambridge University Press, 2012), pp. 124–126).

distinguish between better and worse reasons and hence the objectivity of our value-norms. The articulation of reasons cuts across the normative-objective distinction in Nietzsche in that it allows us to articulate the point of view of all value-norms and also distinguish between which of those value-norms are ultimately supported by good or bad reasons, where the differentiation between good and bad reasons is to be understood in terms of degrees of power.

In sum, my argument is that Nietzsche puts forward a metaphysically laden account of value that holds that values are dispositional and normative properties of psychic drives that act in and interact with the dispositional fabric of reality and can be deemed objective, or not, in terms of their capacity to manifest their natures in cooperation with what the dispositional fabric of reality affords. Understood thus, values are, for him, metaphysically continuous with the dispositional fabric of reality itself and can be supported by conscious reason-giving and the causal efficacy of consciousness. This argument will be developed across five chapters as follows.

Structure of the Argument

Chapter 1 offers a negative argument in favour of the need for objective value by considering the viability of non-objectivist and metaphysically neutral accounts of our values as potential responses to nihilism and finds them deficient. The chapter considers three versions of value non-objectivism and one argument in favour of a metaphysically neutral account of the objectivity of our values. These include two arguments for value fictionalism, an argument in favour of value non-cognitivism and, finally, in response to the latter, a reconfiguration of non-cognitivist and cognitivist approaches to value in support of a metaphysically neutral account of the phenomenal objectivity of our values.

Although I argue that Nietzsche is not *ultimately* a fictionalist about value, there is no escaping the fact that he certainly sounds like a fictionalist at various points in his writings. However, the reasons why he is a fictionalist at these points and the character of this fictionalism are not always clear. It is easy to attribute a Humean influence, and whilst there are elements of a Humean flavour to Nietzsche's fictionalism, the ultimate source of this fictionalism lies in his philosophical engagement with Kant's idealism. This engagement, which is not always critical but ultimately becomes so, sees Nietzsche adopt two different versions of value fictionalism in his writings. The first, idealistically inspired, account of value fictionalism sees him run together the mind-dependent constitution of empirical reality with the constitution of human value. Although our values in this specific sense are fictions because they fail to correspond to things-in-themselves, this idealistic account nonetheless secures the intersubjectivity-cum-objectivity of our values to the extent that the constitution of empirical reality by the mind is a cogent philosophical thesis. But, although Nietzsche ultimately rejects the cogency of Kant's idealism, he does not immediately reject fictionalism. Rather, his earlier account of value fictionalism metamorphoses into a Humean account through a commitment to the fact-value distinction brought about by his critical reflections on Kant's idealism and the implications of this criticism for the status of empirical science and the role of the constitutive or creative-artistic mind. Since Nietzsche consistently understands values analogously to artistic creations throughout his writings and also describes the constitutive idealistic mind in such terms, Chapter 1 examines the development of his thinking with regard to value fictionalism in the context of his changing views on the relation between art and science in selected texts from Nietzsche's canon.

The chapter examines the historical source and development of Nietzsche's fictionalism with a view to highlighting and extracting the logic of his arguments with regard to fictionalism from two texts, TL and HAH. The arguments of these two texts will be highlighted not with a view to suggesting that they are in direct conversation with one another but rather with the distinct aim of extracting and bringing the logic of their respective arguments to bear on the issue of value fictionalism in Nietzsche. However, it will be seen that both forms of fictionalism, when assessed on their logical merits, are found wanting. Specifically, it will be argued that fictionalism can work in practical terms only if 'honest illusions' can motivate us to act. However, whilst this might be possible under the terms and conditions of Nietzsche's early commitment to Kantian idealism, it ultimately proves implausible in light of his criticism of idealism and his acceptance of a more Humean account of value in HAH. Finally, attention will be given to the viability of adopting a non-cognitive alternative to value fictionalism in addition to an argument for phenomenal – metaphysically neutral – objectivity. However, it will be concluded that both non-cognitivism and phenomenal objectivity succumb to the same practical difficulties as fictionalism.

In light of the failure of both non-cognitivism and the phenomenally objective alternative to the fictionalist position of HAH, Chapter 2 takes up the issue of the objectivity of our values in the aftermath of Nietzsche's conclusion in that book. There Nietzsche derived his conclusion about the non-objective status of our values by juxtaposing evaluative inventions to scientific accounts of the natural world and claiming that the latter were untainted by subjective preference or volition. According to Nietzsche, the particular phenomenological or affective quality that, in his view, characterizes our evaluative judgements precludes them from being objective in the specific sense of corresponding to the empirical world as it is constituted independently of our human experience of it. Informing Nietzsche's position here is the presupposition that objectivity entails adopting an external point of view, which is capable of discovering mind-independent and non-evaluative facts and which is to be contrasted with the 'subjective' features of human-lived evaluative experience. According to this view, because perspectivity, affectivity and relationality are taken to be the markers of both subjective judgements and properties, the attainment of an objective point of view must involve the ability to escape all perspectives or points of view.

Although Nietzsche often argues that the subjective status of our values should not count against their existential and practical importance, this conclusion sits uncomfortably with his own philosophical pronouncements and value judgements, which often presuppose the objectivity of those pronouncements and judgements. However, it is arguably the case that all our values are merely subjective rather than objective only if we accept the cogency of the idea of extra-perspectival knowledge divorced from affective or commendatory responses and by taking correspondence or verisimilitude as our standard of objectivity. Nietzsche ultimately doesn't accept the cogency of these ideas, which has the consequence of making his perspectivism compatible with an alternative account of value. An extended examination of his later appeal to the possibility of perspectival objectivity in particular (GM, III, 12) will reveal that objectivity, for him, must include perspectivity, affectivity and relationality. Moreover, it will be argued that perspectival objectivity entails the adoption of a comprehensive perspective arrived at through the consideration of multiple perspectives and that the adoption of a comprehensive perspective, for Nietzsche, is not metaphysically neutral but rather implies the metaphysics of the will to power.

Chapter 3 engages in a sustained examination of the historical context in which Nietzsche proposes his will to power thesis and the manner in which it is founded on an argument in favour of understanding the mind-independent world as comprising intrinsically constituted causal powers or dispositions. The chapter thus puts forward a non-Humean interpretation of Nietzsche, contrary to the dominant view that he endorses Hume in both his theoretical and practical philosophy, most particularly by adopting an anti-essentialist approach to questions of causality and value. Of course, one cannot deny that Nietzsche shares much in common with Hume, most notably the latter's naturalism and his attempt to provide a science of human nature by understanding all aspects of human life – our cultural and evaluative concerns – according to naturalistic principles. Despite this important shared philosophical orientation, however, Nietzsche's ultimate position, when rendered consistent and philosophically viable, is ultimately non-Humean in terms of its conclusions.

Focussing on the issue of causality and leaving the issue of value to Chapter 4, we see that Nietzsche offers a decidedly non-Humean and essentialist account of causality. He does this not by engaging with Hume directly but rather by critically examining Kant's response to Hume. It will be argued that Nietzsche critically engages with Kant's philosophy, and although he praises Kant's efforts to respond to Hume on the causal question, he ultimately finds Kant's own denial of intrinsic natures wanting. By examining Nietzsche's critical engagement with Kant's theoretical philosophy, it will be argued that Nietzsche proposes an essentialist metaphysics that puts him fundamentally at odds with the anti-essentialism of Hume and the philosophy of the Enlightenment, including Kant, more generally. Although this argument is made by tracing Nietzsche's engagement with Kant's theoretical philosophy, the primary aim is to use Nietzsche's responses to Kant to highlight the particularist metaphysics of the will to power, with a view to setting the metaphysical stage to his naturalistic but metaphysically laden approach to value and the conscious mind in later chapters, rather than to understand Kant *per se*. His metaphysical-cum-naturalistic approaches to the status of human values and the character of consciousness are taken up in Chapters 4 and 5 respectively.

Chapter 4 draws on the resources of Nietzsche's will to power thesis to examine how, by aligning value with power, Nietzsche adopts a dispositional account of value that undermines Hume's distinction between facts and values. It is contended that the logic of Nietzsche's argument regarding the metaphysical status of our values provides a three-pronged challenge to Hume. First, he emphasizes the role of the agent rather than spectator with regard to values by denying Hume's identification of values with affective responses of observers. Instead, Nietzsche identifies values with causal-dispositional properties of intentionally directed human drives. In so doing, he proposes that values be understood as causes rather than effects. Second, by proposing that values are causal-dispositional properties that are metaphysically continuous with the causal fabric of reality, Nietzsche denies Hume's view that values are projections of affective feelings onto the world. He does this by extending his alignment of value with power to include worldly power. Values, for Nietzsche, are normative by virtue of overcoming internal resistance from subordinate drives to become the dominant drive of the evaluating agent. However, some values are also objective by virtue of a drive's capacity to overcome external resistance from the powerful capacities of the world. In the case of veridical-objective values, it is argued that overcoming resistance takes the form of a cooperation of values with the natural capacities of reality. Nevertheless, all value-norms, whether they prove objective in this sense or not, are characterized by their active or reactive forms of action in and engagement with the world and are not, therefore, to be understood as reducibly ideal or dualistically apart from the world. Rather, our very engagement with the world is normative through and through. Third, Nietzsche's rejection of the fact-value distinction is sealed by arguing that the preceding dispositional account of value is compatible with the normative and potentially objective character that he attributes to value. It is shown by appealing to an independent argument that norms operate according to the same dispositional modality as the causal processes of nature. Nietzsche's argument that our capacity to formulate explicit value judgements supported by consciously articulated reasons is metaphysically continuous with nature's causes is also examined. Contrary to recent suggestions in the secondary literature, it is concluded that whilst the causal efficacy of conscious reflective thought is not a necessary condition for agential activity *per se*, it is nonetheless a necessary condition for human autonomy[23] and is demarcated from non-human nature not in terms of kind but rather in terms of degree. That is, the causal efficacy of conscious reflective thought is metaphysically continuous with the rest of nature but also demarcated from it in terms of its increasing our power and therefore our agential capacities. Yet the idea of understanding conscious reflective thought as a contributor to human agency and as causally efficacious is a contentious issue in the context of Nietzsche's writings. This is because despite his presupposition of the causal efficacy of consciousness at various junctures in his writings, Nietzsche also claims that it is epiphenomenal. The fifth and final chapter takes up this issue and by appealing to the metaphysics of the will to power offers a resolution to the problem.

---

[23] This is argued contrary to Katsafanas's argument in his *Agency and the Foundations of Ethics*, pp. 241–242.

The final chapter examines how Nietzsche's account of the relation between mind and world informs his views on the causal efficacy of conscious thought. The chapter seeks to reconcile a tension in his writings between his fatalism and its presupposition that our actions are governed by non-conscious mental states and the further, incompatible, presupposition of the causal efficacy of consciousness, which is arguably a necessary condition for the possibility of autonomous agency. By employing the same historical analysis and logical reconstructive methodology that is employed in the earlier chapters, this chapter argues that Nietzsche's naturalistic account of the mind stems from his engagement with both Leibniz and Kant. Nietzsche's endorsement of Leibniz's appeal to the principle of continuity in his denial that consciousness is the mark of the mental informs his adoption of a non-Cartesian and non-eliminativist account of the mind. However, Nietzsche oscillates, without explicit acknowledgement, between two non-eliminativist accounts, which, I argue, is responsible for his confusion about the causal efficacy of conscious mental states.

The first, which I shall for convenience call the 'containment' thesis, holds that human minds share a metaphysical boundary with non-human nature. As I interpret it in the context of the resources afforded by the metaphysics of the will to power, the containment thesis entails that human minds share the capacity for phenomenal conscious feeling with non-human animals and the capacity for non-conscious intentional behaviour with all of nature. Human minds, although metaphysically continuous with non-human minds and nature, more generally, can be demarcated from them by the capacity for reflective conscious and linguistically articulated thought. However, although the containment thesis facilitates the possibility of causally efficacious conscious thought, it proves problematic because by making the intentional the marker of the physical, consciousness becomes, contrary to Nietzsche's initial anti-Cartesian stance, the marker of human minds.

The second non-eliminativist account of the mind that Nietzsche considers bears similarities to some versions of the contemporary higher-order theory of consciousness, and whilst it avoids the relapse into Cartesianism, it does so by denying the causal efficacy of consciousness. Through a process of rational reconstruction, however, I argue that Nietzsche's power metaphysics provides him with the necessary conceptual and metaphysical resources to overcome the problem. The reconstruction sees Nietzsche hold that consciousness is an acquired causal power. As acquired, it is extrinsic to the mental *per se*, and as causal, it is metaphysically continuous with the causal constitution of reality itself. Nevertheless, I conclude that although this reconstruction is arguably cogent in philosophical terms and although the seeds of the reconstruction are evident in Nietzsche's texts themselves, it nevertheless sees him take the intentional to be the mark of dispositional-causes and hence of both the physical and the mental.

There is a deep and, I think, unavoidable tension in Nietzsche on this issue. If, as in the containment thesis, he holds the intentional to be the marker of the dispositional and the physical, then he has to allow that consciousness is the marker of the mental. However, if he is to consistently maintain that consciousness is extrinsic to the mental, then he may have no option but to concede panpsychism. Even if one were to argue that panpsychism entails the attribution of consciousness and not just intentionality to non-human nature, we still encounter a tension in Nietzsche's writings in relation to the issue of re-enchanting nature. I argue that despite the best efforts of some commentators, most notably the admirable endeavours of Paul Loeb, to save Nietzsche from the charge of panpsychism, the tension in Nietzsche between wanting to avoid re-enchanting nature (GS, 109) and arguing that consciousness is extrinsic to the mental but still causally efficacious is ultimately insurmountable. Moreover, I conclude that despite Nietzsche's discomfort at the prospect of re-enchanting nature, he shouldn't be so worried. To see why, it is apposite before I embark on the project outlined in earnest that I comment on the type of naturalist that I take Nietzsche to be and how this naturalism is compatible with the metaphysics of the will to power.

Nietzsche and Naturalism

Brian Leiter argues that we should understand Nietzsche as a substantive and methodological naturalist. He is a substantive naturalist, according to Leiter, because he rejects supernatural explanations that transcend existence in space and time. However, Nietzsche is also a methodological naturalist in the specific sense that he thinks that philosophical inquiry should be continuous with the results of both the human and non-human natural sciences.[24] Specifically, this means, for Leiter, that Nietzsche seeks to explain human phenomena in terms of their causal determinants or what he describes as psycho-physical type-facts about a person.[25] According to Leiter, Nietzsche proposes that we need to appeal to natural facts and dispositions about human

---

[24] Brian Leiter, *Nietzsche on Morality* (London: Routledge, 2002), p. 11.   [25] Ibid., p. 8.

beings to explain why they hold the beliefs that they do or behave as they do. What Leiter calls an 'explanation' of human phenomena amounts to a reductive, 'quasi-speculative theory of human nature',[26] modelled on empirical science's appeal to causal determinants of natural phenomena.[27] Although I agree that Nietzsche can be fruitfully described as a substantive naturalist and whilst I also agree with Leiter that Nietzsche is very much interested in the causal determinants of human behaviour, I take Nietzsche's interest in causes to be rather more wide-ranging than Leiter does. This is because, although Nietzsche is certainly interested in methodological issues and considers such issues to be scientific (AC, 13, 59), his explanation of human psychology and behaviour in terms of psychological-biological causal determinants is not an empirical science *per se* but rather results from Nietzsche's attempt to offer a broader view of the place of the human being in nature than can be attained by taking the evidence of the senses at face value or the perspective of the empirical sciences as privileged.[28] To take the senses at face value, for Nietzsche, is to reduce explanations in the natural sciences to mere empirical 'descriptions' of natural phenomena, which, in turn, reduces what counts as real to the narrowly outside perspective of that which can be 'seen and touched' (BGE, 14). But to genuinely explain natural phenomena entails thinking further than the surface 'appearance of things' (BGE, 12) to penetrate to a 'darker' shade and 'degree' of appearance (BGE, 34). To see what Nietzsche might mean by this, let me consider how he employs the term 'science' in his writings.

Nietzsche employs two notions of science in his writings, both of which stress substantive naturalism as Leiter defines it. The first is empirical science. However, Nietzsche complains that empirical science in some of its guises has presented itself as an extra-perspectival, purely descriptive and dogmatically reductionist form of inquiry that eliminates the human from an objective picture of the world altogether. Although Nietzsche undergoes a period of being enthralled by the supposed objectivity of the natural sciences in HAH, he ultimately contends that inquiry in the empirical sciences is coloured by human interests by virtue of being perspectival and interpretive (GM, III, 24, 25). He criticizes the unreconstructed version of empirical science for being a manifestation of the ascetic ideal (GM, III, 25), for having pretensions to extra-perspectival knowledge (GM, III, 24, 25; GS, 344), for the narrow descriptive focus of its empiricism (BGE, 12, 14, 252) and for its bungling naturalism (BGE, 12). Although Nietzsche demonstrates considerable respect for the natural sciences once they are

[26] Ibid., p. 10.   [27] Ibid., p. 8.   [28] Ibid., pp. 14, 20.

released from their 'convictions' about their privileged status as forms of knowledge (GS, 344; AC, 13, 59), he nonetheless demarcates the practices of the empirical sciences from his own methodological task, which he also describes as scientific in a second sense.

The second view of science goes by the name of Philosophy in Nietzsche's writings, and its scientific nature stems from its adoption of a very particular methodological aim, which is informed by the aesthetic demands for parsimony and simplicity of explanatory principles (BGE, 13, 36).[29] Nietzsche describes genuine philosophy as an experimental and critical science (*kritische Wissenschaft*) that incorporates 'the certainty of standards, the conscious use of a unified method' (BGE, 210). Whilst restricted to giving an account of the empirical world in space and time, it nonetheless seeks to broaden the scope of scientific inquiry beyond that of a mere empirical account of one aspect of nature, whether non-human or human nature, to include a comprehensive, non-reductive and non-eliminativist account of the empirical world and the human being's place in it.[30] Now, it might be argued that Nietzsche's account of the empirical sciences in the first sense is not reductive or eliminativist because he includes the human sciences, such as psychology, in his reconstructed version of empirical science.[31] However, Nietzsche's interest in human psychology extends beyond a mere description of the psychological-physical causes of our behaviour to include an account not just of the manner in which the human being is immersed in nature but also of the respect in which human psychology 'unnaturally' (GS, 355; GM, III, 25) exceeds non-human nature. Accordingly, the mere inclusion of the 'soft' or human sciences in his account of empirical science does not save him from the problem of descriptivism or reductionism.[32]

---

[29] Leiter differentiates the role of science and philosophy in Nietzsche by taking science as a privileged form of objective knowledge that respects the senses and empirical facts whilst taking philosophy to be concerned with the creation of values (ibid., p. 22).

[30] Nietzsche also describes philosophy as a 'gay science'. What I describe here as the task of Philosophy, that is, of ascertaining the continuity of the human self with nature, is a gay science to the extent that it is concerned with the existential consequences of knowledge and not knowledge for its own sake. As we will see in Chapter 2, a gay science, for Nietzsche, entails a combination of scientific knowledge and artistic invention (GS, 113). It entails the creation of life-affirming values on the basis of knowledge of the physical world (GS, 335). For these reasons, I will not address the issue of a gay science as a 'third' conception of science in Nietzsche but rather will view it as a consequence of what he describes as the philosophical practice of combining knowledge with the determination of value (BGE, 211).

[31] Leiter, *Nietzsche on Morality*, pp. 6 ff.

[32] Although Leiter describes Nietzsche's naturalism as offering causal explanations of human phenomena, to the extent that it restricts its analysis to psycho-physical facts about human beings and to the extent that it takes the evidence of the senses and the empirical sciences as privileged (Leiter, *Nietzsche on Morality*, p. 22), it arguably fits into the category of explanations that are descriptions of phenomena.

Nietzsche's philosophical science amounts to more than offering an empirical description of the character of the world and of human beings such as those offered by the empirical sciences of biology, physics and empirical psychology. And it entails more than an acknowledgement that the practices of these sciences are really interpretive and perspectival. Rather, for Nietzsche, philosophical science must provide an explanation of how things hang together in a broad or general sense. Rather than taking the empirical sciences as privileged, Nietzsche instead proposes that we should adopt a philosophical and evaluative perspective towards empirical science. However, this is not to suggest that he reduces philosophy to normative reason-giving activity where such activity is thought to operate independently of the causal sphere of nature, leaving the findings of empirical scientific inquiry untouched, as it has already been suggested that some contemporary approaches to the issue of naturalism and norma-tivity are wont to do when they distinguish the sphere of scientific descrip-tion from that of normative reasons. This is exactly what Kant had done when he reduced philosophical inquiry to critical science alone without, in Nietzsche's view, combining criticism with experiment (BGE, 210). That is, according to Nietzsche, Kant reduced philosophy to a theory of cogni-tion (BGE, 204, 210) by taking the task of philosophy to be concerned with the conditions that make human cognition of the world possible, thus separating the sphere of norms from the sphere of mechanistic causes. However, Kant's project has the effect, in Nietzsche's view, of leaving the dominant mechanistic science of the period of Enlightenment intact, seeking to merely justify the mechanistic conception of nature on the grounds of the character of human cognition rather than offer a revision of it. Accordingly, in a similar manner to his criticism of Kant for having attempted 'to prove, in a way that would dumbfound the common man' that the common man's Christian view of the world was right (GS, 193), Nietzsche implies that Kant's project of appealing to a non-naturalistic sphere of normativity has the consequence of preserving the mechanistic scientific practice of taking the senses at face value (BGE, 14) and thus restricting our knowledge to the world as it is observed by us, precluding insight into the inner character of things-in-themselves.[33] In so doing, Nietzsche suggests that Kant's project ultimately fails to overcome the

---

[33] Nietzsche is of the view that the world of mechanical science is, for Kant, a constitution of the human mind and ultimately divorced from how things are in themselves. His criticism of Kant's allegiance to mechanistic science, however, is a criticism that is targeted at Kant's account of the empirical-phenomenal world, specifically, and not just the distinction between phenomena and things-in-themselves.

deficiencies of raw empiricism (BGE, 252), and despite the a priori character of his appeal to the sphere of norms and its obvious differences from Hume's account of the naturalistic-sentimental basis of our values, it perpetuates the distinction between the sphere of empirical facts of mechanistic science and the sphere of human normativity.

However, by adopting a philosophical perspective towards empirical science, Nietzsche means to offer an explanatory account of the metaphysical continuity of our human values and reason-giving capacities with the causal processes of nature itself, where continuity entails metaphysical explanation from the inside by appealing to the metaphysical character of the world and our immersion in it instead of mere descriptions of observed correlations from the outside. As explained earlier, metaphysical continuity allows that human beings and their cognitive-cum-normative capacities are part of nature, partaking of its essential character, without being reducible to it. Yet some will claim that Nietzsche is guilty of doing a priori philosophy here or that any appeal to explanation as capturing things from the inside goes beyond what is permitted by naturalism. Leiter, for example, contends that naturalism entails a repudiation of first philosophy or 'a philosophical solution to problems that proceed a priori, that is, prior to any experience or empirical evidence'.[34] However, Nietzsche's appeal to explanation does not operate independently of empirical evidence but instead seeks to incorporate it into a comprehensive perspective of the nature of things as a whole.

It is in this specific sense of offering a comprehensive perspective of things as a whole that I will argue that Nietzsche's will to power is a naturalistic thesis. Its comprehensive scope and naturalistic standing is evident in his appeal to the will to power as an explanation of both human and non-human natural phenomena and in his appeal to the will to power as pertaining to the common inner, essential, nature of those natural phenomena. Thus, we find him appealing to the will to power in the context of returning the human being to nature (BGE, 230) and describing it as the 'essence' of the world in the context of a discussion of morality (BGE, 186).[35] It will be argued that to the extent that power is instantiated empirically,

---

[34] Leiter, *Nietzsche on Morality*, p. 3.

[35] Leiter describes Nietzsche as a causal essentialist and denies that the appeal to essences is incompatible with naturalism (ibid., p. 26). Whilst I think this is correct, Leiter restricts his account of essences to refer to the essential natures of human beings and would reject my extension of the will to power to non-human reality and my description of essences as capturing the inner nature of things. Although he initially identifies an essence with a thing's nature he then proceeds to define it in terms of Quinean predicates that are basic to a theory (ibid., p. 26). Essences, as I understand them in Nietzsche, pertain to the nature of a thing and are not reducible to basic predicates in a theory.

there is no reason, apart from evaluative bias in favour of the Enlightenment view of inert, power-less, matter, to understand the will to power thesis in non-naturalistic terms or, indeed, to worry, as Nietzsche himself sometimes does, about adopting a revisionary account of the character of the Enlightenment's conception of nature. The Enlightenment is a period of intellectual history of which he is generally critical. In many places he specifically targets the very fundamentals of Enlightenment thinking, with its emphasis on, for example, democratic politics in addition to mechanistic science. According to Nietzsche, mechanical science reduces causality to a description of observed correlations instead of the operation of causal powers (BGE, 22). Moreover, the democratic politics of the Enlightenment is, in his view, just a secularized version of the Christian principle of equality and sameness (BGE, 202) and is ultimately detrimental to a flourishing culture based on a hierarchy of values (BGE, 257). And an understanding of the role of causal powers is necessary, he argues, to appreciate such an evaluative order of rank. We will have cause to reflect on Nietzsche's criticism of the period of the Enlightenment again at the end of our inquiry, but with the preceding sign-posts to guide us, we now turn to Chapter 1 to begin our investigation in earnest.

CHAPTER I

Nihilism and the Problem of Objective Value

This chapter sets in motion the first step of our investigation into metaphysics and value in Nietzsche by arguing that, despite statements from him to the contrary, our values must be objective and their objectivity cannot be divorced from metaphysics. Although it will be the task of the rest of the book to make good on this claim in a positive sense, the argument is executed negatively here. I aim to show by giving a fair hearing to the opposition and in spite of the fact that Nietzsche sometimes argues in favour of the opposition that both non-objectivist and metaphysically neutral accounts of value are unfeasible. I demonstrate the unviability of these arguments, specifically, by examining them as potential responses to nihilism and finding them deficient.

The issue of nihilism looms large in Nietzsche's thinking and is inextricably intertwined with questions about the implications of scientific knowledge for the possibility of offering a metaphysical support to our values. Nihilism, according to Nietzsche, is rooted in the Platonic and Judeo-Christian idea that objective values are metaphysically grounded and mind-independently instantiated in the world, where 'world' means the traditional notion of the 'real' or 'true' world that is other than the empirical one (WP, 7 KSA 13: 11 [100]). According to the value realism that informs nihilism, *our* values are objective if they correspond to mind-independent values or value-properties *in the world*. That is, value-properties must be mind-independent from a metaphysical point of view and *our* values must correspond to them from an epistemic point of view to be considered objective. The nihilistic value realist runs together the metaphysical and epistemic points of view on the basis of the presupposition that the objective valuer adopts a God's Eye perspective, such that how a value-property is *known* corresponds to how it mind-independently *is*. It is for this reason that values that correspond to the world and mind-independently instantiated values or value-properties are considered synonymous.[1] For the value realism that informs nihilism, the epistemic and metaphysical points of view collapse into one another. Nihilism culminates, however, in the realization that our hitherto highest human ideals and values are incapable of this realist metaphysical support, and it manifests itself in psychological symptoms such as a loss of faith in previously held values and finally the psychological disorientation and despair that ensues from recognizing that these values are metaphysically groundless (WP, 13 KSA 13: 11 [99]).[2]

Referring to 'God's mortal terror of science', Nietzsche contends that science plays a significant instrumental role in undermining the metaphysical presuppositions of Platonism and Judeo-Christianity (AC 48). He uses the term 'science' to denote the empirical, descriptive and causal account of the natural world offered by natural science, which undermines the notion of there being a metaphysical support to our values by precluding the possibility of our acquiring knowledge of a metaphysical ground in a true world beyond the empirical. The impossibility of our knowing such a ground through the empirical methods of the natural sciences is tantamount, in Nietzsche's view, to its refutation and abolition (TI, 'Real World'). However, the difficulty is not just that our values are not grounded in a 'true' world; they are not to be found in the empirical world of our acquaintance either.[3] Nietzsche writes that '[w]e see that we cannot reach the sphere in which we have placed our values; but this does not by any means confer any value on that other sphere in which we live: on the contrary, we are *weary* because we have lost the main stimulus' (WP, 8 KSA 12: 7 [8]).

The *problem of nihilism*, for Nietzsche, entails that without the traditional metaphysical support that Platonism and Judeo-Christianity purported to offer, to value at all is tantamount to willing nothingness, and it is this realization that brings about the ultimate devaluation of our highest

---

[1] Thus, Nietzsche describes the Platonic system as running together Plato's metaphysics and his presupposed God's Eye access by declaring, 'I, Plato, *am* the truth' (TI, 'Real World').

[2] For a recent discussion of nihilistic disorientation and despair, see Bernard Reginster, *The Affirmation of Life: Nietzsche on Overcoming Nihilism* (Cambridge, MA: Harvard University Press, 2006), Chapter Two.

[3] The will to truth, which initially forms the basis of the traditional appeal to the notion of a true world ultimately turns on this metaphysical presupposition and reveals our highest values to be without a metaphysical foundation (WP, 5 KSA 12: 5 [71]). Science, for Nietzsche, embodies the will to truth and is itself called into question to the extent that it sets itself up as a successor to the notion of a true world by believing in the absolute value of its own claims. Moreover, by describing the empirical world as value-less, the 'faith' in science leads to the positing of '*another world*' than the world of life, nature, and history'. That is, when science mistakes regulative hypotheses for convictions, it proves to be as nihilistic as Christianity (GS, 344; GM, III, 24, 25).

values and the consequent existential and cultural crisis that threatens the very foundations of Western culture (GM, III, 28). According to the Nihilist, our values have meaning only to the extent that they are objective and metaphysically grounded in a true world (WP, 5 KSA 12: 5 [71]). The problem of nihilism arises when it is revealed that our value perspectives are simply that and do not correspond to the world because values do not belong to the fabric of the mind-independent world at all (WP, 5 KSA 12: 5 [71]). Scientific knowledge, which depicts a disenchanted world devoid of value, lies at the heart of the problem of nihilism because it rules out the possibility of our value judgements corresponding to value properties instantiated mind-independently in a metaphysically true world or the empirical world knowable by science.

Although the denial of value realism in the sense described previously informs the problem of nihilism, the problem cannot be overcome, in Nietzsche's view, by illegitimately attempting to place values mind-independently back into the world. The acceptance of the illegitimacy of such an attempt makes it tempting to argue that responding to nihilism involves treating values separately from the world and according to purely internal criteria of assessment that are divorced from the character of mind-independent reality. At times, Nietzsche's response to nihilism exhibits this tendency to separate values from the world on the grounds of their having no mind-independent instantiated object to which they correspond. Such a strategy is tantamount to arguing, contrary to the Nihilist, that our values can be meaningful in the absence of a metaphysical support. Accordingly, it is generally thought that Nietzsche's response to nihilism is a *practical* one in the sense of maintaining the irrelevance of supposedly purely theoretical – metaphysical and scientific – knowledge of the character of the world for the practical meaningfulness and efficacy of our values.[4] On the back of the view that knowledge of the character of mind-independent reality is practically irrelevant, it is argued that Nietzsche's response to nihilism entails either denying that our values are objective or redefining objectivity in a metaphysically neutral way, that is, not just in terms other than correspondence to and instantiation in the mind-independent world but, rather, in a way that makes the metaphysical relation of our values to the world irrelevant to their

---

[4] Although the relation between metaphysics and science will be addressed in Chapter 2, where they will be seen to be complementary but non-identical, I run them together here for now on the grounds that since science debunks the idea of a metaphysical world, science becomes the key to knowledge of the metaphysical character of the world where this metaphysical character is understood since the period of the Enlightenment in a decidedly empirical and non-essentialist sense.

objectivity. Both approaches, in different ways, accept the Nihilist's ultimate denial that values are residents of the mind-independent world but contend that this conclusion need not result in disorientation and despair on the grounds that either non-objective values can still motivate us to act in the world or by denying that the Nihilist's claims about the metaphysical instantiation of our values, or lack of a metaphysical relation between our values and the world, count against their objectivity and, in turn, their motivational capacity. I examine both of these approaches. Specifically, I consider three potential non-objectivist responses to the problem followed by a fourth that seeks to redefine what constitutes objectivity. The first two are interrelated fictionalist responses, the third entails non-cognitivism whilst the fourth reconfigures and offers an alternative to the standard non-cognitive and, indeed, cognitivist arguments, to offer a metaphysically neutral account of the objectivity of our values. It is to be noted that what I describe as Nietzsche's fictionalism and non-cognitivism arises from the extent to which he contrasts our values with mind-independent reality. To the extent that he does contrast them and to the extent that our values do not correspond to reality, he declares them to be false.[5] The erroneousness of our values amounts to fictionalism for Nietzsche because he claims that our values are still practically useful despite their falsity and their usefulness resides in their status as honest illusions that have the power to motivate us to act in spite of our knowing that they do not accurately represent the world.[6] Nietzsche's argument in this regard involves appealing to the special ontology of illusions, which, however, when fully drawn out contains the seeds of a potentially non-cognitive and alternative response to the problem of nihilism. The non-cognitive potential of his appeal to illusion is realized in contexts where Nietzsche does not contrast our values with mind-independent reality and declares that our values have no relationship

---

[5] Of course, Nietzsche's fictionalism contains epistemic, semantic, metaphysical and psychological components. Nietzsche claims that our values are false but we don't realize this because language tends to refer to entities that don't actually exist (TI, 'Reason' 5, 'Improvers', 1) and, psychologically, we needed to believe that these values are real (HAH, I, 32; WP, 12 KSA 13: 11 [99]). However, despite the many components to his claim that our values are false, the metaphysical one is paramount. Nihilism arises because the meaning of our values hinges on them being metaphysically grounded in a 'true' world coupled with the revelation that our values do not exist mind-independently in the world. It is primarily by virtue of contrasting our values with reality that they are false (TI, 'Improvers', 1). That the metaphysical issue of values informs his fictionalism will be seen from the fact that in TL, for example, his fictionalism is grounded in his account of the mind-dependent metaphysical status of our values and, indeed, the empirical world.

[6] Nietzsche would be properly described as a revolutionary rather than hermeneutic fictionalist in the contemporary literature as a result of his combining error theory with fictionalism. See Nadeem J. Z. Hussain, 'The Return of Moral Fictionalism', *Philosophical Perspectives*, 18, Ethics, 2004, pp. 149–187.

to the world that can be described as true or false. However, Nietzsche tends to blur the lines between fictionalism and non-cognitivism because both views attribute the same ontological – mind-dependent – status to our values and, therefore, unless appropriately reconstructed, are forms of value non-objectivism. My differentiation of them in this chapter, then, is intended only for the purpose of analysing potential alternative practical responses to the challenges posed by the problem of nihilism suggested by Nietzsche's analogy of values with artistic illusion even though Nietzsche himself does not explicitly differentiate between these alternatives.[7]

As already indicated from the outset, my aim in examining Nietzsche's fictionalism and non-cognitivism as forms of value non-objectivism, in addition to a reconfiguration of non-cognitivism in support of a metaphysically neutral account of objectivity, is primarily negative in that by establishing the unviability of non-objectivism and metaphysically neutral accounts of objectivity with regard to our values, we pave the way for the quest in subsequent chapters for a metaphysically laden account of the objectivity of our values in Nietzsche's writings that avoids both re-instantiating our values in the world and cutting them off from it. Whilst all of the responses considered in this chapter concede the unviability of instantiating values mind-independently back into the world, they nonetheless fall short as viable responses to the problem of nihilism as a result of how they treat the metaphysical status of our values idealistically and take idealism to be opposed to realism such that if something is ideal then it must be divorced from the real. However, this treatment of the metaphysical status of our values in the case of the fictionalist, the non-cognitivist and the metaphysically neutral objectivist alternative to non-cognitivism, despite their respective claims to the contrary, deprives values of the requisite motivational efficacy to overcome the existential crisis of nihilism. Since fictionalism is more

---

[7] As Nietzsche describes them, our fictional values may or may not have assertoric force, depending on whether he discusses the ontological falsity of our values from the point of view of us embracing them as honest illusions or whether we have to deceive ourselves or are deceived into believing illusions to be true. This accounts for his blurring the lines between fictionalism and non-cognitivism. For discussions of fictionalism in the contemporary literature, see Richard Joyce, *The Myth of Morality* (Cambridge: Cambridge University Press, 2001). For an argument that blurs the boundaries between fictionalism and non-cognitivism and argues that fictionalism is a form of non-cognitivism, see Mark Eli Kalderon, *Moral Fictionalism* (Oxford: Oxford University Press, 2005). For arguments in favour of the non-cognitivist view that value statements are expressions of non-truth apt attitudes, see C. L. Stevenson, *Facts and Values* (New Haven, CT: Yale University Press, 1963) and A. J. Ayer, *Language, Truth and Logic* (New York, NY: Dover Publications, 1952).

obviously evident in Nietzsche's writings than non-cognitivism,[8] I begin with his arguments for value fictionalism before proceeding to consider the final two responses, which although not explicit in his writings are, nonetheless, implied.

In the first two sections of the chapter, I examine Nietzsche's fictionalism by focussing on his analogy between value and artistic creation and their juxtaposition with scientific knowledge. Fictionalism responds to nihilism by licensing the conscious appeal to ontological untruths in a way that the Platonic and Christian appeal to truth did not. That is, the fictionalist accepts the Nihilist's ontological conclusion – that values are not in the world (in either the metaphysical or empirical sense) – but denies that this should be a cause for despair. Rather, the recognition that our values are fictions affords us the liberty to create new values and to be motivated to act in the world according to these values. According to Nietzsche, the fictional character of our values stems from the fact that they are indexed to the perspectival interests of human beings and have no objective correlates in the world – either metaphysical or empirical – itself.[9] The lack of objective correlates to our values accounts for the manner in which Nietzsche identifies the fictional status of our values with that of dreams, mind-dependency, ontological irreality, artistic creations and the illusory without differentiating between these descriptions.[10]

I examine two sources to this fictionalism: one that emphasizes artistic creation over scientific discovery in a Kantian idealist context and a more Humean version that emphasizes the role of scientific discovery. The first

---

[8] See Nadeem J. Z. Hussain's argument in this regard in 'Nietzsche and Non-Cognitivism' in Christopher Janaway and Simon Robertson (eds.), *Nietzsche, Naturalism and Normativity* (Oxford: Oxford University Press, 2012), pp. 122–131.

[9] Reginster claims that whilst fictionalism can overcome nihilistic disorientation, it cannot overcome nihilistic despair because despair arises from the realization that our values cannot be objective as a result of the inhospitability of the world to their realization (*The Affirmation of Life*, p. 100). Accordingly, Reginster claims that meta-ethics (both the subjectivist and fictionalist varieties that he considers) is limited in its capacity to respond to nihilism and that instead we need to do substantive ethics by engaging with the actual content of our life-denying values. Nadeem Hussain, however, argues in favour of the capacity of fictionalism to respond to nihilism. (See Nadeem J. Z. Hussain, 'Metaethics and Nihilism' in Reginster's *The Affirmation of Life*, *The Journal of Nietzsche Studies*, 43.1, Spring 2012, pp. 99–117.) I will argue that fictionalism is ultimately unsuccessful but that, contrary to Reginster, we do not have to see Nietzsche as giving up on the possible objectivity of our values and that this possibility is brought to light by focussing on the metaphysics of the will to power. This argument will be made in Chapters 2 and 4.

[10] See, for example, BT, 1; HAH, I, 222. Since Nietzsche tends to run his descriptions of values in terms of dreams, mind-dependency, illusions, etc. together, I shall too. Consequently, I will not restrict references to illusion to instances where Nietzsche explicitly uses the term '*Schein*'. Instead, my use of the term will also make reference to instances where Nietzsche's reference to illusion is implied or captured by one or other of his alternative descriptions.

idealistically informed account of fictionalism undermines the disenchanted scientific world view in contrast with which our value illusions are deprecated and rendered meaningless on account of their not being scientifically objective or metaphysically supported. Although Nietzsche's proposal of genuinely honest illusions as an antidote to nihilism arguably succeeds within the strict confines of his idealist running together of the ontological status of the empirical world with that of illusions, it ultimately fails as a result of his own debunking of the idealist backdrop to the argument in subsequent writings and gives way to the second, Humean, version of fictionalism. However, this second account of fictionalism also fails because it leaves the status of science and the disenchanted account of the world in which nihilism culminates intact. In so doing, it draws our attention to the ontology of artistic illusions and reveals why value fictions are unable to motivate us to act by making more pronounced a tension that is evident but obscured in his idealist account between false belief and illusion. Highlighting the tension reveals a weakness at the heart of Nietzsche's fictionalism. This weakness is that we cannot be properly motivated by value illusions unless we adopt false beliefs in relation to them such that the very analogy that Nietzsche draws between values and artistic illusions is undermined.

Nevertheless, Nietzsche's analogy between values and illusions invites an alternative non-cognitive response. The non-cognitive response to nihilism, unlike fictionalism, denies that our values are either true or false and attempts to address the practical implications of the nihilistic problem of the meaningfulness and motivational efficacy of metaphysically unsupported values by inducing an alteration in our evaluative attitudes that does not involve belief, whether false or otherwise. However, non-cognitivism fails as a response to nihilism as a result of running contrary to the phenomenology of value by severing our values from the world. Nihilistic despair, for Nietzsche, is bound up with the fact that we do not experience value as cut off from the world despite the theoretical knowledge that our values are not mind-independently instantiated in a metaphysical or empirical world (WP, 5 KSA 12: 5 [71]). Rather, we experience the world evaluatively and take our values to be subject to constraint and correction by the world such that we experience things as really valuable. Nietzsche concedes as much when he writes that our desires regarding what ought to be are inextricably intertwined with the desire for knowledge of what is (WP, 333 KSA 12: 7 [15]). Now, it might be wondered why Nietzsche must cater for our phenomenological experience of value at all. Shouldn't he, it might be asked, just re-assert his fictionalist argument and maintain that our phenomenological experience of value is globally false?

However, the problems that, I will argue, Nietzsche encounters with fiction-alism caution against adopting this view.[11] Moreover, if the phenomenology of value is globally false, then it doesn't make sense to propose, as Nietzsche does in some of his writings, to take human psychology and experience as our unavoidable investigative starting point (BGE, 23). A perspectival starting point is made inevitable by Nietzsche's ultimate rejection of the possibility of adopting a non-human or extra-perspectival stance in relation to the world and our knowledge and evaluation of it. Still, even if both fictionalism and non-cognitivism fail as responses to the problem of nihilism, it will be argued that we can reconfigure aspects of the non-cognitivist response and cater for the objectivity of our values and hence for the phenomenological experience of value in a metaphysically neutral way. It is in order to consider this final response that I turn to examine what Peter Poellner calls phenomenal objec-tivity. This account denies that our values are fictions or *mere* attitudes and argues that they can be considered by us to be objective in a phenomenal but not a metaphysical sense. However, a close examination of Poellner's proposal will reveal that the phenomenal objectivity of our values leaves them vulner-able to their separation from the world and, consequently, to the same problems faced by both the fictionalist and non-cognitivist, by virtue of not only dissociating objectivity from the requirements of correspondence and metaphysical independence in which nihilism is rooted but also adopting an attitude of indifference to the metaphysical connection of our values to the world. By way of conclusion, I argue that an adequate response to the problem of nihilism requires objectivity in our values but that such objectivity cannot, as Poellner suggests, be metaphysically neutral even if objectivity cannot involve correspondence and the mind-independent instantiation of value properties in the world. The problem of nihilism does not emerge in a metaphysically neutral context. Its solution does not either.

The Kantian Roots to Nietzsche's Fictionalism

The Priority of Art over Science

This section puts in place the first stage of our overall negative argument by showing that Nietzsche's most promising argument for value fictionalism and, hence, value non-objectivism, is grounded in his appropriation of

---

[11] This claim is opposed to Hussain's view that fictionalism preserves the phenomenology of value. See Nadeem J. Z. Hussain, 'Honest Illusion: Valuing for Nietzsche's Free Spirits' in Brian Leiter and Neil Sinhababu (eds.), *Nietzsche and Morality* (Oxford: Oxford University Press, 2007), pp. 172–173.

Kant's idealism and that its viability is ultimately compromised by his own emerging critical reflections on Kant and internal tensions within Nietzsche's argument itself. I focus on how Nietzsche employs the resources of Kant's idealism to prioritize artistic invention over scientific truth in order to keep at bay the ultimate nihilistic collapse of our values in the early unpublished essay TL (KSA 1, pp. 875–890).[12] Although he does not explicitly mention nihilism in this essay, it is nonetheless clear that the criticisms he offers of truth and language there must be understood in the broader cultural context of Modernity. For him, this is the period of Enlightenment and science in which the *'highest values'* (WP, 2 KSA 12: 9 [35]) are shorn of their traditional metaphysical significance and revealed to be illusory (WP, 3 KSA 12: 10 [192]). In this essay, Nietzsche's idealist treatment of the status of science rules out both the possibility of scientific truth and the possibility of knowledge of things-in-themselves as a mind-independent metaphysical support to our values. However, by virtue of ruling out the possibility of scientific truth, Nietzsche also licenses the appeal to illusions by denying that the meaningfulness and motivational efficacy of these values can be deprecated by contrasting them either with the empirical world described by science or a metaphysical world that we cannot know. He precludes the possibility of scientific truth by arguing

---

[12] Nietzsche's interpretation of Kant is heavily influenced by Schopenhauer's interpretation of transcendental idealism as a form of Berkelian empirical idealism. Kant's influence on Nietzsche's thought is evident in other early writings besides TL. For example, it is quite clear in BT, despite Nietzsche's own retrospective judgement that his reliance on the epistemological and metaphysical frameworks of Kant and Schopenhauer obscured the emergence of a non-Kantian and non-Schopenhauerian philosophical standpoint (BT, 'An Attempt at Self-Criticism', p. 10, section 6). Although it is arguably the case that Nietzsche is attempting to escape the confines of Kant's and Schopenhauer's epistemology and metaphysics in BT, such as when he describes the artist that constitutes the world in the non-anthropological terms of a Dionysian world-intellect (BT, pp. 25–26, section 4), his attempt in that book, according to his own retrospective admission, ultimately fails. For example, in BT his concern with the revitalization of modern culture is, similarly to his position in TL, framed in the context of a discussion of the Kantian-Schopenhauerian treatment of appearances and things-in-themselves. This is evident when he identifies Dionysus with the truth about things-in-themselves, whilst Apollo is identified with culture and illusion (BT, pp. 41–42, section 8). Moreover, even the non-anthropological idea of a Dionysian world-artist can be interpreted as a version of Kant's supersensible designer. (See R. Kevin Hill, *Nietzsche's Critiques: The Kantian Foundations of His Thought* (Oxford: Clarendon Press), 2003, p. 99.) Despite the background similarities between BT and TL, I will focus on the latter in order to avoid the interpretive complications of the former. My aim, in so doing, is not to trace the development of Nietzsche's thought from early to late but rather to highlight two accounts of the metaphysical status of value that are evident in his thought and the manner in which those two positions emerge and develop through an engagement with Kant's idealism. My aim, therefore, is to use this historical background as a way of focussing attention on the logic of Nietzsche's arguments in relation to the metaphysics of value. In doing this, I do not mean to suggest that evidence of the later view is not already emerging, however indistinctly, during the early period of his writing but only that certain strands of his thinking are more evident at particular times.

that scientific knowledge is restricted to that of mind-dependent images and that mind-dependent images are false by virtue of failing to correspond to mind-independent things-in-themselves, which ultimately transcend our capacity for knowledge.[13]

Nietzsche formulates the preceding argument by appropriating Kant's idealist 'mind-imposition thesis'[14] and arguing that the forms of our cognition constitute the phenomenal-empirical world of our experience through the imposition of specifically human cognitive-cum-evaluative structures on the data of sense to produce sensory images in the mind (KSA 7: 19 [217]).[15] These cognitive structures, which include space, time, succession and number, are quasi-transcendental in a Kantian sense because they precede and are conditions of the possibility of human perceptual experience. However, unlike Kant, as interpreted by Nietzsche under the influence of Arthur Schopenhauer, they emanate from the human brain (KSA 7: 19 [79]) and therefore have a physiological root. He likens the manner in which the forms of our cognition constitute experience to the process of artistic creation when he writes that 'the *artistic process* [my emphasis] of metaphor formation with which every sensation begins in us already presupposes these forms and occurs within them' (TL, 1, p. 88 KSA 1, p. 886). Images are inventions, he contends, because the imposition of these forms entails the metaphorical transposition of the data of sense by forms which are entirely alien to sense data. Accordingly, in Nietzsche's view, the fundamental unit of cognitive significance is not the 'given' sensation but rather the mind-dependent perceptual image (KSA 7: 19 [217]) to which the empirical world, the object of scientific investigation, is mind-dependently reducible. As a result, for Nietzsche, the empirical world is not metaphysically real but rather is divorced from the mind-independent character of things as they are in themselves. He writes that '[w]e believe that we know something about the things themselves when we speak of trees, colors, snow and flowers; and

---

[13] Note that Nietzsche does not use the word 'mind' in the text but more commonly uses the term 'intellect', which, for him, is a more holistic account of human experience that incorporates emotion and affect. At this stage of his intellectual development, Nietzsche is not entirely clear on how this broader notion of intellect might be incompatible with Kant's idealism. He becomes clearer about this later on (BGE, 15). Despite the interpretive complexities, I will use the more general term 'mind' in my discussion of Nietzsche's account of the constitutive intellect in TL as my aim is to highlight the Kantian-idealist framework in which Nietzsche arguments are formulated there.

[14] I borrow the term 'mind-imposition' from R. Kevin Hill, *Nietzsche's Critiques*. See, for example, p. 170.

[15] Nietzsche makes it clear in TL that our cognitive structures reflect the human organism's need for preservation (TL, 1, p. 79 KSA 1, p. 875) and that our values, such as that of truth or what we conventionally accept as 'truth' reflect our biological and cultural needs (TL, 1, p. 81 KSA 1, pp. 877–878).

yet we possess nothing but metaphors for these things – metaphors which correspond in no way to the original entities' (TL, 1, pp. 82–83 KSA 1, p. 879).

Nietzsche's denial that the mind-dependent world corresponds to mind-independent things-in-themselves is a sceptical conclusion, which bears directly on the issue of the possibility of scientific knowledge and his response to the nihilistic collapse of the meaningfulness of our values. To the forefront of such scepticism is his contention that despite science's belief that it has managed to discover necessary laws in nature, the metaphorical and aesthetic ground to all our knowledge rules out the possibility of such discovery. This is because all that is to be discovered, even through rational analysis using concepts, is what we have put there in the first place (TL, 1, p. 87 KSA 1, p. 885). Moreover, since the idealist account of mind presupposes mind-independent things-in-themselves to which our mind-dependent 'inventions' must fail to correspond, the impossibility of genuine scientific discovery is intimately tied in with the ultimate falsity of scientific descriptions. Nietzsche articulates this point when he writes that if Kant's idealist account of mind is correct, and in TL Nietzsche thinks that in broad outline it is, then natural science is wrong (KSA 7: 19 [125]). It is wrong because science does not deliver knowledge of things-in-themselves but only descriptions of images. Now, whilst the preclusion of genuine scientific knowledge does not overcome nihilism by providing a metaphysical support to our values, it does have the consequence of undermining the possibility of truth, which, in turn, licenses the appeal to values understood as fictional inventions as an existential response to the lack of a metaphysical support.

Nietzsche proposes that since the empirical world of our experience is necessarily a cognitive-evaluative invention constituted by us and since we cannot penetrate beyond the bounds of our own creations, our response should be to embrace these inventions.[16] However, in making this proposal, he points to a tension that he claims exists between the scientific impulse to truth and discovery and the artistic impulse to invention (TL, 2, pp. 90–91 KSA 1, pp. 889–890). He claims that '[t]hey both desire to rule over life: the former, by knowing how to meet his principle needs by means of foresight, prudence, and regularity; the latter, by disregarding these needs and,

---

[16] Nietzsche's argument here mirrors his diagnosis of a twofold path to nihilistic collapse in BT. There nihilistic collapse emerges from a rejection of Socratic optimism where the latter represents a combination of two views: (1) knowledge is possible and (2) such knowledge will bring happiness. Nietzsche here undermines the possibility of knowledge and by appealing to artistic illusion denies that such metaphysical knowledge is necessary for us to be happy.

as an "overjoyed hero", counting as real only that life which has been disguised as illusion (*Schein*) and beauty' (TL, 2, p. 90 KSA 1, p. 889). Nietzsche argues that since the very basis of our cognition is inventive, the scientific impulse can never be satisfied on its own terms. This is because all it will ever discover are our own inventions. Therefore, we should allow the artistic impulse to dominate over life. Such 'mastery' (TL, 2, p. 90 KSA 1, p. 889), however, will entail recognising the scientific impulse to truth and accommodating it by disguising that which has been invented and presenting it as true. In this sense, art's domination entails 'dissimulation' and 'deception' (*Verstellung*) (TL, 2, pp. 90–91 KSA 1, p. 889). According to Nietzsche, science and art, which both deal in illusions, differ not in kind but rather only to the extent that the scientist 'believes' that their illusions are true in the sense of corresponding to mind-independent reality (KSA 7: 19 [43]) whilst the artist instead knows that they are not. Adopting a version of the Platonic noble falsehood, he proposes that only artists and philosophers genuinely understand that the scientist's claim to knowledge, in the sense of having justified true beliefs and where truth corresponds to mind-independent reality, is in fact illusory (TL, 2, pp. 90–91 KSA 1, pp. 889–890; KSA 7: 29 [7] and 29 [8]). Science is revealed to be just as evaluative as art, but whereas the scientist values truth, the artist knows that such truth is not forthcoming.[17]

It is this artist's knowledge that is best placed, in Nietzsche's view, to respond to the problem of nihilism. This is because the artist values illusions more highly than truth, revealing such illusion to be a necessary condition for the possibility of the specifically human form of life that Nietzsche refers to as culture. Artistic illusions are intended to motivate the will despite the metaphysical truth that the status of the human, its cognitive and evaluative needs, is largely insignificant and meaningless (TL, 1, p. 79 KSA 1, p. 875) outside of the invented cultural context that shapes it. Culture, which Nietzsche defines as 'above all, unity of style in all expressions of the life of a people' (DS, 1), presupposes the possibility of shared values, even if it knows that these values are not metaphysically real. Nietzsche articulates this point when he describes culture as a form of lying according to fixed conventions. Peaceful co-existence, he conjectures, entails adherence to 'linguistic conventions' of what constitutes truth and falsity. Societal cohesion, therefore, presupposes understanding human relations and nature as bound by general rules and the sedimentation of

---

[17] On a charitable interpretation of Nietzsche's argument here we can say that the artist knows that our empirical claims to knowledge are false not because the artist possesses special insight into things as they are in themselves but rather because they are aware of the inventive capacity of the human mind.

such rules in language (TL, 1, p. 81 KSA 1, pp. 877–878). Only artistic illusion, Nietzsche concludes, can facilitate the possibility of a culture based on shared values and principles and, in so doing, provide the necessary context for meaningful human action.[18]

The tenability of this proposal clearly rests on whether it is capable of motivating such action. Since only the philosopher and the artist actually know that the empirical world and our values are illusory, then it seems that everyone else, including the scientist, operates under the delusion that what are in fact illusions are real. This opens up a potential tension in Nietzsche's argument because delusions amount to false beliefs rather than the honest illusions that he identifies with artistic creations (KSA 7: 29 [17]; GS, 107; GM, III, 25]. Nietzsche demonstrates an awareness of this tension when he writes that delusions and false beliefs rather than honest illusions are capable of motivating the will (KSA 7: 29[17]). However, he can avoid being inconsistent in his fictionalism if we consider that it is arguably the case that illusions *can* be motivational for the philosopher and the artist who are aware of their status as ontological illusions. That this is so can be seen if we consider that the artistic illusions in Nietzsche's account are practically real even if they are not theoretically or metaphysically so. Our knowing that our values are metaphysically unreal makes no practical difference to their motivational efficacy. Nietzsche secures this argument in TL by running together the possibility of culture and value with the constitution of empirical reality. Accordingly, there is no 'outside' of the illusion that can impact on us in a practical way. The consistency and coherency of our empirical experience arguably preclude such an impact since the thing-in-itself is entirely divorced from the empirical world. For Nietzsche in TL, artistic illusion pervades every aspect of human life. Consequently, value illusions can motivate either when we don't know that they are illusions and are deluded into thinking that illusions are real and in cases where we do know values to be illusions but can nonetheless consider them to be real for our practical purposes.

The plausibility of this argument relies on the idealist scaffold upon which Nietzsche's argument for value fictionalism rests in TL. But, as already indicated, Nietzsche ultimately abandons the idea that the fictional status of our values is tied in with the constitution of empirical reality and its separation from things-in-themselves. That is, he argues, albeit outside the textual

---

[18] Simon Blackburn interprets Nietzsche as a conventionalist rather than fictionalist (Simon Blackburn, 'Perspectives, Fictions, Errors, Play' in Leiter and Sinhababu (eds.), *Nietzsche and Morality*, pp. 281–297). However, the idealist backdrop of the argument in TL makes his conventionalism a form of value fictionalism.

confines of TL, that either the thing-in-itself does make a practical difference or if the notion of the thing-in-itself is genuinely superfluous in practical terms then the distinction between the empirical world as a product of the constitutive activity of the mind and things-in-themselves should be abandoned. Although it is a theoretical possibility that there is a thing-in-itself, we can afford to be indifferent to this metaphysical possibility on the grounds that the argument that the thing-in-itself is theoretically and practically superfluous is tantamount to its refutation (HAH, I, 9; TI, 'Real World', 4–6). One might argue that this gives us what we want because it means that although our values are fictions and their fictional status is bound up with the mind-dependent constitution of empirical reality, there is now nothing outside of the illusion with which to contrast them, thus strengthening the motivational powers of our evaluative illusions. If there is nothing outside the mind-dependent illusion with which to contrast our values, then we can be motivated by them as if they were real. However, according to Nietzsche, if the thing-in-itself is abandoned, then so too is the correlative idea that the empirical world is metaphysically unreal or illusory. According to the terms and conditions of Nietzsche's idealistic argument, if the empirical world is real, then it must be mind-independent in a metaphysical or existential sense even if, as Nietzsche is willing to concede throughout his entire corpus, the conditions of knowing or cognizing the empirical world are mind-correlative. But this alteration in Nietzsche's argument has implications for how he understands the role of science and art. As witnessed earlier, Nietzsche thinks that philosophical idealism and genuine scientific knowledge are incompatible. However, if the empirical world is real, then it can no longer be described in terms of an artistic illusion but must instead be amenable to genuine scientific-empirical investigation and discovery. The illusory, by contrast, must belong to the arena of genuine artistic creations rather than the constitution of the empirically real world. According to this reasoning, the empirical world is real and knowledge of its character through the empirical investigations of the natural sciences can act as a constraint to our values by serving to mark the distinction between the true and the illusory. Once this argument is in place, the idea of there being no 'outside the illusion' that can impact on the motivational power of artistic creations is rendered null and void. It arguably becomes more difficult to be motivated by fictions when their status as fictions is highlighted by virtue of being contrasted with the real or non-illusory. That this is the case can be seen by examining Nietzsche's argument in HAH where his critical engagement with Kant's idealism, articulated through his prioritization of science over art in that book, results in an alternative – Humean – account of value fictionalism. The challenge to

Nietzsche's fictionalist response to the problem of nihilism in HAH is, accordingly, whether the analogy that he draws between values and illusions can be upheld to be motivational when the idealist scaffolding on which it depends in TL is removed. In the next section, the difficulty of being motivated by values that are known to be illusory will be highlighted by drawing our attention to the ontology of artistic illusions in HAH, where we see the tension that exists between the false belief of the scientist and the honest illusion of the artist in TL become more pronounced, such that, in the absence of the support of his appropriation of Kant's idealism, Nietzsche must ultimately conclude that genuine value fictions cannot motivate unless we adopt false beliefs. But, in so doing, the very analogy between artistic illusions and values is undermined and calls out for an alternative, non-cognitive, response to nihilism.

The Second Argument for Value Fictionalism

The Priority of Science over Art

That Nietzsche adopts a non-idealist position in HAH is obscured by his tendency to frame the argument of the text in the terms of reference of Schopenhauerian representationalism. Thus, we find Nietzsche claiming that our knowledge is restricted to the specifically human point of view, which may or may not capture how things are in themselves (HAH, I, 9). On the surface, the argument of HAH differs little from that of TL. However, closer examination reveals that the logic of Nietzsche's argument in HAH points towards a non-idealist conclusion. This conclusion follows from his arguments in relation to the cogency of the idea of the thing-in-itself in addition to his views about the possibility of scientific knowledge and the status of illusions.

Nietzsche runs together two arguments about the thing-in-itself in HAH without adequately distinguishing between them. First, he claims that the idea of the thing-in-itself is a logical possibility to which we can be practically indifferent. Second, he argues that genealogical analysis reveals that the very idea of the thing-in-itself is an invention, which, when revealed as such, is rendered invalid (HAH, I, 9). The first argument is an agnostic one, whilst the second rejects the thing-in-itself as a human invention and hoax. Nietzsche arguably runs the two arguments together on the grounds that they both yield the same practical conclusion. This conclusion is that the object of knowledge for us is the empirical world, which is knowable through scientific investigation (HAH, I, 29). Unlike the argument of TL, however, the idea of the thing-in-itself no longer has sceptical implications for the possibility of genuine scientific knowledge. Rather, Nietzsche goes so far as to describe scientific discourse as "*the imitation of nature in concepts*" (HAH, I, 38), which gives us the 'truth' about the empirical world (HAH, I, 29). The thing-in-itself as something that lies beyond the reach of human knowledge, even in principle, is to all intents and purposes 'refuted' (HAH, I, 9).

The non-idealist logic of Nietzsche's argument in HAH is further bolstered when he rejects the idea that the empirical world is an artistic creation on our part and instead holds that only values should be understood thus (HAH, I, 27). The new age of science, which captures the world from a non-evaluative standpoint, he argues, reveals that our perspectivally informed evaluative judgements (HAH, I, 34, 371) do not correspond to the empirical world. Objective knowledge thus entails the recognition that the empirical world is devoid of value and consequently that human values are in essence subject-dependent rather than real properties of the world (HAH, I, 29). Accordingly, Nietzsche presupposes the possibility of distinguishing between truth and illusion – and, hence, science and genuine invention – from within the empirical world as it shows up for us.[19] Consequently, illusion is a property not of the empirical world but of artistic inventions and, by analogy, our values. He writes that

---

[19] According to Nietzsche, although science works with 'errors', these errors are heuristic maxims only, and are abandoned if shown to be incompatible with the findings of empirical investigation (HAH, I, 19). Scientific, unlike evaluative, discourse, therefore, is 'capable of detaching us from this ideational world – and, for brief periods, at any rate, lift us up out of the entire proceeding' (HAH, I, 16). The reason for this is that science is governed by the intellect, whilst evaluation is dominated by the will. See HAH, I, 29 for Nietzsche's view that science gives us theoretical knowledge of the 'true nature of the world', which can be distinguished from the 'practical' concerns of evaluative discourse. Clark is sensitive to Nietzsche's view that science gives us the truth about the empirical world and that values are errors in HAH when she writes:

> In *Human, All Too Human*, Nietzsche seems to accept a particular version of anti-realism, namely, an 'error theory' of value; for he dubs the coloured world of our concerns 'the world of representation (as error)'. He thus divides Schopenhauer's world as representation into two aspects: first, the empirical world disclosed by science, which *may* be only appearance of the thing in itself but can still be treated as 'true nature of the world' because it is the only world of any *cognitive* or theoretical interest to us, and then the world of our practical concerns, which Nietzsche treats as the world of appearance in the sense of 'error'. (Maudemarie Clark, 'On Knowledge, Truth and Value: Nietzsche's Debt to Schopenhauer and the Development of His Empiricism' in Christopher Janaway (ed.), *Willing and Nothingness: Schopenhauer as Nietzsche's Educator* (Oxford: Clarendon Press, 1998), pp. 37–78, p. 54.)

> ... supposing our visible world were only appearance, as the metaphysicians assume, then art would come to stand quite close to the real world, for there would then be only too much similarity between the world of appearance and the illusory world of the artist (*der Traumbild-Welt des Künstlers*); and the difference remaining would even elevate the significance of art above the significance of nature. – These presuppositions are, however, false ... (HAH, I, 222)

The human subject is a creative one, but the empirical world is no longer one of its creations. The empirical world, therefore, is no longer genuinely illusory.[20] The naturalistic human subject continues to engage in pure aesthetic activity, but its products and projects, although expressing in symbolic form an interpretation of the world, nonetheless can be sharply demarcated from the empirically real.[21]

From the early writings and through his later ones, Nietzsche contends that illusion is the defining characteristic of genuine artistic creations.[22]

---

[20] It might be objected, however, that Nietzsche does not allow for the distinction between semblance and nature and that he incorporates what we call empirical reality or nature within the sphere of semblance even in the later writings. Proponents of this view might appeal to GS, 54 for support where Nietzsche denies that there is any essence beyond semblance. Robert Rethy makes such an argument, maintaining that the reason that Nietzsche talks about illusion (*Schein*) rather than Kantian appearances (*Erscheinung*) is because he is aware of Kant's claim that appearances imply a thing-in-itself or essence beyond and independent of the appearance. (See '*Schein* in Nietzsche's Philosophy' in Keith Ansell-Pearson (ed.), *Nietzsche and Modern German Thought* (London: Routledge, 1991), pp. 59–87.) That Nietzsche puts a lot of emphasis on the language of semblance despite his awareness that once he gives up on the idea of a 'true' world there is no longer any justifiable grounds for describing the empirical world as an illusion can be explained, however, not as a refusal to distinguish between illusion and truth within the world as it shows up for us but rather as a refusal to countenance the need to go beyond the world as it shows up for us to make this distinction.

[21] This argument is not restricted to HAH. Rather, the distinction between mind-dependent illusions and empirical reality also follows from his rejection of idealism. For example, Nietzsche's argument in BGE that idealism and naturalism are incompatible (BGE, 15) results in the view that philosophical coherency on the issue of the relation between mind and world requires a clear demarcation between mind-independent reality and creations of the mind. Clearly, artistic illusions need not be mind-dependent. But Nietzsche seems to include mind-dependent objects in the category of the illusory as a result of his Schopenhauerian-inspired interpretation of Kant and his own earlier commitment to Kant's idealism thus understood.

[22] For a discussion of this understanding of art in a non-Nietzschean context, see Friedrich F. Schiller, *On the Aesthetic Education of Man*, trans. Reginald Snell (New York, NY: Dover Books, 2004), Letters 26–27. See also Susanne K. Langer, *Feeling and Form* (London: Routledge and Kegan Paul, 1979), Chapter Four. Of course, Nietzsche saw himself as offering a very different account of art to that of the 'disinterested' aesthetics of Kant and Schiller. This is arguably because, interpreting Kant through Schopenhauer, Nietzsche failed to realize that by disinterest Kant meant that we appreciate a work of art independently of whether the object actually exists (Immanuel Kant, *Critique of Judgment*, trans. Werner S. Pluhar (Cambridge: Hackett Publishing, 1987, section 5) and instead understood it as entailing a suspension of the will (GM, III, 6). Contrary to 'Kant's' and Schopenhauer's view, Nietzsche argues that art is a form of evaluation and appraisal (TI, 'Reconnaissance Raids', 24). Nevertheless, to the extent that Nietzsche emphasizes the need to

This claim takes on a particular resonance, however, once he abandons the view that the empirical world is a mind-dependent creation. Although he does not explicitly state it, it follows from his prising apart of empirical reality from illusion that artistic illusion must have distinct ontological features that obviously demarcate it from empirical reality and its constraints. Nietzsche describes the genuinely inventive as having such distinct features. As can be discerned from his criticism of realist aims in art,[23] the genuinely inventive does not mirror and has no direct causal relationship with the world but rather, as Nietzsche terms it, the genuinely inventive 'transfigures' without constituting empirical reality.[24] The visual artist might do this, for example, by presenting objects in unusual spatio-temporal configurations. For instance, a visual image might present two objects as spatially contiguous when in reality the objects share a rather different spatial relation. Similarly, the image might present two temporally distinct and heterogeneous events as coincident. This describes how visual art is illusory but Nietzsche claims that music, as an art form, is also illusory.[25] This illusory character can be appreciated if we consider that

distinguish between empirical reality and illusion his account inadvertently shares similarities with Kant and Schiller. See Matthew Rampley, *Nietzsche, Aesthetics and Modernity* (Cambridge: Cambridge University Press, 2000), pp. 177–206 for a useful account of the historical context in which Nietzsche formulates his criticisms of Kant. My interpretation here differs from Rampley's, which sees the role of art as world-constituting throughout Nietzsche's writings (ibid., p. 181). For discussion of the issues of art and illusion in a specifically Nietzschean context, see Alexander Nehamas, *Nietzsche: Life as Literature* (Cambridge, MA: Harvard University Press, 1990) and Aaron Ridley, 'Perishing of the Truth: Nietzsche's Aesthetic Prophylactics', *British Journal of Aesthetics*, 50.1, 2010, pp. 427–437.

[23] See GS, 'Joke, Cunning and Revenge', 55. For a discussion of his criticism of realism in art, see Rampley, *Nietzsche, Aesthetics and Modernity*, pp. 201–204.

[24] The reason for this, it seems to me, is to emphasize the 'artificial' character of invention (GS, Preface 2nd ed., 4, GS, 80, GS, 107), which demarcates it from empirical reality. In BT, Nietzsche draws our attention to the illusory – Apolline – character of Raphael's *Transfiguration of Christ*. In this painting Raphael portrays two successive biblical scenes synchronically. Nietzsche's description of the painting as illusory here, however, is complicated by his dubious metaphysical claim that it is a semblance of a semblance because the empirical world is a projection of a Dionysian world-artist (BT, pp. 25–26, section 4). Nonetheless, we can still extract an important point about the illusory character of the painting. The painting is illusory as a result of its defiance of and freedom from actuality. Such defiance and freedom is evident in the manner in which this Classical painting juxtaposes time and place and is causally unconstrained by the time and place of actual events (BT, p. 26, section 4). See Gary Shapiro, 'This Is Not a Christ: Nietzsche, Foucault and the Genealogy of Vision' in Alan D. Schrift (ed.), *Why Nietzsche Still? Reflections on Drama, Culture and Politics* (Berkeley, CA: University of California Press, 2000), pp. 79–98 for a discussion of Nietzsche's reference to Raphael's painting.

[25] In BT, for example, this claim is informed by a Romantically inspired metaphysics. Describing the ontological status of Dionysian art as a semblance (*Schein*) that is projected by a Dionysian world-artist, he contends that music is only once removed from metaphysical reality whereas Apolline art forms, as a result of their distinct visual and spatial character, are twice removed, rendering their ontological status a semblance of a semblance (*Schein des Scheins*) (BT, pp. 25–26, section 4). In the

music is even freer from the constraints of the empirically real than visual art. For in music we do not recognize references to the spatially actual at all. However, it is arguably the case that all genuine art forms are illusory images that are divorced from the real. Even realist literature that tells us something about reality does so from a particular point of view that gives unity to the narrative but is at a 'distance' from reality (GS, 107).[26]

It is this emphasis on the illusory character of artistic invention that allows Nietzsche to clearly demarcate artistic invention from scientific discovery and truth. Nietzsche did not distinguish between scientific knowledge and illusion in TL because, as a result of the constitutive and impositionist account of mind presupposed in that essay, both nature and human attempts at knowing it were enveloped within the sphere of illusion. However, the non-idealist argument put forward in HAH relies upon a meaningful distinction between artistic illusion and scientific knowledge. Nietzsche still holds that objectivity entails correspondence to the world, but as a result of the distinction between artistic illusion and scientific knowledge made in the book, the world is now identified with empirical reality rather than a non-empirical thing-in-itself, and it is knowable through the empirical methods of the natural sciences.

Nietzsche develops his philosophy of value in HAH within the parameters of these oppositional notions of scientific knowledge and artistic illusion. The illusory status of our values stems from his juxtaposition of evaluative inventions to scientific accounts of the empirical world, which he takes to be untainted by subjective preference or volition. He describes the metaphysical status of values analogously to secondary qualities such as colour and taste when he juxtaposes what he calls 'sensations of value' with the quantitative character of 'scientific' objective knowledge (HAH, I, 16). Nietzsche clearly thinks of these sensations as mind-dependent experiences. Although mind-dependency is not necessarily synonymous with illusion, Nietzsche tends to describe the mind-dependent as illusory as a result of his earlier practice of treating them as identical in the context of philosophical idealism. Besides their mind-dependent status, the illusory character of secondary qualities, for

context of the particular metaphysics put forward in BT, music is closer to metaphysical reality as a result of its freedom from the spatial form of the Apolline principle of individuation that characterizes empirical reality. However, Nietzsche's point about the ontology of music, that it is an illusion (*Schein*), can be upheld independently of the particular metaphysics of BT. Abstracting from this metaphysics and identifying reality with the empirically – spatially – real, we can still give credence to the view that music is illusory.

[26] For a discussion of the ontology of art and the manner in which images are 'distanced' from reality, see Paul Crowther, *Defining Art, Creating the Cannon: Artistic Value in an Era of Doubt* (Oxford: Clarendon Press, 2011), p. 86.

Nietzsche, can be discerned by the fact that unlike primary qualities, secondary qualities are neither in the object nor resemble the empirical object.[27] He contends that evaluative judgements are characterized by a particular phenomenological or affective quality, being experienced as states of favour or disfavour. As a result, our evaluative judgements must fail to correspond to the empirical world (WP, 565 KSA 12: 6 [14]). Our values fail the test of objectivity, according to Nietzsche, because although there is a world that corresponds to empirical scientific description, there is no world that corresponds to human value. Consequently, he describes the Nihilist as 'a man who judges of the world as it is that it ought not to be, and of the world as it ought to be that it does not exist' (WP, 585A KSA 12: 9 [60]). The reason that the Nihilist judges in this way is because he holds to the view that the value properties that we attribute to the world are not real properties but rather anthropocentric projections onto the world. In HAH, Nietzsche endorses this nihilistic conclusion. Similarly to Hume who writes, for example, that '[v]ice and virtue therefore may be compared to sounds, colours, heat and cold, which, according to the modern philosophy are not qualities in the object but perceptions in the mind'[28], Nietzsche describes value in terms of projection. He writes:

> Because we have for millennia made moral, aesthetic, religious demands on the world, looked upon it with blind desire, passion or fear, and abandoned ourselves to the bad habits of illogical thinking, this world has gradually *become* so marvellously variegated, frightful, meaningful, soulful, it has acquired colour – but we have been the colourists: it is the human intellect that has made appearance appear and transported its erroneous basic conceptions into things. (HAH, I, 16)

He also articulates such a view in *Daybreak* when he writes:

> We have thought the matter over and finally decided that there is nothing good, nothing beautiful, nothing sublime, nothing evil in itself, but that there are states of soul in which we impose such words upon things external to and within us. (D, 210)[29]

---

[27] Nietzsche seems to accept the Humean view of secondary qualities as in the mind rather than the Lockean view of secondary qualities as powers in the object. For Locke, such qualities are powers in the object to induce sensations in human perceivers. For Hume, however, the irreducibly phenomenal character of secondary qualities precludes their identification with non-phenomenal properties such as powers. John Locke, *An Essay Concerning Human Understanding*, ed. P. H. Nidditch (Oxford: Oxford University Press, 1975), Chapter VIII, paragraph 10; David Hume, *A Treatise of Human Nature*, ed. L. A. Selby-Bigge, revised by P. H. Nidditch (Oxford: Clarendon Press, 1989, p. 469).

[28] Ibid.

[29] Cf. GS, 301; HAH, I, 1; WP, 12 KSA 13: 11 [99]; WP, 260 KSA 10: 24 [15]; D, 3, 35.

As we have seen previously, the nihilistic conclusion that values do not reside in the world gives rise to an existential dilemma that requires a practical response. The dilemma in HAH hinges on the difficulty of operating with meaningful values given the revelations of scientific analysis (HAH, I, 6, 7). This practical difficulty centres round how we can continue to be motivated by values that are known to be ontologically unreal and that fail to represent the world truthfully. Unlike his argument in TL, Nietzsche cannot now draw on the resources of philosophical idealism to undermine the threat that scientific knowledge poses to the meaningfulness and motivational efficacy of our values. Rather, the contrast between scientific truth and the ontological irreality of our values brings us to the heart of value fictionalism in HAH and also to its ultimate failure as an adequate response to the problem of nihilism.

Nietzsche's fictionalist response in HAH is grounded in the analogy that he draws between artistic illusions and the ontological status of our values. The proposal entails arguing that value, like art, wears its illusory status on its sleeve. However, the analogy between value and art can successfully respond to the existential dilemma raised in HAH only if values have the power to motivate us. Thus, value fictionalism can succeed if we can respond affirmatively to Nietzsche's question 'whether one *could* consciously reside in untruth?' (HAH, I, 34). This question has been an issue of considerable debate amongst Nietzsche's interpreters and the character of the debate is instructive in terms of drawing out the reasons that might support but ultimately detract from any attempt to secure the motivational efficacy of our values on the basis of an analogy between value and artistic illusion. Since Nietzsche's arguments for and against adopting an affirmative answer to his question are a little sketchy, it makes sense to supplement our discussion of his text with a consideration of the more detailed arguments offered by his interpreters, which include both defenders and objectors to the cogency of his value fictionalism as a practical response to the threat to the meaningfulness and motivational efficacy of our values posed by nihilism.

One of the most notable of the affirmative answers to the question of whether we could consciously reside in untruth is that offered by Nadeem Hussain, who likens the motivational capacity of evaluative illusions to the phenomenology of art in his defence of Nietzsche's proposal of value fictionalism. With regard to the phenomenology of art, Hussain claims that art presents its illusions as illusions without undermining their illusory status. He writes:

For example, we see a water jug in a painting. We are aware that before us there is only oil paint on canvas. We can come to know that, say, the precision of the illusion – the way the water jug seems to nestle into the carpet resting on the table – is created by a technique of colouring that when viewed up close presents an image that is out of focus when we step back. We can see the illusion even while knowing that it is an illusion.[30]

However, although Hussain arguably captures the phenomenology of painting in the preceding description, it is not clear how values understood similarly could motivate. That they cannot becomes apparent when, subject to examination, it turns out that Hussain's argument secures the motivational power of value illusions only by altering the initial terms and conditions of the analogy of artistic illusion with the ontology of value itself. Hussain departs from the terms and conditions of the analogy when he contends that value illusions can motivate us to act only by disguising their illusory status and pretending that they are true. He writes:

It can be thought of as a form of make-believe, pretending, or, the non-Nietzschean phrase adopted here, 'regarding – as': S values X by regarding X as valuable in itself while knowing that in fact X is not valuable in itself.[31]

As Alan Thomas has pointed out, the disanalogy between value and artistic illusion that creeps into Hussain's argument pertains to his appeal to the role of error and false belief when accounting for the motivational role of our values. According to Hussain, we have to make-believe that our evaluative fictions are true in order to be motivated to act in accordance with them. But make-believe, as Hussain appeals to it, collapses into delusion and is not the same as perceiving something to be an illusion. Thomas alerts us to the ambiguity in Hussain's argument by appealing to Wollheim's notion of twofoldness. Twofoldness, according to Wollheim, captures the 'phenomenological fact that one can simultaneously see the peasant's shoes in a van Gogh painting while being reflectively aware that one is perceiving a marked surface'.[32] Whilst the notion of twofoldness, according to Thomas, works for illusion, it does not work for Hussain's conception of make-believe. This is because in the phenomenological experience that Wollheim describes as twofoldness, there is no false belief. But what Hussain describes as value fictionalism delivers not illusion but delusion. The disanalogy between aesthetic experience and value is evident in the fact that aesthetic experience does not involve belief and that there is, accordingly, nothing to be honest

---

[30] Hussain, 'Honest Illusion: Valuing for Nietzsche's Free Spirits', p. 169.   [31] Ibid., p. 161.
[32] Alan Thomas, 'Nietzsche and Moral Fictionalism' in *Nietzsche, Naturalism and Normativity*, pp. 133–159, p. 137.

about. Honesty must be directed to a truth-apt content such that one is honest about the truth of that content. But Hussain's fictionalism does not support the idea that honesty is directed to a truth-apt content but only that it is directed to our commitment itself rather than to the content of our commitment. That is, 'the fictionalist stance of entertaining an honest illusion does not take as its object the content itself, but, rather, the attitude in which the content is embedded'.[33] Although Hussain contends that fictionalism involves an 'attitude other than belief towards the same content'[34] and although he distinguishes between entertaining a thought in the spirit of assertion and entertaining a thought in the spirit of pretence,[35] it remains the case, as Thomas argues, that 'this does not identify the intentional content that is the object of one's honesty in the case of an honest illusion. Honesty is towards one's performance, not the thought contents that one entertains as a result of that performance'.[36] As a result, if we accept Hussain's fictionalism, it turns out that we are not being honest about the truth-apt content of our value statements. Rather, we are making-believe that something that is false is true. This is not honest illusion but delusion.

Still, Bernard Reginster offers an argument in defence of the appeal to the motivational power of make-believe that, he claims, upholds the self-proclaimed fictional and hence illusory status of our values. If successful, Reginster's account serves to save Hussain's argument from Thomas's objections.[37] To succeed, the argument must uphold Nietzsche's analogy between values and illusion whilst also allowing that value illusions can motivate and act as a practical antidote to the existential dilemma posed by nihilism. Focussing on what is required to imagine in a belief-like way, Reginster contends that it is possible to act as if one's imaginings are true without actually believing that they are. To demonstrate the plausibility of the motivational capacity of illusions, we are asked to consider a child at play. The child make-believes in the context of a game that he is a Trojan warrior and is motivated to act in accordance with this make-believe whilst knowing that he is not in fact a Trojan warrior. Although this argument has some merit when applied to self-consciously created games, it is arguably more difficult to apply it outside of such contexts. This is because although the child is motivated by the fictional belief within the parameters of the game, it would be a far more challenging task to live one's life this way. Within the boundaries of the game the child is unconstrained by

---

[33] Ibid., p. 138.   [34] Ibid., Hussain cited by Thomas.
[35] Ibid., Hussain citing David Hill in Thomas.   [36] Ibid., pp. 138–139.
[37] Reginster sees Nietzsche as offering both subjectivist and fictionalist responses to nihilism. For his discussion of the former, see *The Affirmation of Life*, pp. 69–85.

reality and so can act heroically and defeat his fictional enemies, but life presents the child with real obstacles that resist the realization of imaginary ideals. For example, the child lacks sufficient physical strength to defeat strong enemies, and even if the child were sufficiently strong, these enemies don't actually exist. Such factors resist the child's aim to be the hero of his dreams in the real rather than the purely imaginary world. These resistances become obstacles rather than stimulants to heroic action in cases where the child lacks the requisite capacity to overcome them. This doesn't matter too much within the context of the game, but outside the game we want objective reasons to assure us that at least some of our ideals are realizable and not mere imaginings.

Thomas also alerts us to the problem of the 'interpenetration'[38] of the actual and fictional worlds for value fictionalism by challenging the feasibility of fictional moral truths that 'are generated by games of prop-oriented make-believe, such that we can interpret fictional truth as truth in a fictional world'.[39] Truth in a fictional world relativizes the concept of truth to the fictional world such that the sentence 'Sherlock Holmes keeps his tobacco in a Persian slipper' is true in the fictional world of Sherlock Holmes but not true or taken to be true in the actual world. Fictionalism might work in this sense if the fiction can be allowed to float free of the actual world. But it is not clear that all fictions can be allowed to do this on the grounds that we seem 'resistant to fictions in which moral truths are violations of moral truths in the actual world'.[40] For example, we resist statements such as 'In killing her baby, Giselda did the right thing; after all, it was a girl', however fictionally presented.[41] Thus fictionalism confronts the problem of 'imaginative resistance', which means that the 'falsity of this claim in the actual world is such that we are resistant even to setting up a fictional world in which it is true'.[42] Hence, pretending or make-believe is subject to moral appraisal in light of genuine rather than purely fictional beliefs that we hold outside the relativized context of specific fictions.[43] Reginster is aware of the potential difficulty that the interpenetration of the fictional and the actual poses for value fictionalism and articulates the problem in terms of the 'fictionalist's ability to interrupt his engagement in the game of evaluative make-believe' such that it must involve 'the ability to ask whether this is a game worth playing in the first place (and whether, in particular, it warrants curbing the "will to truth" to allow the illusion to

---

[38] Thomas, 'Nietzsche and Moral Fictionalism', p. 146.   [39] Ibid., p. 144.   [40] Ibid., p. 145.
[41] Ibid., Thomas cites Kendall Walton here.   [42] Ibid.   [43] Ibid., p. 147.

persist)'.[44] However, he responds to the problem posed by the question whether I should play the game or not by arguing that since all norms are fictions, then the question of whether we should continue playing by the rules of the game can be answered only from within the context of the game framed by fictional norms. The question of the value of evaluative make-believe can be raised only within the context of the game. Thus, he writes that '[w]e may, within the game, ask *piecemeal* questions about the value of this or that aspect of the game, but we cannot coherently ask the *wholesale* question of whether we should play the game altogether'.[45] However, although it is correct that all value judgements are indexed to particular perspectives or contexts, the reduction of all norms to fictions seems incorrect on the basis that if our commitment to normative fictions is unconditional and cannot be questioned except from within the terms and conditions of the fiction itself, then it seems that we collapse what should be considered make-believe and at a remove from the real into the real, such that our fictional beliefs no longer wear their fictional or illusory status on their sleeves but take on the status of delusions. That this is the case can be discerned if we consider Simon Blackburn's argument that the hallmark of games and fictions is that our commitment to playing them is condi-tional and may, at any time, be overridden by our commitments in the actual world and our genuine rather than fictional beliefs. Blackburn writes that 'the "lusory attitude" of the game player is bound to be one of only conditional commitment: among human beings a game is an activity whose pursuit is set as an option within the background matrix of a life with needs and commitments that may at any time trump it'.[46] Fictions,

---

[44] Reginster, *The Affirmation of Life*, p. 96.   [45] Ibid., p. 97.

[46] Simon Blackburn, 'Perspectives, Fictions, Errors, Play', p. 293. Blackburn has offered his 'quasi-realism' as an alternative to fictionalism. Although Lewis contends that quasi-realism is really fictionalism in disguise (David Lewis, 'Quasi-Realism Is Fictionalism' in Mark Eli Kalderon (ed.), *Fictionalism in Metaphysics* (Oxford: Oxford University Press), pp. 314–321), Blackburn argues otherwise and cautions against identifying conventional constructions, which our values are, with fictions (see Simon Blackburn, 'Perspectives, Fictions, Errors, Play', p. 29; for Blackburn's direct response to Lewis, see 'Quasi-Realism No Fictionalism' in Kalderon, *Fictionalism in Metaphysics*, pp. 322–338). Quasi-realism promises to permit our realist evaluative talk without making a realist ontological commitment. Blackburn's view is, then, an argument in favour of a metaphysically neutral account of objectivity. I do not address it here, however, because Poellner's view, which I shall examine shortly, also offers a metaphysically neutral account of the objectivity of value that incorporates a response to Blackburn's quasi-realism, albeit from a phenomenological perspective (for Poellner's qualified endorsement of Blackburn, see Poellner, 'Affect, Value and Objectivity' in Leiter and Sinhababu, *Nietzsche and Morality*, pp. 227–261, p. 253). Since Poellner's argument responds directly to the issue of our phenomenological experience of value, I confine my analysis to Poellner's argument and take the conclusions to apply generally to metaphysically neutral arguments.

however internally coherent, cannot float free of the actual world but are, rather, parasitic on that world. To see that this is the case with Nietzsche's fictionalism and that it ultimately undermines the feasibility of value fictionalism as a response to the problem of nihilism, we can consider that the policy of making believe that things in the world are really valuable when we know that they are not wouldn't matter, as it doesn't in TL, if there was nothing to contrast the illusion with. But, in HAH, our values are contrasted with genuine scientific knowledge of the world. Unlike the argument in TL our evaluative illusions are not practically real. Nietzsche tells us that our values can be taken to be practically real only if we refuse to acknowledge anything 'outside' ourselves with which to contrast our values (HAH, I, 33). If we could engage in such a refusal then we could possibly believe in a dream 'as though it were reality' (HAH, I, 13). But this is tantamount to forgetting that our beliefs are false or else being deceived into thinking that they are true and is rather different from what is meant by an honest illusion.[47] Consequently, if values are to motivate within the context of a dichotomous relationship between value and science for Nietzsche in HAH, then they cannot be openly acknowledged to be illusions. Contrary to Hussain and indeed Reginster, then, the answer to Nietzsche's question whether self-conscious fictions can motivate and act as a practical antidote to the problem of nihilism, must be a negative one.[48]

Although he initially attempts to downplay the significance of the impact of scientific knowledge on our evaluative illusions when he writes that '[r]igorous science is capable of detaching us from this ideational world only to a limited extent – and more is certainly not to be desired – inasmuch as it is incapable of making any essential inroad into the power of habits of feeling acquired in primeval times' (HAH, I, 17), Nietzsche ultimately concedes that the knowledge that science affords will make it impossible for us to be motivated by ideals and values that we know to be illusory. He writes: 'The whole of life is sunk deeply in untruth; the individual cannot draw it up out of this well without thereby growing profoundly disillusioned about his own past, *without finding his present motives, such as that of honour, absurd, and pouring mockery and contempt on*

---

[47] Nietzsche is aware of this tension from his earliest writings. At KSA 7: 29 [17] he entertains the idea that honest illusions cannot motivate the will and considers that only deception (*Verstellung*) (TL, 2, pp. 90–91 KSA1, p. 889) or forgetfulness (*Vergesslichkeit*) (TL, 1, pp. 81, KSA 1, p. 878) can offer a solution to the motivational problem. In his later writings, Nietzsche emphasizes the importance of forgetting (GM, II, 1).

[48] For an account of some of the problems that arise from believing in fictions, see Joyce, *The Myth of Morality*, pp. 234–235.

the passions which reach out to the future and promise happiness in it (HAH, I, 34 my emphasis). Nietzsche's only solution to the failure of the motivational power of values as illusions in HAH is to appeal to a state of mind reminiscent of Schopenhauer's description of aesthetic experience that refrains from making value judgements by merely 'gazing contentedly' at the phenomenon of life (HAH, I, 34). But this response is also unsatisfactory. This is because evaluation, as Nietzsche concedes in his later 1886 preface to the book, is 'inseparable from life' (HAH, I, P: 6). Symbolic forms and value, according to Nietzsche, are intrinsic to human culture and define our activity as human animals (HAH, I, 16, 22).[49]

The reason why fictionalism ultimately fails is because the analogy that Nietzsche draws between the ontology of values and that of artistic illusions doesn't work as an antidote to the existential dilemma posed by the separation of the world of scientific facts from that of values. The reason that the analogy doesn't work and why Hussain, for example, must appeal to delusion is that the phenomenology of value is rather different from the phenomenology of illusion. As in the case of Wollheim, we can experience a painting whilst simultaneously knowing the image projected by it to be an illusion. However, we do not experience values to be illusions. Yet the terms and conditions of the fictionalist account make it difficult for us to appeal to delusions. This is because fictionalism, for Nietzsche, is premised on the dichotomy between that which we know about the empirical world through investigation in the natural sciences and what we need to be the case in terms of our values. This dichotomy makes it very difficult to be deluded in the sense of adopting and acting on false beliefs about the ontological irreality of our values. As indicated earlier, I described Nietzsche's positions in TL and HAH as fictionalism because he claims that our values are illusions and that, although illusions are false to the extent that they are contrasted with what we know about mind-independent reality and to the extent that they are set up in opposition to it, they can nonetheless still be practically useful. The cogency of the latter part of Nietzsche's claim has been called into question, but it could be suggested that his analogy of values with illusions is still viable and capable of acting as a practical antidote to the nihilistic challenge to the meaningfulness and

---

[49] I am not suggesting that this problem is raised only in HAH. As Nietzsche makes clear in GS, 110, for example, the tension between life and knowledge defines the predicament of modernity. However, the difficulty is particularly acute in HAH as it follows from presuppositions that Nietzsche makes in this text, which are not in evidence in other texts to the same degree. For example, in HAH, Nietzsche sharply demarcates the objectivity of science from the non-objectivity of evaluative discourse. In contrast, in GS, 335, he argues that knowledge of physics is a precondition for the creation of value.

motivational efficacy of metaphysically unsupported values. That is, it might be argued that the analogy between values and illusions, contrary to Nietzsche's fictionalism, does not invite a contrast with mind-independent reality such that value illusions should not be considered to be beliefs, whether true, false or merely simulated, but rather they should be considered as non-cognitive attitudes instead. This, it might be further argued, fits better with what it means to be an illusion on the grounds that illusions are ontologically distinct from the real and cannot, for precisely this reason, be contrasted with it. Moreover, it will be contended from some quarters that better success can be had in responding to the nihilistic challenge by identifying our values with these non-cognitive attitudes. What is required to address the problem of the metaphysical irreality of our values informing the existential crisis of nihilism, according to such a view, is to induce an alteration in our attitudes. However, an analysis of such a non-cognitivist response in the next section will show that it also fails to offer an adequate practical solution to the problem of nihilism and that the reason it fails is because it succumbs to the same separation of our values from the world that plagues fictionalism and that runs counter to how we phenomenologically experience value. Although a reconfiguration of non-cognitivism aimed at saving the phenomenology of value by proposing a metaphysically neutral account of the objectivity of our values will then be considered, it too will be found wanting. Critical reflection on the non-cognitivist account and its metaphysically neutral objectivist reconfiguration will bring our overall negative task in this chapter to a close by revealing the ultimate untenability of value non-objectivism and of any alternative objectivist account of value that seeks to divorce the 'inner' sphere of values from the 'outer' world as a response to the problem of nihilism.

Non-Cognitivism and Phenomenal Objectivity

The non-cognitivist, unlike the fictionalist, interpretation of Nietzsche on value denies that our values should be contrasted with mind-independent reality and instead holds that our values are expressions of emotional attitudes that are neither true nor false. There have been some attempts to interpret Nietzsche along these lines as a result of his tendency to discuss values in terms of affect and in the Humean language of projection.[50] The

---

[50] See, for example, Maudemarie Clark and David Dudrick, 'Nietzsche and Moral Objectivity': The Development of Nietzsche's Metaethics' in Brian Leiter and Neil Sinhababu (eds.), *Nietzsche and Morality*, pp. 192–226, pp. 203–204. However, Clark and Dudrick's account succumbs to the same problems as traditional non-cognitivism, which I will discuss in relation to Wiggins later. See also

alignment of Nietzsche's arguments with Hume is not obviously an argument in support of non-cognitivism, as Hume has been interpreted as both a cognitivist and a non-cognitivist and, nonetheless, we saw in the previous section that Nietzsche's appeal to Humean projectionism can be interpreted in fictionalist terms.[51] Moreover, to attribute a role to emotion is not necessarily a non-cognitivist thesis.[52] Nevertheless, as I remarked from the outset, Nietzsche blurs the distinctions between what goes by the names of fictionalism and non-cognitivism in contemporary meta-ethics and he does so on the basis that his real concern is with the ontological irreality and mind-dependency of our values. This blurring of the division is evident in his description of our values as illusions which are false because they do not capture the character of mind-independent reality but which can also be construed non-cognitively on the grounds that illusions can be demarcated from the real and do not represent it, either truthfully or falsely, at all. The non-cognitive aspect of illusion is arguably lost in the problem with make-believe encountered by the fictionalist.[53] Since Nietzsche blurs the boundaries between fictionalism and non-cognitivism and since there is a lack of consensus in the literature about whether he should be interpreted in terms of one or the other, I want to focus on the philosophical issue of whether non-cognitivism can act as a viable alternative to fictionalism by providing Nietzsche with a suitable response to the problem of nihilism rather than the textual issue of whether Nietzsche *really* is a non-cognitivist.

In order to assess the fate of non-cognitivism as a possible practical response to the problem of nihilism, I want to look beyond the immediate confines of Nietzsche's text to a diagnosis put forward by David Wiggins's assessment of Richard Taylor's response to the myth of Sisyphus as a test about the objective meaningfulness of life. Taylor highlights two possible responses to Sisyphus's plight of repeatedly rolling rocks up the hill only for them to roll down again, responses which reflect the predicament of

Nadeem J. Z. Hussain, 'Nietzsche and Non-Cognitivism', pp. 111–132 for criticisms of Clark and Dudrick's argument.

[51] For a discussion of cognitivism and non-cognitivism in Hume, see, for example, Nicholas L. Sturgeon, 'Hume's Metaethics: Is Hume a Moral Noncognitivist?' in Elizabeth S. Radcliffe, *A Companion to Hume* (Oxford: Blackwell, 2008), pp. 513–528.

[52] For an argument in favour of a cognitivist account of emotion, see Martha Nussbaum, *Upheavals of Thought: The Intelligence of Emotions* (Cambridge: Cambridge University Press, 2003).

[53] Unless, of course, we interpret the phenomenon of make-believe non-cognitively rather than in terms of delusion. See, for example, Joyce, *The Myth of Morality*, pp. 195–202. However, as we have seen, there is a tension in Nietzsche's writings between illusion and delusion and whether the former can be properly said to motivate that counts against adopting Joyce's view in relation to Nietzsche. See, for example, KSA 7: 29 [17]; HAH, I, 34.

Nietzsche's Nihilist, who, confronted with the dissolution of another-worldly metaphysical purpose to things, judges of the empirical world and our engagement with it that it is objectively meaningless and devoid of value. Taylor's responses are intended to show that the meaning of life has its origin within us and is not conferred from without. Wiggins's assessment of Taylor's responses, however, serves to highlight how, when one engages in a dichotomy between outer and inner points of view, our account of value must ultimately fall short of how we actually experience it in phenomenological terms.

Taylor's first response to Sisyphus's predicament attempts to point to an objective criterion of value by claiming that if the stones were assembled as an enduring monument at the top of the hill, then Sisyphus's efforts could be deemed objectively meaningful. However, Taylor argues that although a lasting end or *telos* could constitute a purpose for the work, there is in fact, as Nietzsche's Nihilist knows only too well, no permanence (HAH, I, 22) and, even if such permanence were to be a conceivable possibility, Taylor maintains that its point would be 'effectively negated by boredom with the outcome of the work'.[54] According to Taylor, although we have created a meaning for Sisyphus's prodigious labour, the first response falters because it leaves the significance of the human will, the inner point of view, out of account. Consequently, Taylor considers a second response to Sisyphus's plight intended to show that meaning emanates from within rather than from without and that fully acknowledges the centrality of the will in relation to questions of value and meaning. That is, Taylor asks us to imagine that the Gods, as an act of mercy, inject into Sisyphus's veins a substance that influences his character and drives such that Sisyphus is impelled or wants to roll stones. Taylor finds this response more satisfactory, maintaining that the source of value resides in the activity of our wills and emanates from within. He writes that '[t]he meaning of life is from within us, it is not bestowed from without, and it far exceeds in its beauty and permanence any heaven of which men have ever dreamed or yearned for'.[55]

Rather than offering a viable alternative to the failure of Nietzsche's fictionalism, however, Taylor's response is ultimately unsatisfactory. As Wiggins remarks, the promotion of something like Sisyphus's evaluative state as a response to nihilism leaves us in the position where 'the inner view

---

[54] David Wiggins, 'Truth, Invention and the Meaning of Life' in *Needs, Values, Truth* (Oxford: Clarendon Press, 1998), pp. 87–138, p. 94.
[55] Taylor, cited by Wiggins, 'Truth, Invention and the Meaning of Life', p. 95.

has to be unaware of the outer one, and has to enjoy essentially illusory notions of objectivity, importance and significance'.[56] In addition to calling into question the practical realizability of such responses, this is not how we phenomenologically experience evaluative mental states. Wiggins writes:

> To see itself and its object in the alien manner of the outer view, the state as experienced would have to be prepared to suppose that it, the state, could just as well have lighted on any other object (even any other kind of object), provided only that the requisite attitudes could have been induced. But in this conception of such states we are entitled to complain that nothing remains that we can recognize, or that the inner perspective will not instantly disown.[57]

According to Wiggins, '[w]here the non-cognitive account essentially depends on the existence and availability of the inner view, it is a question of capital importance whether the non-cognitivist's account of the inner view makes such sense of our condition as it actually has for us from the inside'.[58] The phenomenology of value is such that values are not experienced by us as being contingent on our merely subjective desires, wishes or preferences.[59] By experiencing values as being more than subjective and contingent, we experience them as being subject to constraint from outside such that the inner sphere of our evaluative experience is not cut off from the outer world. That is, our reasons for commending or pursuing one thing over another or acting in one way over another are experienced by us as being subject to constraint in the sense of being merited or unmerited by the objects of our evaluative assessment.[60] Nietzsche concedes Wiggins's view that we phenomenologically experience value as merited and constrained by the world. In his account of value as will to power, he claims that value judgements can be understood in terms of 'feelings' of strength and weakness in the face of the experience of 'resistance' of the world to our evaluative appraisals (AC, 2). Thus, for him, evaluative judgements are not experienced as mere wishful thinking. However, the metaphysical basis to which we hitherto appealed to establish the objectivity of our values and which was thought to support the phenomenological experience of value as subject to constraint by the world is unjustifiable. And our scientific-empirical accounts of the world are equally unable to offer objective

---

[56] Wiggins, 'Truth, Invention and the Meaning of Life', p. 100.   [57] Ibid., p. 105.
[58] Ibid., p. 98.
[59] See J. L. Mackie, *Ethics: Inventing Right and Wrong* (Harmondsworth: Penguin, 1977), p. 33 for the classical account of the erroneous character of the phenomenology of value.
[60] See Wiggins, 'Truth, Invention and the Meaning of Life', pp. 98–99.

support. This is the source of nihilistic disorientation and despair, which, for Nietzsche, is bound up within the schism between how we experience value and its separation from the character of the world (WP, 5 KSA 12: 5 [71]). Nevertheless, as we witnessed in our examination of fictionalism, we must experience our values as objective if they are to be properly motivational. Although the standard non-cognitive account cannot cater for the objectivity of our values, it might be that the standard account can be reconfigured in order to allow for the objectivity of our values without, however, giving them a mind-independent status. Peter Poellner offers an argument in favour of a metaphysically neutral account of objectivity, which is designed to cater for our phenomenological experience of value. Although he doesn't set his argument up as a reconfiguration of standard non-cognitivism as such, Poellner's argument is of interest to us in this context because, like non-cognitivism, it denies that values are beliefs.[61] Although he argues that values are non-doxastic emotional states that influence our beliefs, he also holds, unlike the non-cognitivist, that values and the judgements that they inform can be objective without instantiating value properties mind-independently in the world. Poellner offers a rational reconstruction of Nietzsche's approach to value that both allows for the possibility of genuine scientific knowledge of the empirical world and concedes the Nihilist's claim that values are not in the world.[62] Nevertheless, Nietzsche can, according to Poellner, hold that values can be objective in a very specific sense that Poellner describes as phenomenal objectivity. If successful, Poellner's argument offers a defence of some aspects of value non-cognitivism without succumbing to the problem of the separation of the inner and the outer that Wiggins detects in non-cognitivism generally and which also informs fictionalism. However, Poellner's argument is ultimately unsuccessful and the reason for its lack of success reveals the need for a more metaphysically engaged account of objectivity that manages to provide a metaphysical ground to our values without illegitimately instantiating value properties in the world.

According to Poellner, value judgements or commitments, such as 'x is good' are informed by affective emotional responses to the '*phenomenally intrinsic value features* of things'[63] and these responses are experienced by us as not merely caused by an object but merited by it.[64] Evaluative emotions,

---

[61] Poellner offers his argument as capturing what is right about both Blackburn's non-cognitive projectivism and non-reductionist cognitivism about value such as that found in non-projectivists such as Wiggins, McDowell and Dancy. Peter Poellner, 'Affect, Value and Objectivity', pp. 227–261, p. 228n1.

[62] Ibid., p. 255.   [63] Ibid., p. 246.   [64] Ibid., pp. 231–232.

however, are not mere subjective sensations or feelings, as they are in the Humean account, for example, but rather, as perceptions of value, they are the manner in which we experience objects evaluatively.[65] Values, Poellner contends, can be described as phenomenally objective rather than subjective if they can be re-experienced by oneself and others even though, their experienced affectivity makes them ultimately existentially dependent on human valuers. Accordingly, phenomenal objectivity, does not imply metaphysical reality and Poellner claims that Nietzsche is ultimately indifferent to the metaphysical reality of values:

> What is objective in this sense is what is standardly presented as pertaining to the (everyday, phenomenal) object, just as the visible, phenomenal colour of a table appears as a property of the table itself, and not, for example, as a property of an 'inner sensation'. An item is objective, rather than subjective, in this sense (which I shall label *phenomenal objectivity*) just in case its existence and nature is not so exhausted by any particular experiential state which purports to represent it, and it is available for various numerically distinct experiences of it by oneself and others – ready to be experienced, as it were. – However, the claim that an item is phenomenally objective neither prejudges nor replaces the metaphysical issue of whether it belongs to the ultimate furniture of the universe.[66]

According to Poellner, phenomenal objectivity entails the view that phenomenal properties, such as experiences of colour or value, are features of objects populating our life-world, but they may not be properties of things-in-themselves. Crucially for our concerns in relation to Nietzsche's argument in HAH, Poellner claims that phenomenal properties are not incompatible with scientific properties because the former, he argues, strongly supervene on the latter, allowing for a symmetrical relation of co-variance between the two.[67] Since phenomenal objectivity is metaphysically neutral, he maintains that we do not need to ask why phenomenal properties supervene on physical ones. To do so is to seek, contrary to Nietzsche's aims, a metaphysical answer, which is of purely theoretical interest and which, therefore, makes no practical difference to us. As such, phenomenal objectivity is relative to our intersubjective interests and concerns.[68] Distinguishing between value anti-realism and value anti-objectivism,[69] Poellner's argument and interpretation of Nietzsche capture the phenomenology of value by refusing to engage in the

---

[65] Ibid., p. 243.   [66] Ibid., p. 233.   [67] Ibid., p. 255.

[68] For a similar argument, see Béatrice Han-Pile, 'Transcendental Aspects, Ontological Commitments and Naturalistic Elements in Nietzsche's Thought', *Inquiry*, 52.2, 2009, pp. 179–214.

[69] Peter Poellner, 'Affect, Value and Objectivity', p. 249.

metaphysical contrast between our value experiences and the character of the world.

On the face of it, Poellner's argument gives us what we want. But his metaphysical indifferentism must give us cause for concern. Metaphysical indifferentism is a concern because by endorsing it, Poellner's interpretation perpetuates the distinction between appearance and reality that informs the evaluative crisis of nihilism and that emerges from the realization that our values are divorced from the world. Now, one might argue that my concern in this regard is ill-founded on the basis that Poellner's argument is very similar to the one outlined by Nietzsche in TL and that there illusions could be taken as real for as long as the thing-in-itself could not impact on us in a practical way, with the difference, of course, that, for Poellner, scientific knowledge is possible and that value properties and phenomenal properties, more generally, supervene on the physical properties of things detected by science. However, the problem with Poellner's argument begins to show when he allows that it may happen that our evaluative needs and concerns prove to be incompatible with metaphysical knowledge. Should this happen, he argues, Nietzsche's position is that we should, for purely practical reasons, jettison metaphysical knowledge in favour of our phenomenal experience. The adoption of this strategy is conditional on the metaphysical knowledge making no practical difference to how we can experience and conduct ourselves in evaluative terms.[70] However, contrary to Poellner's claim that Nietzsche's criticisms of the notion of the thing-in-itself pertain only to its practical irrelevance, part and parcel of Nietzsche's argument as to why the thing-in-itself cannot impact on us in this way or indeed in any way is that the thing-in-itself is incoherent in that it can only be defined negatively. That is, it can only be defined in terms that are opposed to how things appear to us, which is, he argues, tantamount to nothing at all (HAH, I, 9; GS, 54; TI, 'Real World'). But it is not such a benign or indeterminate notion of things-in-themselves to which Poellner appeals. Along with knowledge of the intrinsic qualitative character of physical forces and issues about the fundamental mind-dependency or mind-independency of the objects of our experience, Poellner includes the causal efficacy of our phenomenal mental states as metaphysical topics that are of no practical concern to us. He gives the example of knowing through a priori means that conscious phenomenal mental states are not causally efficacious and argues that such theoretical knowledge should leave our phenomenal experience and the theoretical

---

[70] Ibid., p. 258.

presuppositions that inform that experience unaffected even if it means that our phenomenal experience presupposes the causal efficacy of conscious phenomenal mental states. In such cases, our phenomenal experience turns out to be an illusion, but only by virtue of the contrast between our phenomenal experience and our purely theoretical-metaphysical knowledge. Poellner thus writes that '[t]he individual who is not beholden to the will to truth has no significant purely theoretical interests and is consequently indifferent as to whether the life-world which engages her practical concerns is illusory by the lights of a purely theoretical metaphysical inquiry.'[71] However, if it is really, metaphysically, the case that 'the conscious what-it-is-likeness of phenomenal properties is not in any way causally efficacious',[72] then Poellner's argument is tantamount to the claim that we know that these mental states are causally impotent but we nonetheless feel otherwise about the matter because we experience these mental states contrary to the theoretical evidence. Poellner concedes as much when he contends that his account of value is a form of projectivism in a metaphysical sense, though not in a phenomenological sense.[73] Poellner claims that theoretical metaphysical knowledge can impact on our experience only if this knowledge brings a change in our evaluative attitudes or turns out to be ultimately verifiable because capable of predictive success.[74] If our metaphysical knowledge is not verifiable in either of these two senses, then it is of a purely a priori nature and practically irrelevant. But, contrary to Poellner, one might argue that such theoretical knowledge should be employed to *correct* our ways of experiencing. It is to be noted in this regard that correction of our phenomenological experience does not entail the global falsification of that experience. Rather, the possibility of correction serves to connect the character of our phenomenological experience with the character of the world, something that Nietzsche ultimately considers to inform the manner in which we phenomenologically experience value as desire subject to constraint (WP, 333 KSA 12: 7 [15]). Whilst it is true that Nietzsche criticizes the idea of appealing to metaphysical knowledge to correct phenomenal experience in BT (BT, 15), in HAH, as we saw earlier, he concedes that conscious knowledge of the metaphysical irreality of our values must result in us losing confidence in those values. One of the reasons that Poellner can reject the latter claim, however, resides in his taking evaluative emotions to be perceptions rather than beliefs.[75] He appeals to this argument in his explanation of the phenomenon of recalcitrant emotions. The phenomenon of recalcitrant emotions is such that we

[71] Ibid.   [72] Ibid.   [73] Ibid., p. 253.   [74] Ibid., pp. 256–257.   [75] Ibid., p. 240.

can, for example, consciously know that dogs are not dangerous and yet continue to be overcome by fear at the sight of a dog.[76] Poellner's argument that our emotions can be intractable despite the evidence of purely theoretical knowledge reduces our evaluative experience to the status of a neurotic recalcitrant emotion. One might hold that this objection won't stick because our emotional-cum-evaluative responses to or experiences of objects are subject to intersubjective constraint. But this response only secures an argument in favour of global ontological neuroticism rather than an alleviation of the problem. This is because, according to Poellner's argument, evaluative emotions, however intersubjectively verified and re-experientiable, can prove recalcitrant to purely theoretical concerns. We decided to explore Poellner's account of phenomenal objectivity to test its viability as an alternative response to the nihilistic problem of the meaningfulness of metaphysically unsupported values than that offered by Nietzsche's fictionalism and standard non-cognitivist arguments. However, it now transpires that Poellner's argument doesn't actually bring us very far beyond the problems that we encountered with value fictionalism or those that Wiggins detects with non-cognitivism because Poellner's metaphysical indifferentism leaves open the possibility that our values are globally divorced from the world in a metaphysical sense.

Moreover, it is difficult to see how indifferentism can provide a remedy to the problem that the fictionalist encountered when trying to explain how values that we know to be illusory by virtue of a contrast between our value experience and the true character of the world can be motivational. Poellner might respond that his appeal to a perceptual account of evaluative emotions sees those emotions as evaluative ways of seeing or intending objects but not as beliefs. The affective character of our evaluative experience, it might be further argued, facilitates the possibility of such motivation. But in cases where our manner of affectively intending an object or how the object affectively appears to us conflicts with the character of the object itself we find ourselves returning to the problem diagnosed by Wiggins in his response to Taylor's non-cognitivism. That is, it follows from Poellner's argument that our evaluative experience is cut off from the true character of the world rather than from how it appears to us as a result of the constitutive character of our evaluative emotions.

Still, one might contend that Nietzsche is not concerned with giving a metaphysical account of value, that, for him, value is just a

---

[76] For such criticisms of cognitive theories of emotion, see Michael Brady 'The Irrationality of Recalcitrant Emotions', *Philosophical Studies*, 145.3, 2009, pp. 413–430.

phenomenal issue and not a metaphysical one. This is one strategy but, as Nietzsche's account of nihilism shows, the problem of value is rooted in the metaphysical issue of how the human mind relates to the world. Moreover, the very practice of arguing that values are irreducibly phenomenal and not in the world is itself a metaphysical claim that must, if it is to be cogent, be informed by knowledge of the metaphysical character of the world. Poellner's metaphysically indifferentist plea leaves the metaphysical question hanging and simply refuses to answer it.

Nevertheless, Poellner is quite correct about one thing. That is, Nietzsche's philosophical methodology stipulates that the starting point of our investigations must be anthropocentric and perspectival. According to Nietzsche in BGE, for example, psychology is the key to fundamental issues (BGE, 23). However, making human experience our starting point does not mean that we need to take that experience at face value. Contrary to Poellner, once Nietzsche abandons the strictly positivist account of science of HAH, it is not obviously the case that he is a verificationist or that his philosophical method is restricted to describing rather than explaining phenomena. Rather, Nietzsche tells us that invention is a necessary component to finding (BGE, 12). Invention entails making conjectures that go beyond immediate sense-evidence in order to explain that evidence and correct inaccurate phenomenal experience. Thus, in BGE, Nietzsche criticizes the empiricists for taking the senses at face value (BGE, 11, 14, 252) and instead praises Boscovich for having won a 'triumph over the senses' (BGE, 12). We can extend this point to the issue of value by arguing that although our emotions reflect our values, values themselves need not be reduced to our feelings or emotional states.[77] Rather, it might be argued that values reveal something more fundamental about how the human mind relates to the world and can be altered in accordance with that relation.

That Nietzsche thinks that our values can conflict with the character of the world and indeed shed light on that character can be discerned from the following:

> On the other hand, it is only this desire 'thus it ought to be' that has called forth that other desire to know what *is*. For the knowledge of what is, is a consequence of that question: 'How? is it possible? why precisely so?' Wonder at the disagreement between our desires and the course of the

---

[77] See Nietzsche's criticism of the proof from pleasure (AC, 50).

world has led to our learning to know the course of the world. (WP, 333 KSA
12: 7 [15])

Moreover, understanding the true metaphysical character of reality proves
to be of vital importance. For, in the end, the objectivity of our values and
our manner of being in the world evaluatively must reflect the real
character of the world. Nietzsche writes:

> It is at this point and nowhere else that one must make a start if one is to
> understand what Zarathustra's intentions are: the species of man that he
> delineates reality *as it is*, he is not estranged from or entranced by it, he is
> *reality itself*, he still has all that is fearful and questionable in reality in him,
> *only thus can man possess greatness*. (EH, 5 'Destiny')

However, ascertaining that some of our values conflict with the character of
mind-independent reality does not mean that all of our values must be out
of touch with the character of the real. Conversely, the latter values need not
be simply found in or reduced to reality. Still, values cannot be allowed to
float free of the metaphysical character of the world. The phenomenology of
value as Nietzsche construes it does not require us to consider values as
instantiated mind-independently in the world. However, it does require that
our values are not cut off from the world. Poellner's view that values
supervene on physical properties, in the absence of an explanation of their
relationship, runs the risk of floating free of the world.

In the chapters that follow, I will take up the metaphysical question
explicitly and argue that, although he does not attempt it and certainly
doesn't achieve it in either TL or HAH, due to his Kantian constitutive
account of mind in the former text and his appeal to the objectivity of
science over artistic-evaluative illusions in the latter, Nietzsche is ultimately interested in reconnecting the evaluative self with the world.
However, this reconnection does not involve reducing one to the other
in typically idealist or realist fashion but rather it entails arguing for
their metaphysical continuity. Metaphysical continuity has the particular advantage that it does not require that we place values in the world
independently of human beings, but it still allows us to appeal to the
character of the world to determine the objectivity of our values and to
distinguish between veridical and non-veridical values. It is in the latter
sense that the determination of values, for Nietzsche, cannot be metaphysically neutral.

In sum, we have seen that Nietzsche must respond to the problem of
nihilism by establishing the objectivity of our values. Fictionalism does not
work and non-cognitivism, along with its metaphysically neutral

objectivist alternative in the guise of Poellner's appeal to phenomenal objectivity, ultimately proves inadequate. In the next chapter, I will take up the issue of the objectivity of our values and argue that Nietzsche has the requisite conceptual resources at his disposal to establish the objectivity of values and that objectivity as he understands it is a particularly metaphysically laden idea.

CHAPTER 2

Value and Objectivity

Throughout his writings Nietzsche demonstrates an acute awareness of how values permeate, and indeed constitute, the very fabric of the human animal's acculturation into society and how values have the power to elevate and diminish human life. He claims, for example, that Christian values have 'waged war unto death – against the *presupposition* of every elevation, every growth of culture' (A, 43). His awareness of the enhancing and diminishing power of values leads him to distinguish higher forms of human life from lower ones and to commend noble over ignoble ways of living. Employing an optical metaphor to distinguish between values that 'see' matters clearly and those that do not, he describes Christianity as a defect of the eyes (CW, Epilogue) because its value perspective is non-veridical whilst suggesting that the noble's contempt for the psychological phenomenon of *ressentiment* represents the evaluative properties of this mental state correctly (GM, I, 10, 13; cf. GM, III, 14). In GS he writes of 'what really has value' (GS, 99), and his appeal to an aristocratic standard according to which we judge 'every elevation of the type "human being"' (BGE, 257) also appeals to an objective measure of value.

All of this counts against value fictionalism. Yet, as we saw in Chapter 1, there is a strand in Nietzsche's thought that considers our values to be globally in error. He contends that values are errors because they are metaphysically groundless, failing to correspond to a non-empirical sphere of reality or thing-in-itself. However, we noticed that Nietzsche's description of human values as erroneous does not disappear even when he comes to regard the idea of a non-empirical metaphysical reality as cognitively insignificant (HAH, I, 9). When he continues to describe values as errors, he presupposes that the quest for objectivity must still be informed by the metaphysical ideal of correspondence, although now what constitutes correspondence is dressed up in naturalistic clothes. Accordingly, objectivity still entails correspondence to the world, although the world is now identified with empirical reality rather than a non-empirical thing-in-itself.

The non-objective status of our values stems from his juxtaposition of them to scientific accounts of the empirical world, which he takes to be untainted by subjective preference or volition (HAH, I, 34, 371). The subjective character of values, which, he contends, is characterized by a particular phenomenological or affective quality, being experienced as states of favour or disfavour, must, he argues, be erroneous because it fails to correspond to the empirical world or object as it is independently of the human point of view (WP, 565 KSA 12: 6 [14]). Contrasted in this way, objectivity entails adopting an external point of view, which discovers facts whilst subjective properties entail reference to the phenomenological features of human lived evaluative experience. Subjective properties are, accordingly, indexed to the experience of human beings. Consequently, perspectivity, affectivity and relationality are taken to be the markers of subjective properties. To attain an objective stance one must be able to escape all perspectives or points of view. Our values are errors, Nietzsche concludes, because they do not correspond to the world as described by the methods and results of value-neutral empirical science. Yet, despite arguing that it is an error, Nietzsche contends that the phenomenology of value is a necessary error and should be upheld as a necessary existential fiction.

However, although Nietzsche is oftentimes swayed by value fictionalism and argues that the subjective and erroneous status of values should not count against their significance for life, these conclusions do not necessarily follow from his other philosophical commitments, and they do not fit with his presuppositions about the objective status of his own value pronouncements. Rather, value fictionalism follows only if we allow that extra-perspectival knowledge divorced from affect and commendation is possible; that is, if we take correspondence or verisimilitude as our standard of objectivity. However, Nietzsche's perspectivism is compatible with an alternative account of value that although not taking the phenomenology of value at face value nonetheless legitimizes it as an unavoidable investigative starting point of all our inquiries. This alternative account, which I shall reconstruct using the conceptual resources available throughout Nietzsche's writings, entails a re-examination of what constitutes objectivity. An extended examination of his later appeal to the possibility of perspectival objectivity in particular (GM, III, 12) will reveal that objectivity must after all include perspectivity, affectivity and relationality, which, far from divorcing us from empirical objects, marks the seal of our unavoidable engagement with them. Whilst he indicates in his criticism of what he calls the proof from pleasure (TI, 'Errors', 5) that he does not take the phenomenology of value to be beyond criticism or correction, it is ultimately the case for Nietzsche that our evaluative experience of the world can be objective.

In the previous chapter, we encountered debates about whether Nietzsche is a cognitivist or non-cognitivist about value. His claim that our values are fictions suggested the former whilst his emphasis on the role of the affects suggested the latter. However, my argument in favour of the objectivity of value in Nietzsche in this chapter will not be framed in these terms. That is, to argue that Nietzsche offers an alternative to value fictionalism is not to suggest that we should interpret him as a non-cognitivist. This is because the distinction between cognitivism and non-cognitivism is not so much of an issue for him. Rather, according to Nietzsche, value discourse contains cognitive and non-cognitive aspects, which, because they are ultimately different only in degree rather than kind by virtue of their metaphysical continuity, cannot be sharply divided into the cognitive and non-cognitive in the manner of contemporary debates.[1] Rather than being beliefs, on the one hand, or mere attitudes, on the other, values, for Nietzsche, are necessary conditions of the experience of objects for us. The issue of the metaphysical continuity of the components of human cognition and value will be discussed in Chapters 4 and 5, whilst the manner in which values are necessary conditions of our experience of objects and can be objective themselves will be discussed in the current chapter.[2]

Nietzsche's argument in favour of the objectivity of our values begins to take shape when he contends in a manner somewhat reminiscent of TL, but without the idealist backdrop to the argument there, that the methods and results of empirical science are not value neutral. Rather, science is informed by our values. This claim, in turn, undermines the notion of objectivity as correspondence. It also invites us to reconsider the status of empirical science and what constitutes knowledge in the sense that empirical science is ultimately considered to be one perspective amongst others and genuine knowledge involves adopting a comprehensive, explanatory rather than descriptive, perspective. In this way, Nietzsche overcomes the schism between the inner and the outer points of view that plagues

[1] Peter Poellner attempts to bridge the gap between cognitivism and non-cognitivism in his account of the phenomenal objectivity of our values, which we examined in Chapter 1. However, Poellner's argument does not address how the cognitive and non-cognitive components of value judgements are metaphysically continuous. I address this issue in Chapter 4.

[2] Bernard Reginster also argues that perspectives are enabling conditions of experience and evaluation. However, his normative subjectivist interpretation denies that values are objective. In contrast, I argue that Nietzsche offers an alternative account of objectivity to that of correspondence or mind-independent instantiation of value properties in the world. See Bernard Reginster, *The Affirmation of Life: Nietzsche on Overcoming Nihilism* (Cambridge, MA: Harvard University Press, 2006), p. 69.

fictionalism. However, it will be seen that the adoption of a comprehensive perspective, for Nietzsche, is not metaphysically neutral but rather implies a distinct but contentious metaphysics. The argument will be structured in two parts. The first outlines Nietzsche's argument in favour of the objectivity of values, whilst the second addresses his argument in favour of identifying objectivity with a comprehensive and metaphysically laden perspective, in addition to considering and responding to potential objections to this argument.

Value Objectivism

In light of his claim that values define our human cultural practices, it is important for Nietzsche to hold onto the inner perspective of evaluative discourse. However, he needs to find some way of reconciling this inner point of view with the point of view of science that does not succumb to the problem with Poellner's argument that we witnessed in Chapter 1. That is, our phenomenological experience cannot be allowed to float free of the metaphysical character of the world. Whilst Nietzsche has the conceptual resources to achieve this aim, a degree of reconstruction is required to bring them into focus.

The reconstruction brings these resources into focus by demonstrating that Nietzsche is committed to three distinct claims that make objective values possible. First, he rehabilitates the status of values by undermining the opposition set up in HAH between evaluative and scientific discourse. Second, and, as a result, he establishes that values, rather than being disconnected from external reality, are in fact necessary conditions of us knowing reality. By reality I mean real, mind-independent – rather than ideal – empirical objects. Thirdly, Nietzsche shows not just that values are necessary conditions of our cognition of external objects but that we can distinguish between those values that are veridical and those that are non-veridical. The achievement of these aims yields the conclusion that objectivity or veridicality (terms that I shall employ synonymously) does not require correspondence and that relationality, affectivity and perspectivity, the hallmarks of our subjective-phenomenological experience of value, can also be conditions of objectivity.

The first step towards rehabilitating the status of values is achieved by Nietzsche's assessment of the status and scope of scientific discourse in his later writings. Here his critique of the ascetic understanding of science undermines the idea that scientific discourse can provide neutral and extra-perspectival access to the world. He writes:

There is, strictly speaking, absolutely no science 'without presuppositions,' the thought of such a science is unthinkable, paralogical; a philosophy, a 'belief' must always be there first so that science can derive a direction from it, a meaning, a boundary, a method, a *right* to existence. (GM, III, 24)[3]

This is a significantly different position to that of HAH where he contends that science can lift us, albeit momentarily, beyond the subjectivity and perspectivity of evaluative discourse (HAH, I, 16). His reconsideration of the claim that science is capable of yielding such a presuppositionless or value-free standpoint follows from his rejection of the coherency of the idea of extra-perspectival knowledge, which is evident in the following passage from GM:

> ... let us guard ourselves better from now on, gentlemen philosophers, against the dangerous old conceptual fabrication that posited a 'pure, will-less, painless, timeless subject of knowledge': here it is always demanded that we think an eye that cannot possibly be thought, an eye that must not have any direction, in which the active and interpretive forces through which seeing first becomes seeing-something are to be shut off, are to be absent; thus, what is demanded here is always an absurdity and non-concept of an eye. (GM, III, 12)

Whilst Nietzsche employs a visual metaphor to highlight the notion of perspective, Heidegger is arguably correct when he warns against taking the ocular metaphor for perspectivism too literally. According to Heidegger, 'The "perspective" is never the mere angle of vision from which something is seen' but rather must be understood as an evaluative condition of preservation and enhancement.[4] A perspective, thus understood, constitutes a 'human *contribution*' to how things appear (GS, 57; GM, III, 12). According to Nietzsche, perspectivism entails adopting an evaluative stance towards the world. He argues that all perspectives, as 'standpoints' (WP, 715 KSA 13: 11 [73]) that we adopt towards the world, are evaluative (WP, 481 KSA 12: 7 [60]).

Nietzsche thus dissolves the distinction between the inner point of view of evaluative discourse and the point of view of scientific discourse on the grounds that scientific discourse is no less perspectival than evaluative discourse. Even at its most descriptive, science describes the world from within a particular theory of how the world is, a theory that is an expression

---

[3] See also GS, 344, where Nietzsche argues against the notion of presuppositionless scientific convictions and in favour of provisional – regulative – scientific hypotheses.

[4] Martin Heidegger, *Nietzsche*, Volume 3, trans. Joan Stambaugh, David F. Krell and Frank A. Capuzzi (New York: HarperCollins, 1991), p. 197.

of values and preferences (WP, 567 KSA 13: 14 [184]). This is not to say that we cannot distinguish between scientific and value discourse, but it is to say that scientific discourse is never value-free. That is, although natural science, for example, is primarily concerned with the causal nexus of the world, in order for it to articulate judgements about causes, it must adopt a perspective about, for example, what should count as good evidential support or justification for a proposition and, therefore, can never be evaluatively neutral. Furthermore, Nietzsche denies that the affective or commendatory character of value discourse demarcates it from scientific discourse. This is because, for Nietzsche, affect is the mode in which we interpretively and evaluatively encounter the world. He writes of '[t]he world seen, felt, interpreted [*ausgelegt*] as thus and thus so that organic life may preserve itself in this perspective of interpretation [*dieser Perspective von Auslegung*]'. Affect is perspectival, and written into the idea of perspective, for Nietzsche, is the idea of praise or blame (HAH, I, 34; WP, 267 KSA 12: 2 [178]). According to this argument, then, physics and natural science (BGE, 14, 22), and indeed rational thought itself (WP, 552 KSA 12: 9 [91]),[5] is no less interpretive or evaluative than morality (GS, 359).[6] For Nietzsche, to the extent that we make a distinction between scientific and evaluative discourse, the distinction must be understood to be one of degree rather than kind.[7] It is no longer the case that physics, for example,

---

[5] Nietzsche emphasizes the interconnection of affect and rationality when he denies, contrary to what he calls the 'misunderstanding of passion and reason', that reason is an 'independent entity' and argues instead that it is properly understood as 'a system of relations between various passions and desires' (WP, 387 KSA 13: 11 [310]). He makes a similar point in GS, 333, when he denies that '*intelligere*' is extra-evaluative ('something conciliatory, just, and good . . .') and 'opposed to the instincts'. Rather, reason is, he claims, '*a certain behaviour of the instincts toward one another*'.

[6] See also TI, 'Improvers', 1; WP, 1 KSA 12: 2 [127]; WP, 5, 114 KSA 12: 5 [71], WP, 228 KSA 11: 44 [6]; WP, 258 KSA 12: 2 [165]; WP, 270 KSA 12: 10 [121]. For further discussion of such issues in a non-Nietzschean context, see Hilary Putnam, who also denies that scientific judgements are non-affective or non-commendatory. See Hilary Putnam, *Realism with a Human Face* (Cambridge, MA: Harvard University Press, 1990), p. 138. Additionally, Putnam contends that there is no intrinsic difference between scientific and evaluative judgements (ibid., p. 171).

[7] Maudemarie Clark and David Dudrick have recently argued that perspectivity and objectivity, for Nietzsche, are not mutually exclusive. However, their interpretation adopts a strong distinction between the status of scientific and evaluative discourse. Whilst they correctly, in my view, take justification in the sphere of value to entail a connection to the drives (Maudemarie Clark and David Dudrick, 'Nietzsche and Moral Objectivity: The Development of Nietzsche's Metaethics' in Brian Leiter and Neil Sinhababu (eds.), *Nietzsche and Morality* (Oxford: Oxford University Press, 2007), pp. 192–206, p. 216), it is my contention that Nietzsche holds, at least some of the time, that justification in science also entails a relation between the drives. For example, in GS, 333, he denies that knowledge is opposed to the instincts. This follows from his claim that scientific investigation is perspectival and directed by our interests. It is for this reason that I have refrained from discussing Nietzsche's account of science and value in the context of the debate between cognitivism and non-cognitivism. Nietzsche's rejection of philosophical oppositions in general militates against such a

can be considered to discover causes in a value-neutral way and that the investigations of physics can be considered to be distinguished from the normative domain of evaluative discourse. Rather, according to Nietzsche, our values reach down into and permeate the very activity of scientific discovery.

However, Nietzsche's claim that interpretation, perspective and, hence, value are fundamental to investigations in the natural as well as the human sciences might, if taken at merely face value, be understood to mean that our knowledge in these domains is irreducibly anthropocentric and entirely divorced from mind-independent empirical objects.[8] For example, Nietzsche writes of what he takes to be the physicist's notion of the lawfulness of nature that:

> ... it is not a factual matter, not a 'text', but rather no more than a naïve humanitarian concoction, a contortion of meaning that allows you to succeed in accommodating the democratic instincts of the modern soul! ... someone could come along with the opposite intention and interpretative skill who, looking at the very same nature and referring to the very same phenomena, would read out of it the ruthlessly tyrannical and unrelenting assertion of power claims. (BGE, 22)

Understood at face value, one might take Nietzsche here to be claiming that our interpretive engagement with the world entails unconstrained projection onto the world such that our interpretations are self-referential, reflecting ourselves rather than external objects. However, this result is averted when Nietzsche shows that values are necessary conditions of the experience of objects. This brings us to the second step of his rehabilitation of the status of values. Its successful execution follows from a rejection of a theory-independent conception of world and objects, a rejection that is already implied by Nietzsche's perspectivism.

The theory-independent conception holds that the world stands over and above our epistemic claims as a neutral standard of objectivity and correctness, and as a correlate of the God's Eye view, it entails the idea that reality cannot be adequately captured by our perspectival manner of

distinction in kind and points instead to a distinction of degree. See also Clark and Dudrick's discussion of these issues in their 'The Naturalisms of *Beyond Good and Evil*' in Keith Ansell Pearson (ed.), *A Companion to Nietzsche* (Oxford: Blackwell, 2006), pp. 148–168.

[8] It is a general tendency amongst postmodern interpreters to conclude that Nietzsche is proposing an unconstrained proliferation of interpretations. I do not interpret him in this way. For postmodern interpretations, see David B. Allison, *The New Nietzsche: Contemporary Styles of Interpretation* (Cambridge, MA: Massachusetts Institute of Technology Press, 1985), and *Reading the New Nietzsche* (Lanham, MD: Rowman and Littlefield, 2000).

describing it. I use the term 'theory' not just in the narrow sense of a theoretical framework (although it may mean this in special cases) but rather to denote that our engagement with the world is always interpretive and formed against the background of various presuppositions and interests. Arguing that all our descriptions are interpretive or perspectival (BGE, 22), Nietzsche denies that we can meaningfully talk about knowing reality independently of a point of view. Rather, he claims that we operate within the realm of perspectival appearance, stressing that his reference to appearance does not entail a reference to anything beyond appearance (GS, 54).

For Nietzsche, appearance refers to the world as perspectivally presented, a point that he illustrates with an example from perception. Human perception is perspectival, and central to its perspectivity is the role of the imagination, which, he argues, actively contributes to the perception of objects rather than passively mirroring them. In BGE he draws our attention to the centrality of the imagination in determining these features of perception by outlining, in terms resembling Kant's account of the imagination in synthesis and schematization, how we come to have perception of objects. According to Kant, the imagination is 'the faculty for representing in intuition an object that is *not itself present*'.[9] Nietzsche agrees, although he articulates it in different terms. Perception, Nietzsche tells us, relies on a certain fabrication or invention performed by the imagination. He argues that the imagination plays an important role by filling in the gaps of immediate sense-impressions. For example, to use Nietzsche's own illustration, when I perceive an object, such as a tree, I do so from a particular angle that precludes the possibility of registering all of the features of the tree. Nonetheless, I recognize the object *as* a tree. How is this possible? Nietzsche contends that it is the imagination that makes this possible. He argues that when it comes to knowledge, whether perceptual knowledge of an object or interpretive knowledge of another person's conversation, the imagination always 'adds' something. In the case of perception it is the features of an object that we do not actually see, or, in the case of conversation we attribute beliefs to the person that they do not explicitly articulate (BGE, 192).

By 'fabrication' and 'invention' Nietzsche means the supplementary role that the imagination plays in facilitating perceptual experience and recognition of objects. Fabrication as the term is used here, however, does not entail a projection of qualities or properties onto the object that the object does not have, but rather it refers to the act of interpreting visual data

---

[9] Immanuel Kant, *Critique of Pure Reason*, trans. Norman Kemp Smith (London: Macmillan, 1929), B151.

according to a schema that selectively focuses on particular features of the object. Nietzsche uses the language of 'lying' to convey the idea that, in the case of perceptual recognition of objects, the interpretive schema focuses on particular features of the object, which are those general features that the object shares with other objects that resemble it. Nietzsche can avoid the invention-discovery dichotomy because 'invention', strictly speaking for him, does not preclude 'finding' (BGE, 12), but rather the former makes the latter possible.

However, it might be argued that Nietzsche's appeal to the role of invention is intended to preclude finding. For example, in GS, 301 he emphasizes the role of artistic invention in relation to evaluative discernment, an emphasis that has led some to argue that he perpetuates rather than rejects the error theory of value of HAH in that passage.[10] But it is important to recognize that Nietzsche's aim in this passage is to warn us against thinking that our values are reducible to the world in the sense of being simply found through the medium of perceptual experience. Instead, he emphasizes that values belong to the domain of the higher animals and that values are creations of human beings. Independently of human beings, he argues, 'nature is always value-less, but has been *given value at some point, as a present – and it was we who gave and bestowed it*' (GS, 301). However, although values belong to the domain of the higher animals, they are not divorced from the world but rather are necessary conditions of our experience of it. In a passage close to GS, 301, he draws our attention to the central role that values play in our interpretive engagement with the world. Comparing the activity of valuing to that of an artist but in a way that avoids reducing our values to illusions as in HAH, he tells us that the artist presents objects in the world by highlighting or selectively focussing on particular features of the object from a specific point of view. Nietzsche writes:

> *What one should learn from artists.* – How can we make things beautiful, attractive, and desirable for us when they are not? – Moving away from things until there is a good deal that one no longer sees and there is much that our eye has to add if we are still to see them at all; or seeing things around a corner and as cut out and framed; or to place them so that they partially conceal each other and grant us only glimpses of architectural perspectives . . . (GS, 299)

---

[10] See Nadeem J. Z. Hussain, 'Nietzsche and Non-Cognitivism' in Christopher Janaway and Simon Robertson (eds.), *Nietzsche, Naturalism and Normativity* (Oxford: Oxford University Press, 2012), pp. 111–132.

Rather than perspectival values being simply discovered through perceptual experience, Nietzsche argues that they condition our experience of objects through a process analogous to that of artistic framing. That is, for Nietzsche, we experience the world in a highly focussed and stylized way (GS, 290), highlighting some features of the object and downplaying others. The world as it appears to human perception is thus a 'picture' (although not a mind-dependent representation, as Nietzsche makes clear in BGE, 36) in that it is 'presented' or 'framed' in a particular evaluative way (GS, 299). It does not follow from this that our values are unconstrained projections onto the world. Rather, one might argue that our evaluative framing of the world serves to highlight particular features of the world. Just as we might position ourselves spatially in such a way that particular features of the world become perceptually available to us, the fact that such features become thus available is not an act of choice on our part but rather reflects real properties of the object. Thus, Nietzsche's argument implies that the activity of valuing permeates our perceptual and cognitive processes and has the particular result of highlighting or drawing our attention to these features of the object. The features thus highlighted are those properties of objects that are of interest or significance for beings such as ourselves. As a result, our values cannot be reducible to mere desire or wishful thinking but rather must be world-involving in a significant sense.

According to Nietzsche, then, in perception and knowledge the eye/mind 'frames' objects by presenting them perspectivally. Similarly to Kant, Nietzsche denies that we are acquainted with the sensory given as given, arguing instead that our cognition of the world is inextricably interpretive. Against the positivist, he writes, there are no facts, only interpretations (WP, 481 KSA 12: 7 [60]; GS, 57). The object of knowledge, he argues, is perspectivally presented to us and therefore is theory-dependent. That is, we always view or know the world from a particular perspective and the idea of trying to articulate a contentful conception of the world independently of a perspective is incoherent (GS, 374). He thus claims that perspectives are necessary conditions for something to be recognized as something or to mean anything to us (GM, III, 12).[11] Since perspectives constitute an evaluative horizon that conditions our encounter with the world, it follows then that values must be necessary conditions for us to have experience of the world at all. Nietzsche writes:

---

[11] For Nietzsche's explicit identification of perspective with value, see, for example, the 1886 preface to HAH, where he writes of 'the sense of perspective in every value judgement – the displacement, distortion and merely apparent teleology of horizons...' (HAH, I, P: 6).

The apparent world, i.e., a world viewed according to values; ordered, selected, according to values, i.e., in this case according to the viewpoint of utility in regard to the preservation and enhancement of the power of a certain species of animal.

The perspective therefore decides the character of the 'appearance'! As if a world would still remain over after one deducted the perspective! (WP, 567 KSA 13: 14 [184])

But just as Nietzsche warns that values are not reducible to the world, the claim that value perspectives are necessary for us to have experience of objects in the world does not translate into the idea that value perspectives constitute objects. That it does not follows from Nietzsche's mature view that the idea of there obtaining a thing-in-itself, inaccessible to and unknowable by our perspectives, is a contradiction in terms (GM, III, 12) and that such a thing-in-itself can be conceived only in opposition to the predicates that we ascribe to the empirical world (GS, 54). The idea of the thing-in-itself and the constitutive mind, for Nietzsche, go hand in hand. If there is no thing-in-itself, then the empirical world is the real world.[12] Free of the thing-in-itself, Nietzsche can hold that perspectives, rather than constituting the world, are instead positioned in the empirical world and access that world, albeit partially and never completely. The empirical world is mind-independent but amenable to our perspectival knowledge of it. Nietzsche's argument in favour of such a position rests on the claim that our perspectives, which condition how things appear to us, are situated within and actively engage with the dynamic character of reality (WP, 636 KSA 13: 14 [186]).[13] With this argument in place, Nietzsche can consequently satisfy the second aim to demonstrate that value-laden perspectives are necessary conditions of cognition in addition to denying that there is any metaphysical remainder to the world as it might appear to or be experienced by us.

Moreover, Nietzsche's ability to satisfy the third aim to distinguish between veridical and non-veridical values follows from his appeal to perspectives as conditions of cognition and his acceptance of a theory-dependent conception

---

[12] Nietzsche writes in GS: 'What is "appearance" for me now? Certainly not the opposite of some essence: what could I say about any essence except to name the attributes of its appearance! Certainly, not a dead mask that one could place on an unknown *x* or remove from it' (GS, 54). In BGE, 54, he proposes that we speak in terms of lighter and darker shades of appearance rather than in terms of an opposition between truth and falsity. In TI, he writes: 'We have abolished the real world: what world is left? The apparent world perhaps? – But no! *with the real world we have also abolished the apparent world!* Elsewhere, he writes: 'The antithesis of the apparent world and the true world is reduced to the antithesis "world" and "nothing"' (WP, 567 KSA 13: 14 [184]).

[13] See also Nietzsche's praise for Hegel on conceptual change and Becoming at GS, 357.

of world. This is because what ultimately determines the veridicality of our values and perspectives, according to Nietzsche, is not their correspondence to the world but rather their relations to other perspectives and values (WP, 530 KSA 12: 7 [4]). The consideration of values and perspectives in relation to one another involves the practice of what Nietzsche calls 'intellectual conscience' (GS, 2), or the consideration of the best reasons for and against a point of view (GS, 319; GM, III, 12). It follows from Nietzsche's argument that perspectives are conditions of knowledge for us that metaphysical claims cannot be prioritized over epistemic ones. His appeal to a theory-dependent conception of world entails that our epistemic claims are value-laden and that they share a relationship of reciprocal dependency with ontological claims. Reciprocal dependency entails, as outlined previously, the idea that the empirical world is knowable by but metaphysically independent of us. Its knowability depends on us contributing interest-directed forms of knowledge, which, however, should not be understood to constitute the empirical world in a metaphysical sense. Only such a position can allow Nietzsche to hold that values are realistically constrained without committing him to the idea of an unknowable metaphysical remainder. Our knowledge of objects is manifested through perspectival presentations of them, which have objects partially in view. This allows Nietzsche to conclude that our values can be both perspectival and objective. He thus writes that '[t]here is *only* a perspectival seeing, *only* a perspectival "knowing"; and *the more* affects we allow to speak about a matter – that much more complete will our "concept" of this matter, our "objectivity" be' (GM, III, 12). From this, we can see that perspectives, as evaluatively informed points of view, do not float free of the world and that, therefore, the mutually constraining influences of perspectives on one another represents a realist constraint. Objectivity, redefined thus perspectively, has a distinctive realist but relational character.

Such a redefined account of objectivity is important for making sense of Nietzsche's evaluative appraisal of, for example, *ressentiment*. His claim that the *ressentiment* subject misrepresents its own and the noble's relationship to the world presupposes that some values can be objective. According to Nietzsche, the *ressentiment* subject misrepresents the features of the world upon which it selectively focusses its attention, which in this case is the noble or any external thing that resists its efforts. Of *ressentiment*, Nietzsche writes that 'it must be a kind of provisional expression, an interpretation, formula, arrangement, a psychological *misunderstanding of something* whose actual nature could not be understood for a long time . . . ' (GM, III, 13, my italics).

The *ressentiment* subject, despite its protestations to the contrary, apprehends the noble as hateful precisely because the noble is capable of what the *ressentiment* subject is not, that is, effective action in the world. This also leads the *ressentiment* subject to misrepresent the world such that he will represent the empirical world of change and the senses as an 'error', pointing to an extra-natural standard of truth and reality (GM, III, 12). The *ressentiment* subject, whose mode of engagement with the world is reactive rather than effectively active (GM, I, 10), compensates by projecting its negative emotions onto the object of its revenge and by pursuing what Nietzsche calls an 'imaginary revenge' (GM, I, 10). Since, for Nietzsche, reaction is a form of action (GM, I, 10) that is subject to insurmountable obstacles or resistance, the reactive evaluative perspective of the *ressentiment* subject is characterized as such by its interaction with, and negative experience of resistance in, the world.

However, Nietzsche's suggestion that *ressentiment* gives birth to the ascetic ideal[14] and that the ascetic ideal ultimately dissipates according to its own internal rationale (WP, 2 KSA 12: 9 [35]; WP, 5 KSA 12: 5 [71]) presupposes that whilst values cannot ultimately be divorced from the world, the non-veridicality of *ressentiment* values must be assessed according to internal reasons rather than by correspondence to the world. He stresses that the judgement that *ressentiment* values are distorted ones is made from within our irrevocable acculturated position, a position in fact brought about by the ascetic priest, in whom *ressentiment* as a psychological and evaluative mental state is given expression (GM, III, 12). According to Nietzsche, the ascetic priest is responsible for the fact that human beings are self-aware (GM, II, 1–3), a capacity, he argues, that is closely aligned with the acquisition of linguistic and conceptual competencies and which is the hallmark of human society and culture (GS, 354). Consequently, it is, paradoxically, the ascetic priest's practice of 'reversing perspectives', of presenting that which is base as noble and vice versa, that, in principle, equips us to consider multiple perspectives in relation to one another and thus to distinguish between distorted and veridical perspectives (GM, III, 12).

Nietzsche presupposes, then, that to consider a value in the context of multiple perspectives is to subject that value to a realist constraint. Some values misrepresent the world, he suggests, whilst others are merited by it. The *ressentiment* subject misrepresents both the noble and the character of

---

[14] According to Nietzsche, suffering gives rise to *ressentiment* (GM, III, 15), and the ascetic ideal gives a meaning to suffering (GM, III, 17).

the world. The reason for this, according to Nietzsche, is that although the ascetic priest's reversal of perspectives involves acknowledging the existence of other perspectives, this reactive and revengeful viewpoint ultimately considers only its own viewpoint as valid, lacking sufficient 'strength' to highlight the role that opposing or alternative perspectives might play in bringing the distortions of its own viewpoint to light.[15] As a result, the evaluative stance of the *ressentiment* subject selectively focusses on features of the world but is not merited by them. That is, our values, whilst formulating the perspectival 'horizon' in which we interpret the world, are nonetheless also constrained by the world. Nietzsche secures the objectivity of the phenomenology of value, therefore, not by placing values mind-independently in the world but rather by subjecting the affective, relational and perspectival character of our values to constraint from the world and possible correction in light of that constraint.

The preceding argument undermines the threat that the prioritization of science as an extra-perspectival and extra-evaluative form of inquiry posed to the objectivity of our values in HAH by mobilizing the conceptual resources in Nietzsche's writings other than that text to deny that natural science is more objective than evaluative discourse and by holding that value perspectives are a necessary condition for us to have experience or knowledge of the empirical world. On the basis of this conclusion, Nietzsche revises what he means by objectivity and knowledge. That is, if the methods and results of natural science are not value-free, then the perspective of the natural sciences alone can no longer be legitimately upheld as the standard of objective knowledge. Rather, in line with his view that objectivity entails the consideration of multiple perspectives (GM, III, 12), Nietzsche redefines objective knowledge to comprise the adoption of a comprehensive explanatory perspective that includes but is not reducible to the perspective of the natural sciences. According to Nietzsche, scientific knowledge should have a broader, more comprehensive meaning than just entailing the knowledge

[15] Nietzsche attributes to the priest, the instigator of *ressentiment* values, the 'power' to see multiple perspectives that characterizes the nobles and which the slaves, as followers of the priest, lack. Thus, Nietzsche attributes to the priest both noble and slave traits (GM, I, 6–7). Still, the ascetic priest is ultimately weak because his form of seeing multiple perspectives fails to get at these perspectives from the inside and merely reverses values instead of adopting ones that more adequately reflect the character of reality. In contrast, Nietzsche's value-legislating philosopher adopts a comprehensive perspective from a height (BGE, 211). Nietzsche writes of what he calls 'justice' or objectivity that it is 'in the long run the opposite of what all revenge wants, which sees only the viewpoint of the injured one, allows only it to count – from now on, the eye is trained for an ever *more impersonal* appraisal of deeds...' (GM, II, 11). According to Nietzsche, the 'precondition' for the education of the philosopher or creator of values is the ability to consider multiple perspectives from within and to abandon nook perspectives for broader, more adequate ones (BGE, 211).

afforded by the perspective of the natural sciences. The appeal to a more comprehensive conception of science undoes the oscillation between the supposedly inner and outer points of view of evaluative and scientific discourse that informed Nietzsche's argument for value fictionalism in HAH.

Since Nietzsche thinks that evaluative perspectives are both world-involving and – reciprocally – constrained by the world, it shouldn't come as a surprise, despite suggestions to the contrary in the secondary literature, that Nietzsche's adoption of a comprehensive explanatory perspective is not ultimately metaphysically neutral. Whilst he clearly thinks that all metaphysical claims are fallible and revisable (BGE, 22) and although his argument in favour of adopting a comprehensive perspective does not stand or fall with the cogency of any particular metaphysical account of the world, there is a very specific instance in Nietzsche's writings where his adoption of a comprehensive perspective leads him to a very particular and, indeed, contentious metaphysics. This is the metaphysics of the will to power, and it has implications for how we should understand the relation between our values and the world. Specifically, I want to examine the manner in which it proposes that our human values are metaphysically continuous with the causal fabric of reality. This is because the realist constraint that our values are subjected to, for Nietzsche, ultimately arises from the metaphysical continuity of our values with the world. Being metaphysically continuous with the world rules out the possibility that our values can float free of the world without theoretical and practical repercussions. Consequently, metaphysical continuity does not mean we give a causal-mechanical explanation from the outside of how our various values have come to be.[16] Rather, metaphysical continuity appeals to causality from the inside and concludes that values themselves, in a metaphysical sense, are causes.

Nietzsche does not arrive at this conclusion by appealing dogmatically to the causal character of the world and then arguing for the metaphysical continuity of our values with it. Equally, since he thinks that investigation in the natural sciences is evaluative, he must avoid dogmatically presupposing an 'inner', specifically human, point of view that will lead to the 'outer' point of view of the natural sciences. Rather, although he adopts the methodological strategy of beginning provisionally with our

---

[16] This is contrary to Maudemarie Clark in 'On Knowledge, Truth and Value: Nietzsche's Debt to Schopenhauer and the Development of His Empiricism' in Christopher Janaway (ed.), *Willing and Nothingness: Schopenhauer as Nietzsche's Educator* (Oxford: Oxford University Press, 1998) pp. 37–78, p. 53.

inner – psychological-phenomenological – perspective on the grounds that extra-perspectival knowledge is not to be had and that we must begin from somewhere, ultimately he incorporates both the perspective of the natural sciences and the inner point of view in order to see more comprehensively than either perspective alone will allow. In the next section, I contend that an argument of this shape is implied though not always explicitly articulated in a number of Nietzsche's mature texts and that by overcoming the schism between the inner and outer points of view that informs value fictionalism, it undoes the basis for understanding our values as global errors in favour of understanding them as capable of being veridical or non-veridical. I will begin by illustrating what Nietzsche means by a comprehensive perspective and how it implies the metaphysics of the will to power. I will then proceed to show how he offers a metaphysically laden and non-fictionalist account of value, followed by a consideration of possible objections to my argument.

Comprehensive Science

In GS, Nietzsche contends that scientific knowledge must be understood more comprehensively than in terms of a narrow and extra-evaluative quest for knowledge for its own sake (GS, 113). A comprehensive conception of science entails more than giving an account of the operations of the non-human physical world and must include an account of how the human being – its phenomenological experience of value, consciousness and agency – fits into that world. It is the knowledge that is yielded by this comprehensive perspective with which Nietzsche is concerned and which will form the basis of his argument that values are metaphysically continuous with and constrained by the causal fabric of nature.

He proposes that a comprehensive rather than narrow compass of science takes shape when the 'artistic energies and practical wisdom of life – join with scientific thinking to form a higher organic system . . . ' (GS, 113). The achievement of a broader perspective, such as he describes here, entails stressing the results of natural science not for their own sake but for their existential significance and the improvement of health and culture (GS, 382).[17] Nietzsche calls this a 'gay science', and it is properly described as the task of philosophy rather than natural science alone. However, the idea of appealing to a more comprehensive perspective is not restricted to GS. It is evident early on when in SE he writes of a 'higher organic system'

[17] In GS, 335, Nietzsche writes that value creation requires knowledge of physics.

that offers what he describes as a 'regulatory total picture' that presents a 'picture of life as a whole' (SE, 3). Later, in AC, he appeals to the notion of a 'uniform science' (AC, 59), and in BGE, he emphasizes the need to avoid 'nook' perspectives (BGE, 230) in favour of perspectives from a height that have more comprehensive scope. In the latter text, Nietzsche appeals to the notion of a comprehensive perspective by way of rejecting what he calls 'an unseemly and hierarchical shift between science and philosophy' that reduces philosophy to a mere 'theory of cognition' (BGE, 204). Rather, according to Nietzsche, the genuine philosopher must '*be able* to look with many kinds of eyes and consciences from the heights into every distance, from the depths into every wide expanse' as a 'precondition' for the determination of values (BGE, 211).[18] Moreover, of the philosopher whose job it is to determine values, he writes that '[t]heir "knowing" is *creating*, their creating is law-giving, their will to truth is – *will to power*' (BGE, 211).

In BGE, the will to power results from Nietzsche's efforts to offer a comprehensive and 'uniform' (AC, 59) perspective on things and to establish the continuity of the self with the causal fabric of the world by drawing on Boscovich's force physics in addition to providing an account of the self that is consonant with this physical view (BGE 12). In relation to the former, Nietzsche praises Boscovich for having offered a more refined account of causal connection than that supplied by mechanical atomism. He writes:

> ... the Pole Boscovich ... along with the Pole Copernicus achieved the greatest victory yet in opposing the appearance of things. For while Copernicus convinced us to believe contrary to all our senses that the earth does *not* stand still, Boscovich taught us to renounce the last thing that 'still stood' about the earth, the belief in 'substance', in 'matter', in the bit of earth, the particle, the atom: no one on earth has ever won greater triumph over the senses. (BGE, 12)

Rather than understanding causal connection in terms of the physical contact of two material bodies and the consequent discontinuous change of velocity in the two bodies, Boscovich construed causal influence in terms of action at a distance and a continuous rather than discontinuous change in the velocity of objects.[19] However, despite his praise for Boscovich,

---

[18] See GS, 301, for Nietzsche on the higher human animal's ability to see comprehensively. What distinguishes the higher human being from the lower and the human being in general from non-human animals, he argues, is the extent to which we see.

[19] See Rom Harré and E. H. Madden, *Causal Powers: A Theory of Natural Necessity* (Oxford: Basil Blackwell, 1975), p. 169.

Nietzsche warns against taking the results of the natural sciences at face value, arguing that to the extent that we do take them at face value we get only descriptions of things from the outside (BGE, 14). Nietzsche levels this charge at Boscovich notwithstanding his commendation of him for having refused to accept the evidence of the senses unquestioningly. Boscovich is guilty of coming at things from the outside in his account of physical force, in Nietzsche's view, because he captures only the external relations between forces rather than their genuine causal efficacy or power, thus reducing force to a functional element in a mathematical formula.[20] Coming to the issue of force metaphysically from the inside, however, allows us to attribute genuine causal efficacy to force. Consequently, Nietzsche describes force as a particular quantum of power (GM, I, 13) and proposes that we ascribe to the concept of physical force an inner will to explain its causal efficacy. His proposal of an inner will is made on the basis of an argument from analogy with our own phenomenological experience of willing and is bolstered by his familiarity with the notion of a creative striving force informing organic development in non-Darwinian evolutionary theory in nineteenth-century biology. According to Nietzsche, physics must be metaphysically continuous in the sense of being subject to the same metaphysical explanations even if they are not identical in all particulars.[21] The appeal to the inner causal efficacy of force, however, is ultimately framed within and licensed by the argument from analogy, as is evident from the fact that his proposal of the will to power thesis in BGE, 36, begins with reference to human phenomenological experience. On the basis of this argumentative strategy, he describes 'effective energy' in terms of the will to power, which, in turn, is described as '[t]he world as it is seen from the inside, the world defined and described by its "intelligible character"' (BGE, 36). Elsewhere he writes:

> The victorious concept 'force', by means of which our physicists have created God and the world, still needs to be completed: an inner will must be ascribed to it, which I designate as 'will to power', i.e., as an

---

[20] Nietzsche writes, 'It is an illusion that something is *known* when we possess a mathematical formula for an event: it is only designated, described; nothing more!' (WP 628 KSA 12: 2 [89]; WP 624 KSA 12: 7 [56]).

[21] Gregory Moore, 'Nietzsche and Evolutionary Theory' in Keith Ansell Pearson, *A Companion to Nietzsche* (Oxford: Blackwell, 2006), pp. 517–531. Christian Emden argues, however, that Nietzsche is more of a Darwinian than he acknowledges. See Christian J. Emden, *Nietzsche's Naturalism: Philosophy and the Life Sciences in the Nineteenth Century* (Cambridge: Cambridge University Press, 2014). Nietzsche's appropriation of nineteenth-century biology will be discussed further in Chapter 3.

insatiable desire to manifest power; or as the employment and exercise of power, as a creative drive. (WP, 619 KSA 11: 36 [31])

However, the argument from analogy is designed not only to compensate for an explanatory deficit in physical science's concept of force but also to provide a provisional investigative starting point for Nietzsche's attempt to establish the metaphysical continuity of the human being with the causal fabric of non-human reality. That is, it must serve to explain how the sphere of the human – its phenomenological experience of value, consciousness and agency – is metaphysically continuous with the causal fabric of the natural world. The first step towards achieving this involves arguing that the human self is metaphysically continuous with the causal character of reality understood as will to power. Nietzsche contends that the human self must not be understood as a traditional substance but rather is better construed as a hierarchical structure of drives and affects that vie for dominancy or power over the other drives. This conclusion is reached by including an atomistic conception of the self in his rejection of mechanical atomism, more generally. He writes:

> However, we must go even further and declare war, a merciless war unto the death against the 'atomistic need' that continues to live a dangerous afterlife in places where no one suspects it (as does the more famous 'metaphysical need'). The first step must be to kill off that other and more ominous atomism that Christianity taught best and longest: *the atomism of the soul.* (BGE, 12)

Although he rejects the idea that the self is 'something ineradicable, eternal, indivisible, a monad, an atom' and proposes that 'science must cast out *this* belief' (BGE, 12), he nevertheless stresses that the alternative to the traditional view of the self is not to eliminate the self, which, he claims, 'the bungling naturalists tend to do' (BGE, 12). Rather, Nietzsche argues that the rejection of the atomistic conception of the self makes possible 'new and refined versions about the soul', such that, 'in future, concepts such as the "mortal soul" and the "soul as the social construct of drives and emotions" will claim their rightful place in science.'" (BGE, 12) The mortal self that he describes here is a hierarchically structured construct of drives and affects. Moreover, the drives that make up the self, in their essential desire to rule the other drives (BGE, 6), according to Nietzsche, seek to 'philosophize' (BGE, 6), by which he means that the drives seek to determine values (BGE, 211). The self, understood on the model of the will to power, is, then, an evaluative self. Since the self is to be understood as metaphysically continuous with the causal-powerful character of non-human reality, so too must our values.

We get a glimpse of how Nietzsche understands human values to be continuous with the causal fabric of reality from the manner in which he argues that values, understood along the lines of the will to power, should be construed naturalistically in the chapter called 'Our Virtues' in BGE. There he rejects the non-naturalistic – moralistic – account of virtue offered by Kant. In section 215 of the text, Nietzsche envisages a planet orbiting two different stars of two different colours; the planet is illuminated sometimes by one of the stars and sometimes by the other and yet again sometimes by both. According to Nietzsche, the parable illustrates that 'we modern men, because of the complicated mechanism of our "starry sky" – are defined by *differing* moral codes; our actions shine with differing colours in alternation, they are rarely clear – and there are a good many cases when we perform *many-coloured* actions' (BGE, 215). With this parable Nietzsche responds to Kant, who had written in the conclusion to his *Critique of Practical Reason* that '[t]wo things fill the mind with ever new and increasing admiration and reverence – the starry sky above me and the moral law within me'.[22] In particular, Nietzsche takes issue with Kant's sharp demarcation of the sphere of morality from the sphere of nature. According to Kant, we are subject to natural causal laws in the sphere of nature; as natural beings our actions are unfree and determined by such causal laws. As moral beings, however, Kant argues we are free and can act independently of natural causal influences.[23] According to Nietzsche, an honest examination of the notion of virtue dissociates it from Kant's moral trappings by giving a naturalistic account of virtue. A naturalistic account, in his view, aligns virtue with the will to power. On the basis of such an alignment, he contends that human action is 'fated' rather than uncaused. This is because all virtues or values are expressions of our natures as will to power. As such, our virtues express our natures as weak or strong, master or slave, active or reactive.

Nietzsche explicitly aligns human values with the will to power when he writes:

> What is good? All that heightens the feeling of power, the will to power, power itself in man.
> What is bad? – All that proceeds from weakness.

---

[22] Immanuel Kant, *Critique of Practical Reason*, trans. Werner S. Pluhar (Cambridge: Hackett Publishing Company, 2002), 5:162, p. 203.

[23] Nietzsche denies, contrary to Kant, that values 'point back or down to another, metaphysical world' and argues instead that values are grounded in physiological conditions (WP, 254 KSA 12: 2 [190]; BGE, 187).

What is happiness? – The feeling that power *increases* – that a resistance is overcome.

Not contentment, but more power; *not* peace at all, but war, *not* virtue (*Tugend*) *but proficiency* (virtue in the Renaissance style, virtù, virtue free of moralic acid) [Tugend, sondern Tüchtigkeit (Tugend im Renaissance-Stile, virtù, moralinfreie Tugend)]. (AC, 2)

In this passage Nietzsche puts forward a naturalistic account of value that draws on the Renaissance notion of virtue where virtue is understood naturalistically as a capacity, ability or power. Hanna Pitkin describes what is meant by the Renaissance notion of virtue in the following:

> In the Renaissance, it was often used, for instance to mean something like power or motive force. It appears in Leonardo's notes on dynamics as more or less equivalent to physical motive power. The Italian term derives etymologically from the Latin term *virtus*, on the root *vir*, meaning 'man'. *Virtus* thus meant something like manliness, energetic strength, and was one of the traditionally admired Roman virtues along with *dignitas* and *gravitas* and the others ... These earlier uses of the concept of virtue remain only in occasional English forms like 'by virtue of,' which clearly implies not morality but force, or 'virtuosity,' which is a matter of skillfulness and achievement, not of good motives or good behaviour.[24]

Nietzsche appeals to this Renaissance notion of virtue in BGE when he argues that all virtues are expressions of the will to power and when he argues that power should be understood as motive force (BGE, 36). Here Nietzsche describes the will to power in terms of 'efficient causality' and describes efficient causality as *Kraft* (force). Later, in BGE, 224, he refers to 'how the authority of values relates to the authority of active energies (*wirkenden Kräfte*)'. And, in BGE, 230, Nietzsche claims that his thesis that human values are expressions of the will to power follows from his efforts to 'return man to nature'. What the alignment of virtue with the will to power entails specifically is the view that virtues and values are expressions of natural human capacities and that these capacities are experienced by us as feelings of power. Our virtues, then, are a reflection not just of what we actually do but also of what we have the dispositional capacity or power to do by virtue of our immersion in nature.[25]

---

[24] Hanna F. Pitkin, *Wittgenstein and Justice: On the Significance of Ludwig Wittgenstein's Social and Political Thought* (Berkeley, CA: University of California Press, 1972), p. 309. Cited by David Owen, *Nietzsche, Politics and Modernity* (London: Sage Publications, 1995), p. 140.

[25] As Nietzsche's account of how the noble individual has been deceived into thinking that the same values that apply to the slave also applies to them shows, we do not always manifest our capacities. Sometimes, as with the case of nobility in Modernity, these capacities lie dormant as dispositional potentials. This is why Nietzsche addresses BGE, for example, to potential nobles of the future. For

According to Nietzsche, then, physical causes and values have something metaphysically in common. What they have in common, he argues, is that they both can be explained as will to power, which, for Nietzsche, means that their continuity emanates from the inside, from their metaphysical natures, rather than from outward observable correlations and their subsumption under general and descriptive laws of nature. His alignment of value with power and feelings of power is significant because it preserves the objectivity of value instead of fictionalizing it or divorcing it from the world and placing it beyond criticism or correction in light of the character of reality. Instead, human values and their 'subjective' phenomenological – affective, perspectival and relational – character are metaphysically continuous with nature by virtue of being explained in terms of natural capacity or force and are, accordingly, subject to constraint by reality.

Still, if this non-fictionalist and metaphysically laden interpretation of Nietzsche's account of value is to be secured, it must be able to accommodate his description of values as creative wills to power. He describes power on our part in terms of invention or creation, especially the creation of values (BGE, 211; Z, Part One, 'Of the Thousand and One Goals'). This description follows directly from his denial that values obtain mind-independently and are simply there in the world awaiting discovery. The challenge is to explain how Nietzsche can deny that our values are realistically unconstrained and yet not simply to be found. I will hazard the following response as a sketch, which for the moment must remain speculative but will be developed further and in more detail in the chapters that follow.

Virtues, understood as will to power, are capacities. As human capacities ('power itself in man'), for Nietzsche, they have an affective-feeling dimension, and they are intentionally directed to manifesting themselves through the overcoming of resistance (AC, 2). The interrelated affective-intentional aspect of value discernment equates with the 'subjective' side of value, which entails the active projection of wants and needs through an artistic projection and glorification of how we would like the world to be (GS, 85, 109; BGE, 9). However, affective value feelings also respond to and are constrained by 'objective' or external resistances to their efforts exerted by the powerful character of reality (WP, 636 KSA 13: 14 [186]). For Nietzsche, then, values are dispositional capacities on the part of human beings, which are constrained by capacities on the part of mind-independent reality.

---

instance, the chapter 'Our Virtues' attempts to teach the dormant nobles that the idea of a universally applicable table of values is a myth.

Valuing, which, according to Nietzsche, manifests itself in affect or feeling (AC, 2) is the distinctively human activity of potentially realizing or bringing to fruition ideals that are commensurate with powerful dispositional features of the world.[26] According to the logic of this argument and in contrast to the position adopted in HAH, values are neither artistic illusions nor scientific truths but rather aspirations that can be either veridical or non-veridical.[27] Consequently, the world appears to us evaluatively, but our phenomenological-cum-evaluative experience of the world, whilst acting as a necessary starting point for our investigations, can be subject to correction in light of the character of reality itself. This is not to cast the phenomenology of value into global error, but rather it is to say that better or worse, or lighter and darker shades of appearance, are possible (BGE, 34).

The preceding argument that Nietzsche's description of the will to power in terms of value creation does not entail value fictionalism has been presented in broad brush strokes and will necessarily require further development in subsequent chapters. Nonetheless, unless explicitly and immediately addressed, my argument will be thought to be vulnerable to a number of objections, which, if upheld, might have the effect of calling the need for further development of the argument into question. The first of these objections is that my non-fictionalist interpretation is a distinctively metaphysically laden one, based largely on a reading of particular passages from BGE and passages from other texts where Nietzsche explicitly aligns value with the will to power. Although this description of my argument so far is accurate, it is not necessarily an objection to it. This is because my

---

[26] Although valuing is, strictly speaking, the process of realizing values, which are dispositional, valuing and values are metaphysically indistinct for Nietzsche. As we will see in Chapter 4, their metaphysical indistinctness pertains to Nietzsche's view that valuing is the activity whereby value dispositions strive to manifest their powerful natures. Now, R. Kevin Hill argues that dispositions are not the same as powers on the grounds that dispositions are causal tendencies and that powers are abilities that are normative on the grounds that they have 'better or worse ways of working themselves out' (R. Kevin Hill, *Nietzsche: A Guide for the Perplexed* (London: Continuum, 2007), p. 69). However, I will argue in Chapter 4 that dispositions and powers are modally identical and that normativity has a dispositional ground.

[27] The aspirational character of our values fits with the phenomenology of value and with Heidegger's warning against taking Nietzsche's analogy between perspectives and vision too literally. J. N. Findlay, in his phenomenology of value, warns of a disanalogy between perceptual and evaluative properties. Whereas perceptual properties are simply given, he argues, value properties must be realized by us (J. N. Findlay, *Values and Intentions* (London: George Allen and Unwin Ltd. and New York: The Macmillan Company, 1961), p. 208). On the basis of the idea that we often fail at a practical – what is the case – level to do what we ought, evaluations are best described as rational aspirations or wants that are intentionally directed to the objective realization of these evaluative wants and desires through action (Findlay, *Values and Intentions*, Chapter V).

metaphysically laden and non-fictionalist interpretation can be supported beyond the textual confines of BGE by considering that the notion of a comprehensive perspective is also evident in GS, for example, and that, although it is not immediately obvious, Nietzsche reaches similar conclusions about the phenomenology of value in that book that are no less metaphysically laden than the one presented earlier. That is, despite drawing on an analogy between valuing and colouring in GS (GS, 301), Nietzsche provides reasons for rejecting the idea that all values are fictional inventions and in favour of the view that our values are both metaphysically continuous with and constrained by the causal character of reality. Moreover, the logic of Nietzsche's argument in the text points to an understanding of reality as will to power even in places where the will to power is not explicitly mentioned.[28]

We can substantiate this interpretation, firstly, by considering some comments that Nietzsche makes about Hegel in GS. Although Nietzsche is critical of Hegel's religious divinization of nature (GS, 357), he nonetheless praises Hegel's appeal to the possibility of conceptual change for overcoming the distinction between appearance and reality. However, Nietzsche's praise for Hegel is not restricted to the epistemic notion of conceptual change but also includes the latter's view that reality develops or becomes according to a logic that belongs to the fabric of reality itself and is not simply a human imposition upon it ('we are not inclined to concede that our human logic is logic as such or the only kind of logic' (GS, 357)). Nietzsche's particular appropriation of this idea entails that reality is dispositional, being endowed with natural powerful capacities that resist illegitimate projections onto it. That Nietzsche understands reality as causally powerful in GS can be discerned from the fact that in the very same passage that he praises Hegel, he also praises Kant for having overcome Humean scepticism with regard to causality. Not only this, but in GS, 113, Nietzsche rejects the notion of causal connection understood as that between discrete events in favour of understanding causality as a continuum, and in GS, 360, he develops his denial in GS, 113, that causality is a conditional affair and argues instead that causal powers act spontaneously by giving the example of explosive powder and arguing that its explosive power emanates from the causal nature of the powder itself rather than being dependent on the extrinsic stimulus of a match (GS, 360).

Now, Nietzsche combines the Hegelian notion of the possibility of subjecting our concepts to correction and change with the metaphysical

---

[28] It is implicit in GS, 110, for example, in Nietzsche's rejection of the notion of 'enduring things'.

idea of reality as causally powerful in the text when he discusses how values may be projected onto reality and, for a time, come to be taken for the essence of things. He contends that where these projections are 'foreign' (GS, 58) to the – dispositional – character of reality, they need to be revised in favour of values that more accurately reflect the nature of reality and the human being's relation to it. Such revisions, he claims, entail the need for new evaluative creations (GS, 58). These new creations, Nietzsche allows, can be judged to be better or worse than their previous counterparts in the sense that values that are not foreign to reality undo the distinction between appearance and reality.[29] However, in making this claim, Nietzsche is not arguing that human minds constitute the empirical world. Rather, he is claiming that objective values are ones that are realized in cooperation with what the dispositional-causal fabric of reality allows and that non-veridical values are ultimately resisted by reality. This does not make mind or world reducible to one another, but it does indicate that there is a potential reciprocity between them by virtue of their metaphysical continuity.

This is all to say that, according to Nietzsche, we experience reality interpretively, as an 'appearance' that reflects our interests and concerns. We will that the world reflect these concerns and attempt to project our concerns onto the world, taking our specifically anthropomorphic interests as a measure of reality, as its fundamental essence (GS, 58). However, reality is not always compliant with our wills and indeed 'resists' illegitimate projections onto it. Such resistance comes to light, according to Nietzsche, not through an extra-perspectival comparison between our value perspectives and reality but rather through an internal tension within our value perspective itself such that the perspective comes to be seen to lack internal coherence. In the case of Christian values, Nietzsche argues, this internal tension emerges from the fact that it espouses a will to truth, which ultimately reveals that what it takes to be the truth is in fact a falsehood founded on a dishonest interpretation of reality (WP, 5 KSA 12: 5 [71]). As we saw earlier in relation to the *ressentiment* subject, Christian values, according to Nietzsche, are illegitimate interpretations that do not reflect the character of mind-independent reality (GS, 357). When reality resists our evaluative efforts, however, it is not enough, in Nietzsche's view, for us to expose their error. Rather, new values must be created ('How foolish it would be to suppose that one only needs to point out this origin and this

---

[29] Non-veridical values, as capacities, are 'weaker' than their veridical counterparts and cannot overcome resistance to their realization.

misty shroud of delusion in order to *destroy* the world that counts for real, so-called, "*reality*." We can destroy only as creators ... ' (GS, 58)). We can surmise that the reason that the pinpointing of error is insufficient here is because in pinpointing error we do not thereby reveal reality naked. Rather, we continue to interpret it evaluatively because it is impossible for us to do otherwise. However, although the process of replacing errors does not reveal reality in the way just described, the measure of the 'strength' of the new creations is not the extent to which they cover up reality but rather the extent to which they overcome the gap between appearance and reality – between how we would like the world to be and the character of reality itself. Such an overcoming is achieved, according to Nietzsche, through the correction of historically inherited viewpoints and values ('the whole primal age and past of all sentient being continues in me to invent, to love, to hate, and to infer' (GS, 54; cf. GS, 57)) in light of the 'consistency and interrelatedness of all knowledge' (GS, 54). Correction, then, involves acknowledging that the old values are false in light of our knowledge of ourselves and reality. We may retain the names of our old values (such as truth, goodness, etc.) due to the limitations of language, but the intentional content of these terms alters in light of our ever increasing and comprehensive knowledge of our own natural capacities and the natural capacities of reality itself. Nietzsche tends to use the terms 'revaluation of values' and 'creation of values' inter-changeably despite the fact that they do not necessarily mean the same thing. Revaluation suggests the retention of the older values but the adoption of an altered view towards them. Creation, however, suggests that newer values replace the older ones. However, the two descriptions are arguably compa-tible if we take revaluation to entail the retention of some of the names of the old values and creation to signal a change in the intentional content of those terms. Revaluation, therefore, can entail both the retention of older values and their replacement if the latter are understood as involving the replace-ment of the old intentional content with more adequate intentional con-tent.[30] We see this in Nietzsche's description of goodness, not in terms of Christian meekness and obedience, for example, but rather in terms of power. According to Nietzsche in GS, the creation of values is 'our best

---

[30] Simon May suggests that Nietzsche revalues old values rather than replacing them. He writes that 'Nietzsche accepts many of the values, concepts and attitudes which feature in traditional Christian or secular morality – such as "altruism" and "truthfulness", "responsibility" and "soul", "asceticism" and "guilt", "pity" and "god" – provided they can have life-enhancing functions' (Simon May, *Nietzsche's Ethics and His War on Morality* (Oxford: Oxford University Press, 1999), p. 5). However, in cases where Nietzsche retains some of the old values, he radically alters the content and meaning of those values.

power' (GS, 301), where power is understood as a natural capacity and where the latter claim follows from his adoption of a comprehensive perspective in that book. Although the logic of his argument has been pointing to the causal metaphysics of the will to power, he mentions it explicitly by name when in book five of the text he contends that when the natural scientist comes out of his 'nook', he is forced to realize that 'in nature it is not conditions of distress that are *dominant* but overflow and squandering – in accordance with the will to power . . . ' (GS, 349).

However, it is conceivable that my efforts to demonstrate that Nietzsche adopts a similar metaphysically laden and non-fictionalist approach to value in both BGE and GS might still be called into question by singling out the metaphysically laden and non-fictional components for individual and separate critical attention. The non-fictionalist component might be singled out for criticism in the following way: one might argue that the 'new creation' of values mentioned previously in relation to Nietzsche's position in GS represents not a more adequate evaluative paradigm but, rather, the replacement of previous errors with new errors. Such an objection, if correct, would count in favour of the fictionalist interpretation. Evidence for the objection might be sought from GS, 58, by interpreting Nietzsche as claiming that errors that are arbitrarily projected onto 'reality' are taken to be its essence such that with errors that are consistent and uniform there is no distinction to be made between appearance and reality. However, this interpretation is belied by Nietzsche's criticism of Christian values as 'indecent and dishonest' (GS, 357) and his demand that we 'scrutinize our experiences as severely as a scientific experiment' (GS, 319). The view that all values are errors is also inconsistent with his criticism of those that 'tolerate slack feelings in his faith and judgements and – does not account *the desire for certainty* as his inmost craving and deepest distress – as that which separates the higher human beings from the lower' (GS, 2). Yet it might still be objected that Nietzsche's distinction between 'higher' and 'lower' is a distinction not between veridical and non-veridical values but between preferred ways of life. But Nietzsche makes it clear that the values of the higher individuals must be founded on knowledge when he writes that the 'nobler spirits' (GS, 381) must also be scholars (GS, 384). These healthy 'argonauts of the ideal', he claims, experience a 'burning hunger in our conscience and science (*In Wissen und Gewissen*)' (GS, 382).

The non-fictionalist component of my argument can be defended from criticism, then, by recognizing that, for Nietzsche, some ways of life are better than others. And what makes them better is the extent to which they promote values that reflect an appreciation of the true rather than false manner in which the human valuer is embedded in nature. In GS, Nietzsche contrasts such veridical values with the values taught by those he calls the ethical teachers, for example, which presuppose and require transcendent, non-naturalistic support. The ethical teacher, he contends, in appealing to a transcendent metaphysical support for values, 'invents a second, different existence and unhinges by means of his new mechanism the old, ordinary existence' (GS, 1). In contrast the values of the free spirit capture 'reality *as it is*' (EH, 'Destiny', 5, 3; GS, 110; BGE, 230) and reality for Nietzsche in both BGE and GS is will to power (BGE, 36; GS, 349). The human evaluating self is immersed in and metaphysically continuous with nature by virtue of sharing the same essential nature of reality (BGE, 186) as will to power (BGE, 12, 36, 230). The non-fictionalist component of my argument is, accordingly, reciprocally dependent on Nietzsche's causal metaphysics of the will to power. Still, it may be objected that my interpretation of the objectivity of value in Nietzsche oscillates between a cognitivist and non-cognitivist account of Nietzsche's non-fictionalism. That is, it will be contended that I oscillate between describing values as capable of being veridical or non-veridical in the first part of the chapter and describing them as causal powers or dispositional capacities in the latter part. Correlatively, it might be worried that I operate with two different accounts of objectivity or veridicality, that is, objectivity as the consideration of multiple perspectives and objectivity as the cooperation of a value with the dispositional fabric of reality itself. But there is no inconsistency here. This is because although values are, for Nietzsche, causes or dispositions, these causes or dispositions, through their interaction with and constraint by the causal fabric of mind-independent reality, generate reasons in support, or not, of their objectivity or veridicality. The generation of reasons facilitates the adoption of a comprehensive perspective or the consideration of multiple perspectives in relation to one another amongst those with sufficient intellectual conscience to determine the objectivity of a value.[31] As remarked earlier, epistemology and ontology, for Nietzsche, are reciprocally dependent. Consequently, we can say, along with the cognitivist that our values can be veridical or non-veridical and yet we can also say, along with the non-cognitivist, that values do not mirror or

---

[31] Nietzsche denies that all evaluating agents are sufficiently strong to adopt a comprehensive perspective from a height to determine the objectivity of their values and that they instead remain caught within their narrow, nook, perspectives. Consequently, although they provide reasons for their beliefs, they are bad or weak reasons. See, GM, II, 11.

correspond to the world. Rather, for Nietzsche, values direct our interaction with the world instead of corresponding to it.[32]

Nevertheless, the metaphysical component to the argument might also be singled out for criticism by virtue of the fact that a possible objection to it is lurking in the shadows. That is, it might be objected that the appeal to a comprehensive perspective entailing an explanation of reality and value as will to power in support of a non-fictionalist account of value unnecessarily commits Nietzsche to a revisionary account of science and of nature. A more economical and metaphysically neutral interpretation would be to argue that Nietzsche leaves natural science alone and takes its – mechanical – account of nature at face value. The objection here is that Nietzsche's emphasis on artistic creation in relation to value, whilst not entailing that human minds constitute the empirical world of our experience, can and should nonetheless be demarcated from the empirical sphere of causes that is the proper subject matter of the natural scientist and not the value creating philosopher. Proponents of this view, such as Clark and Dudrick, agree that value creation in the sense discussed by Nietzsche in GS, 301, for example, is not a statement in favour of value fictionalism, but they argue that it should be understood in somewhat similar terms to the contemporary distinction between causes and reasons.[33] According to their interpretation, Nietzsche is committed to the idea that values can be distinguished from the natural sphere of causes and consequently that the spheres of the natural sciences and human values are to be distinguished in kind after all.[34] Whilst this view is not wholly incorrect in terms of the acknowledgement that it affords of Nietzsche's emphasis on the need to give reasons in support of our values

---

[32] This claim will be further illustrated and justified in my account of value as will to power in Chapters 4 and 5.

[33] Clark and Dudrick write that 'what many later philosophers learned from the work of Wilfrid Sellars, Nietzsche learned from Afrikan Spir'. See Maudemarie Clark and David Dudrick, *The Soul of Nietzsche's Beyond Good and Evil* (Cambridge: Cambridge University Press, 2012), p. 124. They understand Spir's influence differently to Michael Steven Green, *Nietzsche and the Transcendental Tradition* (Urbana, IL: University of Illinois Press, 2002).

[34] See Clark and Dudrick, *The Soul of Nietzsche's Beyond Good and Evil*, p. 235. See also Clark, 'On Knowledge, Truth and Value', p. 53. That Clark and Dudrick must consider the distinction between causes and reasons to be a metaphysically discontinuous difference in kind, despite their non-cognitivist interpretation elsewhere ('Nietzsche and Moral Objectivity', p. 201), is evident from their support for the following statement from Spir:

> For our bodily organization can certainly contain the physical antecedents or causes of our judgments, but not their logical antecedents (the principles) of cognition. A principle or law of cognition is the inner disposition to believe something of objects, and as such it can never be a product of physical causes, *with which by its very nature it has nothing in common* (my emphasis). (Spir cited by Clark and Dudrick, 'The Naturalisms of *Beyond Good and Evil*', p. 160)

(GS, 2, 319) and although it agrees with mine in interpreting Nietzsche as a non-fictionalist with regard to value, it is, nevertheless, incomplete.

According to Clark and Dudrick, consciousness, agency and normativity capture the sphere of reason-giving[35] and is to be demarcated from the sphere of nature (that is not constituted by us).[36] The argument is that Nietzsche allows that science affords knowledge of the natural world but denies that 'everything can be explained scientifically'.[37] What cannot be explained scientifically is our capacity for giving reasons in support of what we 'ought' to do, a process that is bound by certain constraints about what we are justified or permitted to value. That Nietzsche allows for this capacity is not in question here. However, the manner in which he takes the sphere of values to be continuous with the sphere of natural causes is. As part of their argument to preserve the continuity of our reason-giving capacities with nature, Clark and Dudrick interpret these capacities as non-cognitive attitudes where these attitudes are not mere preferences but rather commitments that express 'a disposition the person regards as justified, as supported by reasons'.[38] They present this argument contrary to what they see as a flaw in John McDowell's cognitivist distinction between the normative space of reasons and the space of scientific description, which, in their view, allows the space of reasons to float free of the space of causes.[39] Nevertheless, I am not convinced that Clark and Dudrick succeed in avoiding the problem. This is because Clark and Dudrick's placing of our reason-giving capacities in the sphere of nature entails merely giving a causal explanation from the outside of how these capacities have arisen but it does not consider reason-giving capacities as causes within nature itself and hence metaphysically continuous – from the inside – with nature. As a result, despite their claim to be able to give a naturalistic explanation of our reason-giving capacities, their account is subject to a tension, which has the effect of separating our values from the world and highlighting the metaphysical discontinuity presupposed in their argument. That is, if they persist in the claim that reasons are non-cognitive attitudes that are neither true nor false and that do not represent the world, then it is difficult to see how our values can be, without further qualification, subject to constraint and irreducible to

---

[35] Clark and Dudrick, 'The Naturalisms of *Beyond Good and Evil*', p. 164.
[36] Clark, 'On Knowledge, Truth and Value', p. 77. Here she claims that perspectives do not constitute objects but, rather, reveal them.
[37] Clark and Dudrick, 'The Naturalisms of *Beyond Good and Evil*', p. 168.
[38] Maudemarie Clark and David Dudrick, 'Nietzsche and Moral Objectivity', p. 214.   [39] Ibid.

mere preferences.[40] And if, on the other hand, they take reasons to be cognitive beliefs, then they fall prey to their own criticism of McDowell by running the risk of being unable to explain how our capacity to give reasons is naturalistic. An intermediate position is required that allows us to make the distinction between causes and reasons but that none-theless considers the two capacities as metaphysically continuous rather than distinct. According to my interpretation, we can still make a distinction between causes and reasons, but contrary to Clark and Dudrick, we find that such a distinction doesn't come metaphysically cheap. Rather, it presupposes a dispositional metaphysics.

Interpretations such as Clark and Dudrick's arise from the presupposi-tion that Nietzsche holds to a broadly Humean disenchanted view of nature, which sharply demarcates the sphere of facts from the sphere of values.[41] Although Nietzsche certainly worries about re-enchanting nature (GS, 109), it is not clear that this worry commits him or that he is in fact committed to the Humean view. Rather, there is considerable evidence that Nietzsche is critical of Hume's account of causality and understanding of laws of nature in terms of observed correlations of events rather than in terms of causal powers (BGE, 22; GS, 112).[42] If we don't accept that Nietzsche is committed to the Humean view, then we are licensed to understand what he means by seeing things more comprehensively (GS, 301) as broadening rather than leaving alone the dominant conception of natural science as a description of value-free facts about inert matter. Nietzsche suggests as much when he writes that the natural scientist should cast off their narrow, nook, perspective and recognize the will to power as an account, not just of the workings of human psychology and value but also of the operations of 'nature' more generally (GS, 349). Nature, Nietzsche argues, revolves 'around power – in accordance with the will to power which is the will to life' (GS, 349).

Yet it will be counter-argued that Nietzsche's caution against 'thinking that the world is a living being' in GS, 109, counts against the applicability of the will to power thesis to physical inorganic nature and that his description of nature as will to power in GS, 349, applies to organic nature

---

[40] For an argument that Clark and Dudrick's non-cognitivism succumbs to similar problems to standard non-cognitivist positions, see Nadeem J. Z. Hussain, 'Honest Illusion: Valuing for Nietzsche's Free Spirits', in Leiter and Sinhababu (eds.), *Nietzsche and Morality*, pp. 157–191.

[41] Clark and Dudrick, *The Soul of Nietzsche's Beyond Good and Evil*, p. 235.

[42] It might be objected that Nietzsche rejects the objective applicability of the concept of causality (BGE, 21). However, whilst he rejects the mechanical account of causality (GS, 112; BGE, 12), he does not reject the concept of causality *per se* (BGE, 36) but rather construes causality on the model of a continuum (GS, 112).

only. However, Nietzsche's caution is a little ambiguous on two grounds: in the same passage in which he issues the caution (GS, 109), he also advises, contrary to scientific mechanism, against describing the world as a machine, in addition to proposing the idea that the living and the dead are not metaphysical opposites. Nietzsche's denial that inorganic nature should be understood as a machine that is opposed to life belies the idea that he adheres to the conception of inert, powerless, matter in that passage. Moreover, in response to the issue of whether the world should be described in purely mechanistic terms or whether it should be described anthropomorphically in terms of life, Nietzsche argues in favour of the metaphysical continuity rather than opposition of the latter description with the former. He writes, 'Let us beware of saying that death is opposed to life. The living is merely a type of what is dead, and a very rare type' (GS, 109). The preceding two factors allow Nietzsche to claim that the will to power is the will to life and still describe inorganic nature in terms of the will to power because inorganic nature understood as will to power is metaphysically continuous with, rather than identical to, organic life. The metaphysical continuity of inorganic with organic nature resides in its essential causal activity, its will to power, even if this activity is not to be understood solely in a biological sense. The argument of GS, 109, then, does not rule out and indeed seems to rule in a revisionary account of science and the metaphysics of the will to power. Yet how are we to understand Nietzsche's initial caution? It seems to me that when he warns against understanding the world as a living being, he cautions us not against the general applicability of the will to power thesis but rather against the illegitimate anthropomorphization of nature. But Nietzsche's appeal to metaphysical continuity in GS, 109, avoids such anthropomorphization on the grounds that although he understands the inorganic world to be metaphysically continuous with the organic one, he does not reduce one to the other in the form of a reductive realism or idealism. According to Nietzsche, it is perfectly legitimate to describe the physical world and organic life as will to power without entailing that they are identical with or reducible to one another. That this is the case may be discerned further from his claim that the world operates according to inner causal powers but not according to laws of nature (GS, 109; BGE, 22). The idea of there obtaining laws of nature which are imposed upon nature from outside and which it obeys is, in Nietzsche's view, nothing more than an 'aesthetic anthropomorphism' (GS, 109). The argument here is very similar to that of BGE, 22, where he claims that we should describe the 'mechanical' world not as conforming to nomological and ultimately anthropomorphic laws of nature but rather as operating according to a necessity that emanates from within nature and which can be described as will to power (BGE, 22). A close examination of GS, 109, then, indicates that Nietzsche's concern with the issue of illegitimately anthropomorphizing nature does not lead him to accept the mechanical account of inert, powerless matter or a Humean account of causality and that, accordingly, his concerns in that passage do not count against the logic of accepting the argument for the comprehensive applicability of the will to power thesis.

Still, I have a certain sympathy with interpretations such as that of Clark and Dudrick in that they want to capture the respects in which Nietzsche thinks that the human being, its capacity for conscious, normative and evaluative thought, is irreducible to nature. However, I don't think that one needs to commit Nietzsche to a Humean account of causality from the outside and a non-causal account of normativity and value to achieve this. Nonetheless, this is not to say that the will to power thesis is unproblematic and more certainly needs to be said in relation to the issue than has been said here. The focus of the current chapter has been to establish that there is a line of thought in Nietzsche's writings that commits him to a non-fictionalist and metaphysically laden account of value that captures the phenomenology of value by maintaining that values reflect human beings and their particular manner of engaging with the world but are nonetheless subject to a realist constraint and the possibility of correction in light of that constraint. The attention given to the will to power thesis reflects Nietzsche's argument that our values are subject to a realist constraint by virtue of their metaphysical continuity with nature. However, further examination of the will to power and its implications for the metaphysics of value will be undertaken in the chapters that follow.

The next three chapters will take on board this task by arguing, first, that despite the contentious character of Nietzsche's will to power thesis as a characterization of reality in both philosophical and textual terms, it can, nevertheless, be seen to be supported by a coherent and justifiable rationale. This rationale, I argue, can be unearthed by considering the will to power thesis as a response to Kant's idealistic epistemology and metaphysics. Nietzsche's engagement with Kant will be seen to be a way, on Nietzsche's part, of criticizing and responding to Hume's scepticism regarding causality and for developing a distinctively non-Humean account of causal power. Secondly, I examine the implications of Nietzsche's appeal to the will to power for understanding the metaphysical status of our values. Specifically, I argue that by holding that values are metaphysically continuous with the causal fabric of reality, Nietzsche puts forward a dispositional account of value that abandons Hume's distinction between facts and values. Thirdly, and finally, in Chapter 5, I examine how Nietzsche's appeal to the will to power caters for the causal efficacy of consciousness and allows for the possibility of meaningful human agency.

CHAPTER 3

The Will to Power as a Response to Kant

In the previous chapter, we saw that the will to power thesis is implicated in Nietzsche's appeal to a comprehensive perspective and in our reconstructed account of his argument for the objectivity of value. However, an independent justification of the will to power thesis that shows how Nietzsche intends the will to power to secure the metaphysical continuity of the human mind with the world is needed. The appeal to metaphysical continuity must overcome the distinction between appearance and reality by allowing that we can capture the character of the world from the inside rather than as a *mere* appearance from the outside. The aim of this chapter is to respond to the need for an independent justification that satisfies the preceding requirements by demonstrating that the will to power emerges from and is justified within the context of Nietzsche's critical reflections on Kant's idealism. Although we have already indicated that Nietzsche abandons his early endorsement of Kant's idealism, the specific reasons for the rejection and the direct link between these reasons and the justification of the will to power have not been made explicit. It is necessary to make Nietzsche's justification explicit because the will to power is a much maligned thesis in the Nietzsche literature and in philosophical circles more generally. Whilst many commentators are willing to accept the thesis in a restricted form as a description of human psychology, Nietzsche's extension of the thesis beyond the human domain has been met with considerable interpretive and philosophical resistance. For example, according to Clark and Dudrick, 'That he called attention to the importance of power relations in human life is certainly to Nietzsche's credit. But the doctrine put forward and defended in BGE is that life, human psychology, and perhaps even reality itself are fundamentally to be understood as will to power, and this claim has done little to enhance his reputation among philosophers. Nietzsche's reputation continues to grow among serious philosophers, but always in spite of the doctrine of the will to

power, never because of it.'[1] According to some, Nietzsche's metaphysics of
the will to power as a thesis about the character of mind-independent
reality amounts to a 'crackpot metaphysics'.[2] However, even those commentators that do take the metaphysical version of the will to power
seriously tend to confine their examinations to a description of the thesis
rather than offering a justification of it.[3] In the absence of an appropriate
justification, Nietzsche's view that the continuity of the human mind with
the world entails metaphysical continuity from within and is not restricted
to the idea that our human abilities and activities can be explained according
to external causal impacts from without remains philosophically suspect.
However, an appropriate justification will be offered and the appeal to
metaphysical continuity secured by arguing that Nietzsche's critical engagement with Kant's idealism culminates in an essentialist and non-Humean
proposal that empirical reality is constituted by mind-independent, intrinsic
but relational causal powers. Although we are ultimately interested in the
implications of the will to power thesis for Nietzsche's understanding of the
metaphysics of value, focussing on the will to power thesis as an account of
mind-independent reality provides the necessary background for understanding how Nietzsche construes human values as metaphysically continuous with but irreducible to the causal fabric of the world.

Nietzsche's critical interpretation of Kant is, of course, very much influenced by his reading of neo-Kantian thinkers, most notably Kuno Fischer,
Friedrich Albert Lange and Arthur Schopenhauer.[4] His understanding

---

[1] Maudemarie Clark and David Dudrick, *The Soul of Nietzsche's* Beyond Good and Evil (Cambridge: Cambridge University Press, 2012), p. 5.
[2] Brian Leiter, 'Nietzsche's Naturalism Reconsidered' in Ken Gemes and John Richardson (eds.), *The Oxford Handbook of Nietzsche* (Oxford: Oxford University Press, 2013), pp. 576–598, p. 594.
[3] See, for example, John Richardson, *Nietzsche's System* (Oxford: Oxford University Press, 1996).
[4] For a discussion of the importance of Fischer, Lange and Schopenhauer on Nietzsche's understanding of Kant, see R. Kevin Hill, *Nietzsche's Critiques: The Kantian Foundations of His Thought*
(Oxford: Clarendon Press, 2003), pp. 13–19. Nietzsche began reading Schopenhauer's *Die Welt als
Wille und Vorstellung* in 1865. He continued to read this book along with others by Schopenhauer in
the following years. For a discussion of Nietzsche's reading of Schopenhauer, see Thomas Brobjer,
Nietzsche's Philosophical Context: An Intellectual Biography (Urbana, IL: University of Illinois Press,
2008), pp. 29, 31–32, 47–49, 55, 66–70, 72, 191–198 and 211–212. Nietzsche read the first edition of
Lange's *Geschichte des Materialismus und Kritik seiner Bedeutung in der Gegenwart* in 1866 and again
in 1868 and 1873. See Brobjer, *Nietzsche's Philosophical Context*, pp. 33–35, 192, 195 and 206, for further
discussion. Nietzsche read the fourth and fifth volumes of Fischer's *Geschichte der neuern Philosophie*
and his commentary on Kant, *Immanuel Kant und seine Lehre*, by 1868. See Brobjer, *Nietzsche's
Philosophical Context*, pp. 37 and 49. Nietzsche also purchased a copy of Überweg's *Grundriß der
Geschichte der Philosophie von Thales bis auf die Gegenwart* in 1867. See Giuliano Campioni, Paolo
D'Iorio, Maria Cristina Fornari, Francesco Fronterotta, Andrea Orsucci and Renate Müller-Buck,
Nietzsches persönliche Bibliothek (Berlin: De Gruyter, 2003), pp. 641–642 and Brobjer, *Nietzsche's
Philosophical Context*, pp. 37, 49, 194–195 and 205. There is evidence that Nietzsche was familiar with

of Kant was influenced by Fischer's emphasis on a priori conditions of knowledge in Kant and the sceptical implications that followed for the possibility of our knowing the thing-in-itself. Nietzsche's interpretation of Kant was also coloured by Lange's account of how our knowledge is made possible and limited by psychological and physiological idealist conditions in addition to his abandonment of the idea of genuine metaphysical knowledge in favour of understanding metaphysics as a form of conceptual poetry. Nietzsche was particularly influenced by Schopenhauer's idealist distinction between appearances constituted by the forms of space, time and causality and the thing-in-itself as a blind will to which our own experience of willing gives us access. Although Nietzsche is ultimately critical of each of these neo-Kantian positions, as is evident from his disapproval of Kant's non-empirical transcendental self and a priori conditions of knowledge that are emphasized by Fischer and in his criticism of attempts to consistently combine idealism with a physiological or empirical self as in Lange and Schopenhauer (BGE, 15) and, further, in his rejection of Schopenhauer's view that the will is either immediately known or simple (BGE, 16), it is nonetheless the case that he draws on these criticisms in forming an assessment of Kant's idealism more generally, taking them to be indicative of tensions and ambiguities that lie at the heart of Kant's idealism even if, as some have suggested, Nietzsche's acquaintance with Kant's texts was second-hand and mediated by neo-Kantian authors. That he takes various neo-Kantian interpretations as shedding light on Kant's arguments themselves perhaps accounts for why Nietzsche often presents himself as responding to Kant rather than to neo-Kantian sources primarily. This would explain his tendency to name Kant as one of his principal interlocutors rather than those neo-Kantians that clearly influenced his interpretation of Kant.[5] This tendency can be further

---

Afrikan Spir's *Forschung nach der Gewissheit in der Erkenntniss der Wirklichkeit, Denken und Wirklichkeit* and *Versuch einer Erneuerung der kritischen Philosophie*. See Brobjer, *Nietzsche's Philosophical Context*, pp. 71–72, 203 and 207. Michael Steven Green and Maudemarie Clark and David Dudrick give conflicting accounts of the influence of Afrikan Spir on Nietzsche's thought. See Michael Steven Green, *Nietzsche and the Transcendental Tradition* (Urbana, IL: University of Illinois Press, 2002) and Maudemarie Clark and David Dudrick, 'The Naturalisms of *Beyond Good and Evil*' in Keith Ansell Pearson (ed.), *A Companion to Nietzsche* (Oxford: Blackwell, 2006), pp. 148–168. For a discussion of the role of Eugen Karl Dühring on Nietzsche's understanding of Kant's Antinomies, see Hill, *Nietzsche's Critiques*, pp. 142–143. For further discussions of Nietzsche and neo-Kantianism, see George J. Stack, *Lange and Nietzsche* (New York: de Gruyter, 1983); Claudia Crawford, *The Beginnings of Nietzsche's Theory of Language* (Berlin: de Gruyter, 1988), Chapter Six; Christian J. Emden, *Nietzsche's Naturalism: Philosophy and the Life Sciences in the Nineteenth Century* (Cambridge: Cambridge University Press, 2014), pp. 20–33.

[5] R. Kevin Hill notes that Kant is the third most mentioned philosopher in Nietzsche's writings, after Plato and Schopenhauer (Hill, *Nietzsche's Critiques*, p. 5n8).

accounted for by Nietzsche's practice of employing philosophical figures to highlight philosophical issues that are of concern to him. That it is the issue that is of overriding importance rather than the scholarly source of the issue is evident from the fact that Nietzsche often discusses philosophical issues pertaining to Kantian idealism without naming either Kant or neo-Kantian sources. The latter practice is evident, for example, in BGE, 15, where Nietzsche offers a *reductio ad absurdum* argument against the practice of combining idealism with an empirical account of the self but where neither Kant himself nor neo-Kantian assessments of Kant are explicitly mentioned. According to Nietzsche, scholarly analyses of texts have an important role to play in bringing to light some issue of philosophical significance, but for him, it is the issue that is of overriding importance (GS, 366). Consequently, although neo-Kantian influences undoubtedly lurk heavily in the background and colour how Nietzsche views Kant and how he thinks that Kant's arguments should be modified, these historical specifics do not alter the logic of Nietzsche's engagement with Kant, as he understands Kant. Thus, whilst I will make pertinent references to some of these neo-Kantian sources in the course of the chapter, I will follow Nietzsche's lead by placing the emphasis squarely on the issue under discussion and use Nietzsche's references or implied references to Kant to highlight these issues.

The chapter will be structured in three parts. The first focusses on Nietzsche's later qualified praise but ultimate criticism of Kant's idealism. Although we have addressed Nietzsche's endorsement of Kant's idealism in TL and his criticism of it in HAH in the specific context of how he understands and alters the relation between art and science, we will explore Nietzsche's praise and ultimate criticism of Kant in more detail here, paying particular attention to how Nietzsche interprets Kant's success in responding to Hume. Nietzsche's qualified praise of Kant comes in the guise of his approval of Kant's aim to establish, contrary to Hume's scepticism, the objective applicability of the concept of causality. However, Nietzsche is disappointed that Kant's account of synthesis, in his view, falls short of bringing this aim to a successful resolution despite a promising stance adopted in Kant's pre-critical writings in response to the *vis viva* debate. The second section assesses how Nietzsche's will to power thesis responds to the shortcomings of Kant's project by offering a naturalization of Kant's account of synthesis. Nietzsche puts forward an argument, contrary to Kant, as he sees it, in favour of the mind-independent but knowable character of the world, an argument that culminates in the thesis that the fundamental constituents of reality, relational powers, are also intrinsic.

Having examined Kant's influence on Nietzsche's will to power thesis, I turn, finally, to consider how the conclusions of this examination can be used to make sense of Nietzsche's claims regarding the will to power in BGE, 36, in addition to responding to Clark and Dudrick's objection to interpreting this passage as a serious articulation of the will to power as a metaphysical thesis. Clark and Dudrick's objection also serves to call into question my argument that Nietzsche arrives at the will to power as a result of sustained critical engagement with Kant rather than, as they claim, acceptance of his demarcation of normativity from the sphere of mechanical nature. Since the issues at stake in this discussion are of considerable textual and philosophical importance and carry significant implications for how we should understand not just Nietzsche's account of the metaphysical character of the world but also his account of the metaphysical status of our values in relation to it, particular care will be taken to outline and respond to Clark and Dudrick's textual and philosophical arguments in detail. Nietzsche's will to power thesis can hardly be expected to be taken seriously as a metaphysical thesis outside of Nietzsche studies if it is not taken seriously within it. Therefore, it is with a view to highlighting the logic of Nietzsche's justification of the thesis that we examine it as a response to Kant and seek to defend it from the strenuous objections of Clark and Dudrick.

Nietzsche's Qualified Praise for Kant's Idealism

That Nietzsche is engaging with Kantian themes is evident from his earliest to his late writings. In particular, he singles out for praise what he sees as Kant's efforts to overcome rationalist dogmatism by restricting our knowledge to the empirical world of space, time and causality and denying the possibility of pure conceptual access to things as they are in themselves. This is evident, for example, in BT, where he writes:

> The hardest-fought victory of all was won by the enormous courage and wisdom of *Kant* and *Schopenhauer*, a victory over the optimism which lies hidden in the nature of logic and which in turn is the hidden foundation of our culture. Whereas this optimism once believed in our ability to grasp and solve, with the help of the seemingly reliable *aeternae veritates*, all the puzzles of the universe, and treated space, time, and causality as entirely unconditional laws of the most general validity, Kant showed that these things actually only served to raise mere appearance, the work of maya, to the status of the sole and supreme reality... (BT, p. 87, section 18)

Although this passage is taken from Nietzsche's first published book, he praises Kant's efforts to restrict our knowledge to the empirical world in both his early and late writings. But there is a difference in his praise across these periods. In the early writings, Nietzsche endorses Kant's idealist method and the sceptical implications that he thinks follows from it. Thus we find him embracing a constitutive account of mind, arguing that the relation between the mind and the empirical world must be understood in terms of the dependency of the latter on the former. In these writings, though, he wavers between different accounts of the constitutive mind. As we have already witnessed, in the unpublished TL, he adopts what he takes to be a position faithful to Kant's idealism, holding that the empirical world is constituted through the imposition of human cognitive forms on the data of sense. Whilst in BT, Nietzsche endorses the idea that the empirical world is mind-correlative, the mind which is responsible for its constitution is not a human mind but rather a quasi-divine world artist that projects the forms of the empirical world (BT, pp. 25–26, section 4). Despite these differences in the description of the constitutive mind in the two texts, Nietzsche agrees that the world of our empirical experience is dependent on mind and divorced from the intrinsic, mind-independent, character of things-in-themselves.[6] Kant's restriction of our knowledge to the empirical world, for Nietzsche, entails a sceptical dissociation of things-in-themselves from our human capacity for knowledge.

Whilst he continues to praise Kant in the later writings of the 1880s, this praise is qualified as his focus switches to Kant's response to the dangers of empiricism in addition to the excessive epistemic claims of rationalism. His praise for Kant in this regard leads him to become increasingly critical of Kant's idealism, which, he argues, renders Kant's efforts to respond to the problems with empiricism unsuccessful despite its success in curbing the immoderate tendencies of rationalism. In particular, Nietzsche praises Kant's aim to secure, contrary to Hume, the objective applicability of the concept of causality as an issue of special importance:

> Let us recall . . . *Kant's* tremendous question mark that he placed after the concept of 'causality' – without, like Hume, doubting its legitimacy altogether. Rather, Kant began cautiously to delimit the realm within which this

---

[6] It is to be noted that Nietzsche does not consistently endorse Kant's idealistically informed distinction between appearance and reality. For example in 'On Schopenhauer' [OS] (*Zu Schopenhauer*) (1867–1868, KGW I/4, pp. 421–427), he is critical of the idea of the thing-in-itself, and in PTG (PTG, KSA 1, pp. 801–872), his endorsement of Kant's critical writings pertains to the latter's rejection of philosophical dogmatism rather than an endorsement of his idealism.

concept makes sense (and to this day we are not done with this fixing of limits). (GS, 357)

According to Hume, although we possess the concept of causality, the objective applicability of this concept in a judgement cannot be rationally justified. The reason for this is that whilst the imagination encourages our assent to beliefs and renders us psychologically disposed to believe that the world operates according to necessary causal laws, it operates independently of rational constraints. Devoid of these constraints, we cannot justifiably be assured that the concept of causality is objectively applicable. Hume reduces causality to mere mechanical spatial contiguity and succession in time, denying that we are entitled to attribute causal powers to nature and claiming that our belief in causality as spatial contiguity and succession is founded on psychological habit and custom rather than rational justification. Central to Kant's response to Hume's challenge is his account of synthesis in the Transcendental Deduction section of his *Critique of Pure Reason* [CPR]. Although Kant wrote two versions of the Deduction, Nietzsche doesn't explicitly distinguish between them and instead stresses the role of the psychological faculties in Kant's efforts to demonstrate the possibility of synthetic a priori knowledge generally. He writes:

> But let's think about it, it is high time. 'How are synthetic a priori judgements *possible?*' wondered Kant, and what did he answer? They are *facilitated by a faculty:* unfortunately, however, he did not say this in four words, but so cumbersomely, so venerably, and with such an expense of German profundity and ornateness that people misheard the comical *niaiserie allemande* in such an answer. (BGE, 11)

However, despite the fact that Nietzsche doesn't distinguish between the A and B versions of the Deduction, it is in the A version that Kant formulates his account of synthesis in terms of psychological faculties most strongly. According to Kant, synthesis takes place in three logically separable but practically inseparable stages, where each stage is attributed to a distinct mental faculty. The three stages – apprehension in intuition, reproduction in imagination and recognition in a concept – are performed by the faculties of Sensibility, Imagination and Understanding, respectively. Appealing to synthesis, Kant argues, contrary to Hume, that our beliefs about the world are rationally justified because the imagination's contribution to cognition operates under the rule-governed guidance of the concepts of Understanding.

However, although he praises Kant's aim to secure the objective applicability of the concept of causality, contrary to Hume, Nietzsche maintains
that Kant's account of synthesis is flawed and prevents him from successfully executing this aim. Consequently, he argues that Kant's project has
yet to be brought to fruition. Although he is not explicit about the reasons
for Kant's failure, we can reconstruct his argument by piecing together
remarks that he makes about Kant. When we do this, we find that
Nietzsche detects three problems in Kant's efforts to make the empirical
world a genuine object of knowledge and to establish the objectivity of
causality. The first sees Kant guilty of psychologism and the genetic fallacy.
The second sees Nietzsche turn his back on his own early Kantian position
to criticize what he sees as Kant's argument in favour of the existential
dependency of empirical objects of knowledge on human minds. Finally,
the third focuses on the sceptical implications of the mind-dependency of
objects in the context of Kant's reference to the thing-in-itself. According
to Nietzsche, these problems must be overcome if the true aim of Kant's
project is to be successfully achieved. I will reconstruct Nietzsche's three
criticisms before turning to his response.

Nietzsche contends that Kant mistakes the psychological origin of our
beliefs for a rational justification of them. In response to Kant's argument
in favour of the possibility of synthetic a priori knowledge, Nietzsche
writes: 'But the origin of a belief, of a strong conviction, is a psychological
problem: and a *very* narrow and limited experience often produces such a
belief!' (WP, 530, KSA 12: 7 [4]).[7] He also writes that '"[f]acilitated by a
faculty" – that's what he had said, or at least that's what he had meant. But
what kind of an answer is that? What kind of explanation? Isn't it rather
simply repeating the question?' (BGE, 21). One might attempt to defend
Kant here by pointing out that Nietzsche misunderstands Kant's argument
and that, in particular, he fails to appreciate the constraining role of
transcendental apperception, which as non-empirical and a necessary presupposition for the application of a priori concepts saves Kant from the
charge of the genetic fallacy.[8] Although Nietzsche does not offer a direct

---

[7] That Kant's transcendental account of our knowledge is concerned with origins can be seen from his
claim that 'what can alone be entitled transcendental is the knowledge that these representations are
not of empirical origin' (Kant, CPR, A56/B81). However, in BGE, 21, Nietzsche contends that recent
attempts to establish the necessity of causal laws have revealed more about the psychology and
preference of the author than the world. In BGE, 22, he indicates that necessity does not entail
conformity to extrinsic nomological impositions.

[8] One might object here and hold that it is the a priori character of concepts of the Understanding that
rationally constrain our judgements rather than transcendental apperception *per se*. However,
Nietzsche's criticism of apperception, if correct, would arguably apply to the application of the

response to this criticism, we can nonetheless see that, for him, the transcendental self cannot provide the much-needed constraint. The reason for this is that, in Nietzsche's view, the transcendental self is an empty notion. Nietzsche agrees with Kant's argument against rational psychology in the Paralogisms section of CPR but maintains that its scope should be extended to include a rejection of all non-empirical accounts of the self (BGE, 54, 12). However, rather than abandon the meaningfulness of the concept of self altogether, he contends that we should replace the content-less notion of a non-empirical self with the contentful notion of the 'mortal' self, constituted by hierarchical relations between drives and affects (BGE, 12). Within the context of Kant's account of synthesis, such a view of the self is incompatible with the need for a rational constraint. That is, within the context of Kant's understanding of the relation between mind and world as one where the former constitutes the latter by imposing its cognitive structures on the 'given' data of sense, the empirical self is unable to supply the requisite ingredients of universality and necessity. Although Nietzsche does not overtly address the matter, he appears to be sensitive to an ambiguity between the different levels, empirical and transcendental, on which Kant's account of synthesis is operating and which Kant does not make explicit. Nietzsche interprets synthesis in Kant as empirical rather than transcendental but he is sensitive to the fact that it is supposed to deliver a type of knowledge that is more than contingent (he acknowledges that it is supposed to be synthetic a priori in BGE, 11). Regardless of whether Nietzsche read Kant directly or not, he would have been aware from his reading of Kuno Fischer, for example, of the a priori character of the transcendental unity of apperception in Kant. Fischer defends Kant's account of the a priori character of the transcendental self in Kant's Deductions, unlike Lange and Schopenhauer who both consider Kant's arguments in the Deductions a failure and who, accordingly, seek to abstract Kant's arguments from his appeal to the non-empirical character of his transcendental psychology. Independent of these neo-Kantian influences, the basis for Nietzsche's view that Kant's synthesis operates empirically even though it is supposed to deliver a priori knowledge might be found in the A Deduction where Kant emphasizes the reproductive role of the imagination, although he replaces the account of threefold synthesis in the B Deduction with figurative synthesis that emphasises the a priori and transcendental role of the productive

concepts because Kant writes in a footnote to B134 (p. 154n) that '[i]ndeed this faculty of apperception is the understanding itself.'

imagination. Transcendental synthesis entails the synthesis of both empirical objects and the empirical self. Empirical synthesis, however, entails that
the empirical objects of the spatio-temporal world both affect and are
combined by the empirical self.[9] Although a charitable interpretation
might take the distinction between transcendental and empirical synthesis
as justification of Kant's claim that empirical objects are mind-independent
but that the conditions of their knowability are mind-dependent, Nietzsche
does not interpret it in this way. Rather, he points to what he thinks is the
vacuous character of Kant's appeal to transcendental conditions and emphasizing the empirical account of mind as the only contentful account of mind
available to us, he commits Kant to the view that the mind-dependency of
objects derives from an empirical account of synthesis. This brings us to the
second difficulty that Nietzsche detects in Kant. This problem pertains to
the constitutive role that Kant assigns to the mind and which results, in
Nietzsche's mature view, in an illegitimate reduction of the empirical objects
of our knowledge to mind-dependent representations.

According to Nietzsche, Kant's efforts to harmonize our knowledge
with the world results in the view that the objects of our knowledge
must conform to the conditions of human Understanding. In line with
his interpretation of synthesis as empirical, Nietzsche interprets transcendental idealism as a form of Berkelian empirical idealism. This means that
the empirical objects of our knowledge must be understood as constituted
by and existentially dependent on the human mind. Thus, in Nietzsche's
view, Kant runs together the epistemic conditions of knowing an object
with the existential conditions of its existence.[10] Once again, Nietzsche's
interpretation of Kant's idealism can be accounted for when we consider
that its formulation is heavily influenced by Schopenhauer and other neo-
Kantians who interpret Kant's idealism as entailing the existential dependency of empirical objects on the human mind.[11] Although we have already
seen that Nietzsche endorsed such idealism in some of his early writings, he

---

[9] See Robert Paul Wolff, *Kant's Theory of Mental Activity* (Gloucester, MA: Peter Smith, 1973), pp. 168–170.

[10] Nietzsche describes the status of Kant's empirical world as a ball tossed about in the heads of men (KSA 7: 19 [153]).

[11] Nietzsche was clearly aware of Schopenhauer's identification of the transcendental subject with the brain from his reading of *Die Welt als Wille und Vorstellung*, 2nd ed. (Leipzig: Brockhaus, 1844), Erster Band, Anfang. Kritik der Kantischen Philosophie. See Arthur Schopenhauer, *The World as Will and Representation*, Volume I, trans. E. F. J. Payne (New York, NY: Dover, 1966), p. 418. Despite differences between Fischer's, Lange's and Schopenhauer's interpretations of the transcendental subject in Kant, these neo-Kantians are agreed in their view that Kant's idealism is a form of Berkelian subjective idealism. See Hill, *Nietzsche's Critiques*, pp. 13–19.

was nonetheless aware of its sceptical implications in a Kantian and neo-Kantian context.[12] For example, in 'Schopenhauer as Educator' (1874), he writes that '[i]f Kant ever should begin to exercise any wide influence we shall be aware of it in the form of a gnawing and disintegrating scepticism and relativism . . . ' (SE, 3). This sceptical threat is to be initially detected, in Nietzsche's view, in the relativized account of objectivity implied by Kant's argument that the world as it is known by us is constituted by the human mind. In this context the empirical world of our knowledge is reduced to a mere 'appearance' and our knowledge is relativized to our human point of view. In his defence it may be argued that relativized objectivity is unproblematic for Kant on the grounds that his constitutive account of mind secures universal and necessary knowledge and that such hallmarks secure the intersubjective validity of human knowledge. As long as we combine this with metaphysical indifferentism,[13] it might be suggested, we need not worry about whether our experience of the world fulfils the non-relative standard of metaphysical correspondence.[14] One might go so far in support of this argument to point out that Nietzsche himself seems to propose a version of it in HAH, I, 9. As we saw in Chapter 1, in the latter book he argues that metaphysical knowledge, to the extent that it cannot make a practical difference to us, should not be allowed to interfere with our empirical knowledge. As long as our empirical experience is coherent, uniform and intersubjectively testable, the additional question of whether it fulfils the requirements of metaphysical correspondence is superfluous.[15] However, this argument is ultimately unsatisfactory when we consider its proposals in light of Nietzsche's interpretation of Kant. This interpretation, as we have seen, downplays the significance of Kant's appeal to the universality and necessity of our intersubjective empirical knowledge on the grounds that such universality and necessity cannot be secured by

---

[12] Nietzsche's sceptical interpretation of Kant's thing-in-itself is influenced by Fischer but also by his reading of Lange and Otto Liebmann, both of whom promoted a return to the epistemic caution of Kant's denial that we can have knowledge of the thing-in-itself. Nietzsche probably read Liebmann's *Zur Analysis der Wirklichkeit. Eine Erörterung der Grundprobleme der Philosophie* and the first part of *Gedanken und Thatsachen*. See Brobjer, *Nietzsche's Philosophical Context*, pp. 33–36, 221, 226–227.

[13] This is Peter Poellner's term in 'Perspectival Truth' in John Richardson and Brian Leiter (eds.), *Nietzsche* (Oxford: Oxford University Press, 2001), pp. 85–117, p. 111.

[14] Beatrice Han-Pile interprets Nietzsche's early writings in this way. See her 'Transcendental Aspects: Naturalistic Elements and Ontological Commitments in Nietzsche's Thought', *Inquiry*, 52.2, 2009, pp. 179–214.

[15] This position is similar to that adopted by Poellner in his argument for phenomenal objectivity, which was discussed in Chapter 1, and it is unsatisfactory for the reasons outlined there. Moreover, it is not Nietzsche's final word on the matter. For example, in GS, 54, he contends that our empirical experience may be compared to a uniform and coherent dream but denies that this experience may legitimately be contrasted with the notion of a thing-in-itself.

the empirical level on which Kant's account of synthesis operates. Although Kant appeals to transcendental levels of both the self and its activity in synthesis, for Nietzsche the transcendental self is an empty concept and is therefore unable to offer the rational constraints and guarantees needed to secure the argument in favour of relative, but inter-subjectively valid, objectivity. Moreover, the problem of scepticism and relativism is compounded, in Nietzsche's view, by the third problem that he detects in Kant. This is the problem surrounding Kant's combination of empirical idealism with a reference to the thing-in-itself.

According to Kant, the empirical objects of our knowledge belong to the world of space and time, which is a world of external relations. This means that the properties of an empirical object are not intrinsic to it but are characterized by its spatial relation to other objects. However, in Kant's view, these relations, constituted by the human mind, are 'only the relation of an object to a subject, and not the inner properties of the object in itself' (CPR, B67).[16] That is, these relations, constituted by the human mind, are not ultimately real and therefore require ontological support from intrinsic prop-erties or mind-independent properties considered 'in themselves' and apart from all relations (CPR, B67). For Kant, although the thought of such a thing-in-itself is implied by the argument of the Transcendental Deduction and its appeal to the relative objectivity of the phenomenal world of our experience, it is nonetheless a 'problematic' idea in that we cannot know it to actually obtain (CPR, A255). However, although there is evidence that Kant intended the distinction between phenomena and noumena to be a distinc-tion between two ways of knowing one and the same object rather than two ontological spheres (CPR, Bxxvii), Nietzsche interprets his reference to the thing-in-itself as a reference to a numerically distinct world that lies beyond our cognitive reach.[17] Moreover, Kant's reference to it, in Nietzsche's view, carries sceptical implications that undermine his efforts to establish the empirical world as an object of knowledge and to establish the objective applicability of the concept of causality, contrary to Hume. When these factors are taken into consideration, according to Nietzsche, it becomes impossible to be indifferent to Kant's thing-in-itself.[18] This is made

---

[16] Kant writes: 'What it is that is present in this or that location, or what it is that is operative in the things themselves apart from change of location, is not given through intuition' (Immanuel Kant, *Critique of Pure Reason* [CPR], trans. Norman Kemp Smith (London: Macmillan, 1929), B67).

[17] That Nietzsche understands the Kantian thing-in-itself in this way is evident from TI, 'Real World', where Nietzsche includes the Kantian thing-in-itself in his history of metaphysical dualism.

[18] Indifference also proves to be impossible for Nietzsche because Kant's reference to the thing-in-itself is not just employed negatively but also plays a positive role in acting as a basis for universal and, in Nietzsche's view, life-denying moral values. See, for example, BGE, 215.

particularly evident when we consider that Kant's transcendental project, which culminates in the argument of the Transcendental Deduction and its account of synthesis, is a product of his on-going pre-occupation with the metaphysical status of 'force' in the *vis viva* debate between the Cartesians and the Leibnizeans. Nietzsche seems to have been aware of this, and his understanding of how Kant responds to it bears consequences for his estimation of the success of synthesis as a response to Hume's scepticism and the issue of causality in addition to forming the background to Nietzsche's own response to Kant in the guise of his proposal of the will to power thesis. It is therefore worth the effort to now turn to a brief rehearsal of Kant's pre-critical and critical response to the *vis viva* issue by way of leading into Nietzsche's proposed alternative to Kant's account of synthesis.

The central issue under discussion in the *vis viva* debate, which began with Leibniz's 'The Memorable Errors of Descartes and Others' (1686), was whether we can intelligibly speak of internal 'living force' in nature distinct from external mechanical force and whether such living force can be measured. The possibility of mathematical quantification was identified with the empirical reality of force. According to Descartes, empirical force is reducible to external dead pressure whose effects are mathematically quantifiable as the product of the quantity of matter and velocity. Force, therefore, for Descartes, must be understood in terms of external motion and motion is to be measured in terms of spatial transfer. Leibniz, however, objected that material substance cannot be defined in terms of extension because it is unable to explain inertia or the resistance of bodies to motion. Rather, Leibniz contends that force is the dynamic essence of matter. However, he argues that whilst the effects of empirical force can be measured as the product of the quantity of matter and the square of velocities, it is reducible to a more primitive internal force which constitutes the substantial form of monadic, non-empirical substances and whose metaphysical reality cannot be empirically instantiated.

Throughout his career Kant struggled to reconcile the relational character of the scientific empirical world operating according to mechanical force with its metaphysical reality or intrinsic nature. Although Nietzsche was aware of the issue of empirical relations and intrinsic natures in Kant through his reading of Schopenhauer on this issue, he seems to side with Kant over Schopenhauer in his identification of force with efficient causality in BGE, 36.[19] Despite the fact that Nietzsche is ultimately critical of

---

[19] For further discussion on this latter issue, see my 'The Kantian Background to Nietzsche's Views on Causality', *Journal of Nietzsche Studies*, 43.1, 2012, pp. 44–56.

Kant's success in handling the issue and bringing it to a successful resolution, his siding with Kant over Schopenhauer in this passage, combined with his seeming awareness of Kant's own treatment of the issue, indicates that Nietzsche's will to power thesis emerges against the specific background of Kant's response to the *vis viva* debate. In an early essay, PTG (1873), Nietzsche indicates in his praise for Kant's pre-critical text *Universal Natural History and Theory of the Heavens* [UNH] that he is aware of Kant's struggle with the concept of force, even if, as has been suggested, Nietzsche's acquaintance with and quotations from Kant's text were second hand.[20] Although he endorses Kant's distinction between appearances and things-in-themselves in some other writings of the same early period, in this particular text Nietzsche praises Kant's pre-critical efforts in UNH to capture within one ontological domain the necessary and intrinsic status of mechanical empirical force:

> Is it not a sublime thought, to derive the magnificence of the cosmos and the marvellous arrangements of the stellar orbits wholly from a single, simple, purely mechanical movement, from a mathematical figure in motion, as it were! Instead of seeing in it the intentions and the intervening hands of a machine-god, he derived it from a type of oscillation which, once having begun, is necessary and predictable in its course and attains effects which are the equal of the wisest calculations of ratiocination; and of the utmost planning of purposiveness – but without being them. (PTG, p. 110)

Kant's argument in UNH that empirical mechanical force is the medium for the self-organizing character of nature differs from his earlier stance on this issue.[21] In 1749 he had attempted to combine the Cartesian and Leibnizean views of force by arguing in favour of the need for both external and internal force. External force, he argued, is required to set a body in

---

[20] See Paul A. Swift, *Becoming Nietzsche: Early Reflections on Democritus, Schopenhauer and Kant* (Lanham, MD: Lexington Books, 2008), p. 116. The quotation may be taken from Nietzsche's reading of Fischer's *Gesichte der Neuern Philosophie*, Volume 5. Nietzsche also cites Kant's UNH in his lectures on the Pre-Platonic Philosophers. He describes his approval of Kant's argument in this text in anti-teleological terms and uses it to criticize Aristotle's appeal to 'final ends' for having failed to pay due regard to 'the simplest forces' (PPP, p. 126). Since Nietzsche identifies force with efficient causality (BGE, 36), he must mean that the action and the aim of force stems from its own efficient nature and is not external to it. The doer and the deed, the efficient force and the final end, are metaphysically identical (GM, I, 13). Their metaphysical identity makes force a 'real property' in PPP (p. 126). But, despite Nietzsche's criticism of Aristotle's final ends, the will to power, by virtue of aiming at an end, is teleological in a sense. However, Nietzsche's identification of the end of the will to power with efficient force arguably saves him from the charge of superfluous teleology (BGE, 13) because the end to which force aims is not external to its efficient causal nature but is instead a manifestation of it.

[21] Immanuel Kant, *Universal Natural History and Theory of the Heavens*, trans. Stanley L. Jaki (Edinburgh: Scottish Academic Press, 1981).

motion, but internal force is required to preserve it in motion.[22] However, Kant changed his mind on this issue when he discovered Newton and the law of inertia. This discovery taught Kant that internal force was no longer required to explain how a body continues in uniform motion despite the fact that no continuous external force is applied. This discovery informs Kant's position in UNH where he appeals to only one type of force and where the Leibnizean notion of internal force is abandoned and external forces become the vehicles for the self-organizing character of mechanical nature. According to Kant in UNH, complex systems evolve from the operations of mechanical forces. Here, for Kant, the empirical and the metaphysical go hand in hand.

However, in his critical writings, Kant denies that mechanical nature can be known to be self-organizing. To claim that the operations of mechanical nature are governed by a self-organizing principle, Kant argues, still involves an illegitimate attempt to capture the inner or intrinsic character of things by dogmatically bypassing the empirical conditions of knowledge and presupposing direct insight into things in themselves. Thus, in the 'Amphiboly' section of CPR, he argues that empirical substance is constituted by external relations in space, and since we would be guilty of an amphiboly, that is, the illegitimate 'confounding of an object of pure understanding with appearance', if we were to claim knowledge of things-in-themselves, our knowledge must, accordingly, be restricted to that of external spatial relations (CPR, A270/B326). Rejecting Leibniz's non-relational noumenal substance, Kant concludes that 'substantia phae-nomenon in space' is 'nothing but relations, and it itself is entirely made up of mere relations' (CPR, A265/B321).[23] If intrinsic natures obtain at all, according to Kant, they must do so at the level of non-empirical and mind-independent things-in-themselves.

Although Nietzsche praises Kant's argument in UNH, he is ultimately less satisfied with Kant's critical position.[24] Once again, we must engage in

---

[22] Immanuel Kant, *Thoughts on the True Estimation of Living Forces* [1749]. Sections 1–11 and 114–115 are trans. John Handyside in *Kant's Inaugural Dissertation and Early Writings on Space* (Westport, CT: Hyperion Press, 1929). The entire text is to be found in Volume 1 of the Academy edition of Kant's works, *Gesammelte Schriften* (ed.) Akademie der Wissenschaften (Berlin: Reimer, later de Gruyter, 1910).

[23] This has the consequence for Kant that 'matter has no absolutely internal determinations and grounds of determination' (Immanuel Kant, *Metaphysical Foundations of Natural Science*, trans. James Ellington (Indianapolis, IN: Bobbs-Merril, 1970), p. 105).

[24] Nietzsche praises Kant's argument in UNH in PTG in 1873, KSA 1, pp. 801–872, the same year in which he subscribes to Kantian idealism, interpreted as subjective idealism, in TL. Yet, in PTG, Nietzsche is critical of the mature Kant's idealism as a result of what he takes to be its dualistic distinction between Becoming and Being. Although Nietzsche praises the mature Kant's criticism of

a degree of reconstruction to formulate the reasons why. When we do, we find that the reasons relate to Nietzsche's dissatisfaction with Kant's idealism and his account of synthesis. According to Nietzsche, Kant's mature writings understand force as a mental 'projection' (WP, 562, KSA 10: 24 [13], BGE, 21). Indeed Kant himself writes that the form of intuition or appearance 'does not represent anything save in so far as something is posited in the mind' (CPR, 67). As such, empirical force captures only external spatial relations that are constituted by the human mind. In so doing, Kant, in Nietzsche's view, fails to capture the intrinsic quality of force. We can appreciate why this might be important to Nietzsche when we consider that Kant refers to this intrinsic quality as the 'causality of their cause' in CPR (CPR, A544/B572). We can surmise that the failure to capture the causal impetus informing causal relations influences Nietzsche's assessment of Kant's ability to respond to Hume on the causal question. That this is so can be discerned from Nietzsche's suggestion that Kant's view that causal relations must be understood in terms of spatial

dogmatism and the idea that pure thought can access a sphere of non-empirical reality independently of sense-experience (PTG 11, KSA 1, pp. 846–847), he nevertheless doesn't subscribe to what he takes to be Kant's appeal to the mind-dependency of empirical reality, and he is also critical of Kant's appeal to a featureless and indeterminate concept of the thing-in-itself. The latter criticism is evident in his discussion of Anaximander's appeal to Being as the 'indefinite', which Nietzsche compares to Kant's thing-in-itself (PTG 4, KSA 1, p. 819) and which he argues can be defined only negatively. Moreover, Nietzsche argues in this text that such a reference to the thing-in-itself serves to undermine the ontological status of the empirical world of our experience, which is rendered a semblance and ontologically unreal (PTG 15, KSA 1, p. 857). In response, Nietzsche traces the arguments of the pre-Socratics as far as Anaxagoras to assess how we might intelligibly go about establishing the reality of the empirical world and avoid ontological dualism generally by domesticating the thing-in-itself and instantiating intrinsic natures at the level of empirical relations. It is in relation to this project that Nietzsche finds Kant's pre-critical argument in UNH more satisfactory than his mature position. Although Nietzsche doesn't develop a detailed discussion of Kant's pre-critical writings but rather embeds it in a discussion of Anaxagoras's account of the source of motion, there is nonetheless sufficient evidence in the text to suggest that Nietzsche sees Kant's pre-critical position in UNH as more satisfactory that his critical position. Nevertheless, one might wonder why Nietzsche presents a position in PTG that is seemingly at odds with and critical of his own endorsement of Kant's idealism in TL, written in the same year as PTG. Although a definite answer cannot be given to this question, it should be noted that it is not unusual to find multiple and sometimes conflicting positions in Nietzsche's early unpublished thought, especially in relation to his appropriation of Kant. For example, despite his references to the Kantian distinction between appearances and things-in-themselves in both TL and BT, in OS (KGW I/4, pp. 421–427), Nietzsche levies a criticism of the notion of the thing-in-itself that closely resembles his negative appraisal of the idea in PTG. Similarly to the latter text, Nietzsche argues in OS that the notion of the thing-in-itself can be defined only negatively in terms of what it cannot be known to be (KGW I/4, p. 423). Although Nietzsche's mature criticism of Kant is prefigured in PTG, the text was never completed. Consequently, I will focus on Nietzsche's criticisms of Kant as they are articulated in his mature writings and mention PTG only to the extent that it sheds light on Nietzsche's praise for Kant's pre-critical thought. This strategy is consonant with my aim to focus on the logic of Nietzsche's arguments rather than to engage in textual exegesis.

contiguity and temporal succession constituted by the human mind fails to contentfully capture the objectivity of real causal relations:

> *Causalism.* – It is obvious that things-in-themselves cannot be related to one another as cause and effect, nor can appearance be so related to appearance; from which it follows that in a philosophy that believes in things-in-themselves and appearances the concept 'cause and effect' *cannot be applied.* Kant's mistakes ... (WP, 554, KSA 12: 2 [139])

Moreover, Nietzsche concludes that despite Kant's efforts to save the legitimacy of the concept of causality, his reference to mind-independent things-in-themselves ultimately underestimates the 'validity of the knowledge attained by the natural sciences and altogether everything that can be known *causaliter*' (GS, 357). From this we can see that Kant, according to Nietzsche, renders force empirically ideal. This charge obviously sits uncomfortably with Kant's view that force is constituted by spatial relations and that spatiality is the marker of the empirically real. Nevertheless, Nietzsche suggests that the fact that spatiality, for Kant, is imposed by the human mind belies this claim and deprives force of genuine causal power. For Nietzsche, if force is to be causally efficacious we must understand it to be both empirically and metaphysically real. That is, even if we can show that space not just is a cognitive structure of the mind but rather is characteristic of mind-independent reality, empirical force must not be reducible to mere relations in space. Rather, causal relations must be relations of *powers* in space. Accordingly, force must be informed by an inner intrinsic nature.

Nietzsche sets out here what is required for Kant to successfully complete the project of establishing the empirical world as an object of knowledge. However, the problems that, in his view, beset Kant's account of synthesis and causal relations ultimately preclude the completion of the project. Therefore Nietzsche proposes an alternative account of synthesis, central to which is a non-impositionist account of mind and an argument in favour of empirically real relations that are informed by intrinsic natures. This alterative account comes in the guise of the will to power thesis, to which I now turn.

The Will to Power as an Alternative to Kant's Synthesis

Nietzsche proposes the will to power as an alternative to Kant's synthesis. His alternative holds that the relational character of the empirical world is informed by intrinsic natures that secure the mind-independence and causal potency of empirical force. According to Nietzsche, the will to power captures the intelligible character of fundamental power-wills that although 'synthetically related to one another' are not 'a delusion in the Berkelian or Schopenhauerian sense' (BGE, 36).[25]

The transition from Kant's synthesis to the will to power is mediated by Nietzsche's critical reflection on Kant's account of self-consciousness, which arises, according to the argument of the Transcendental Deduction, as a result of the activity of the self in synthesis. The active self that accompanies my representations but that cannot be known to be a substance culminates in Kant's rejection of the traditional substantialist and introspective view of the self in the 'Paralogisms'. Nietzsche thinks that this move on Kant's part is significant not simply for its own sake but also because it ultimately serves to undermine the very idea of a non-empirical self whose role is to constitute objects:

> In earlier times people believed in the 'soul' just as they believed in grammar and the grammatical subject. They said that 'I' is a condition that 'think' is a predicate and thus conditioned: thinking is an activity for which a causal subject *must* be thought. And then, with admirable tenacity and cunning, people tried to see whether perhaps the reverse was true: that 'think' was the condition, and 'I' the conditioned; 'I' would thus be a synthesis, which was *made* through the thinking itself. Basically, *Kant* wanted to prove that the subject could not be proved by means of the subject, nor could the object be proved either. Perhaps he was already familiar with the possibility of an *apparent existence* of the subject (that is, the soul), this thought that was once present on earth, tremendously powerful, in the philosophy of Vedanta. (BGE, 54. Cf. BGE, 17)

According to Nietzsche, the removal of the idea of a substantialist self undermines the distinction between non-empirical selves and objects that they constitute. It is a short step from here, he contends, to his own position that the ordering synthetic principle of reality is to be found immanently situated within reality rather than imposed by the cognitive structures of the human mind. This is because idealism, the claim that the objects of our knowledge can be reduced to mind-dependent representations, is defensible only if we can intelligibly appeal to an immaterial substantial self upon which the empirical world, including the human brain and sense organs, existentially depend. Without an immaterial substantial self, idealism, Nietzsche maintains, must collapse into a *reductio ad*

---

[25] It is to be noted that Kant stresses that although our knowledge is restricted to mind-dependent appearances, appearances are not illusions (CPR B67). Nietzsche equates illusion here with mind-dependency.

absurdum that holds that the empirical self in the form of the brain is both an object in and cause of the natural world (BGE, 15).[26] It follows from this, Nietzsche contends, that if Kant is to reject the self of rational psychology in the Paralogisms, then he must, if he is to avoid such a *reductio*, accept that synthesis operates in the natural world independently of human minds. Nietzsche sees himself as bringing Kant's argument to its logical conclusion. He maintains that once we reject Kant's constitutive account of mind that holds that the empirical world of our experience is constituted by forms imposed by the mind, we can understand the relation between mind and world naturalistically. Thus, Nietzsche proposes, contrary to Kant, that knowledge arises through the interaction of the mind with the world such that the translation of the human mind back into nature (BGE, 230) entails that the empirical world is accessible to but ontologically independent of human minds.[27] Rather than constituting the world a priori, the forms of our cognition are rooted in our physiological natures (KSA 12: 7 [4]) and reflect the interest-directed manner in which our physiological drives interact with the world.[28]

---

[26] It may be argued that Nietzsche's argument in BGE, 15, is directed at Schopenhauer rather than Kant. The passage in question is certainly a response to those that Nietzsche calls the 'sensualists'. But, although Nietzsche's claim in BGE, 11, that Kantian philosophy and German idealism in general 'offered an antidote to the still overpowering sensualism pouring into this century from the previous one' indicates that he does not count Kant amongst the sensualists, the argument of BGE, 15, can still be understood as a response to Kant. This is because the argument is that idealism is a coherent philosophical position only if we presuppose an extra-natural and substantial 'I'. Nietzsche indicates that he targets here not just Berkeley and Schopenhauer but also Kant when in BGE, 17, he rehearses an argument similar to Kant's in the Paralogisms against the traditionalist substantialist account of the self (see also BGE, 54). Nietzsche's sensitivity to the transcendental and empirical levels on which Kant's account of synthesis operates is influenced by Fischer's and Lange's respective interpretations of Kant in addition to that of Schopenhauer's. Still, as a result of his rejection of idealism, Nietzsche ultimately abandons the view shared by these neo-Kantians that causality is imposed on the mind by the world.

[27] Nietzsche proposes a version of this view in his early unpublished notes (NL 1872, KSA 7: 19 [153], p. 467, p. 467).

[28] Christian Emden argues that although Nietzsche is critical of Kant's idealist distinction between appearances and things-in-themselves and naturalizes everything that is a priori in Kant (Emden, *Nietzsche's Naturalism*, p. 121), he accepts the neo-Kantian view that the perceived structure of the world is a product of the body. However, Emden denies that this is a form of idealism on account of the fact that the knowing self is a part of the world. Yet, in BGE, 15, Nietzsche indicates that the view that the empirical world is caused by something that is part of it is the *reductio ad absurdum* into which idealism collapses when it takes the self that constitutes the empirical world to be an empirical self. Whilst Emden concedes that Nietzsche claims that the neo-Kantian view is a paradox in this passage, he also claims that Nietzsche 'had no interest in resolving this dilemma' and instead that he rethinks the relationship between the normative and the empirical by 'folding them into each other' (Emden, *Nietzsche's Naturalism*, p. 32). According to Emden, Nietzsche accounts for this interfolding of the empirical and the normative by appealing to reciprocal agency or 'interacting forces' (ibid., p. 179), rather than intrinsic force, at the level of cellular biology as a necessary guide to the

Nietzsche's view that synthesis operates immanently within the world, rather than being understood as an imposition of the human mind, culminates in his claim that the empirical world must be understood in both relational and intrinsic terms. He contends that once we relinquish the distinction between immaterialist substantialist selves and the objects that they constitute we see that the empirical world must be understood in terms of complexes of relational powers:

> If we give up the effective subject, we also give up the object upon which effects are produced. Duration, identity with itself, being are inherent neither in that which is called subject nor in that which is called object: they are complexes of events apparently durable in comparison with other complexes – e.g., through the difference in tempo of the event (rest – motion, form – loose: opposites that do not exist in themselves and that actually express only variations in degree that from a certain perspective appear to be opposites. There are no opposites: only from those of logic do

emergence of life and normativity (ibid., p. 171). Although I agree with Emden that Nietzsche aims to reconcile the natural and the normative and that he took the biological sciences very seriously, as I argued in Chapter 2 I don't see that Nietzsche thought that the empirical sciences stand on their own two feet. Rather, the empirical sciences require a metaphysical explanation. Still, there is no doubting that, at times, Nietzsche toyed with relational non-essentialism. However, as a metaphysical thesis and in the absence of intrinsic force, the appeal to purely relational force, such as Nietzsche describes it at WP, 557 KSA 12: 2 [85], for example, runs into trouble. As Peter Poellner notes in a specifically Nietzschean context and John Foster in the context of a discussion of idealism more generally, this non-essentialist thesis succumbs to the problem of an infinite regress of existential dependency, which can be halted only by adopting a mental or material substrate as a metaphysical support, two notions that Nietzsche explicitly rejects (BGE, 12) and which would commit him to either a reductive realism or idealism (Peter Poellner, *Nietzsche and Metaphysics* (Oxford: Oxford University Press, 1995), p. 283; John Foster, *The Case for Idealism* (London: Routledge and Kegan Paul), 1982, pp. 67–69). For this reason, a more essentialist-metaphysical interpretation of force and causality is to be preferred. Now, intrinsic force does not entail an appeal to powerless substrates but rather to particular quanta of causal powers that can interact with other such powers without being existentially dependent upon them. These powers are genuinely causal in contradistinction to the Humean and Kantian models of causality understood in terms of spatial contiguity and temporal succession, views which Nietzsche claims have an everyday usefulness but are ultimately too crude to capture genuine natural causality (BGE, 12; GS, 112). As a result, the appeal to intrinsic force does not rule out reciprocal action but rather is the very basis of its possibility. Emden may respond to the preceding problem about existential dependency by arguing that it arises only if Nietzsche allows that forces should be understood in terms of relations between pre-existing relata rather than it being the case that relata emerge from reciprocal cellular activity or agency. Whilst this is an interesting idea, it remains the case that Nietzsche was not fully clear about it and can be found discussing relations in terms of relations between relata (WP, 556 KSA 12: 2 [149–152]; WP, 557 KSA 12: 2 [85]). In sum, Emden's Nietzsche holds that we are part of the world we create (Emden, *Nietzsche's Naturalism*, p. 32). My Nietzsche, instead, claims that we are part of the world that we do not create. According to my interpretation, Nietzsche is not merely appropriating neo-Kantian arguments but rather moving beyond them, and the source of these arguments lies with Kant himself despite the influence of the naturalist turn of some of his successors. Even though neo-Kantians were Nietzsche's educators in all things Kantian, Nietzsche maintains that '[o]ne repays a teacher badly if one remains only a pupil' (Z, Part One, 'Of the Bestowing Virtue', 3).

we derive the concept of opposites – and falsely transfer it to things). (WP, 552 KSA 12: 9 [91])[29]

Nietzsche understands the relational powers to which he appeals here in intrinsically causal terms. That is, causality is not reducible to a form of cognition imposed by the human mind nor does it reside in a non-empirical sphere of things-in-themselves, but rather, it belongs to the fabric of the empirical world in which we are immersed and through interaction with which our knowledge develops. According to Nietzsche, his account of causality in the world is supported by the best empirical evidence, which points to a Boscovichean account of causality as action at a distance rather than a mechanical account of causal relations in terms of contact (BGE, 12).[30] However, Nietzsche's argument that Boscovich's appeal to force must be supplemented by an inner will (WP, 619 KSA 11: 36 [31]) reflects the influence of the biological sciences on his thinking and his view that biology and physics can be explained according to a unifying metaphysical principle. In BGE, 36, for example, Nietzsche describes the will to power as the essence of both biological life and 'mechanical events'.

Nietzsche's appeal to the biological sciences in the nineteenth century sees him adopt what he describes as a non-Darwinian form of evolutionary theory that supports his appeal to an intrinsic nature of force in response to both Hume and Kant. His negative comments about Darwin are well known. He argues, for example, that Darwinian evolution, understood as a struggle for existence primarily, is a reactive form of life (WP, 685 KSA 13: 14 [123]; GS, 349; TI, 'Reconnaissance Raids', 14). And, whilst Nietzsche does not deny that organisms interact with and adjust to their environment, such adjustment stems primarily from a drive on the part of the organism to manifest its powerful nature (BGE, 13). Adaptation, understood as the principal generator of evolutionary change, is, for Nietzsche, 'an activity of second rank, a mere reactivity' (GM, II, 12; GS, 349) and superfluously teleological (BGE, 13). He writes that 'adaptation' follows only when 'the spontaneous, aggressive, expansive, re-interpreting, re-directing and for-mative forces' have 'had their effect' (GM, II, 12). Lange was the main source of Nietzsche's negative acquaintance with Darwinian evolution as a

---

[29] For an account of the manner in which Nietzsche's critical engagement with Teichmüller influences his argument here, see Tom Bailey, 'Nietzsche the Kantian' in Gemes and Richardson (eds.), *The Oxford Handbook of Nietzsche*, pp. 134–159, pp. 143–144.

[30] Greg Whitlock points out that Nietzsche embraced Boscovich contrary to both Kant's and Lange's Newtonian accounts of matter. See Whitlock's translator's commentary to PPP, p. 249.

theory of natural selection and adaptation.[31] As Gregory Moore notes, German thinkers such as Lange looked to the appropriation of the concept of *Bildungstrieb* amongst nineteenth-century biologists in promoting evolutionary accounts of organic development. The influence of such views on Nietzsche's thinking accounts for why, despite his critical remarks about Darwin, he nonetheless does not reject evolutionism. The version of evolutionism that he accepts is influenced, for example, by the biologists William Rolph's principle of insatiability and Wilhelm Roux's view that an organism comprises an inner struggle between its parts. Rolph's and Roux's versions of evolutionary theory, which appeal to an internal directive force within nature as the primary instigator of evolutionary development, nonetheless indicate for Nietzsche that Darwinian evolution does not herald in a radically new way of thinking.[32] Rather, Rolph's and Roux's appeal to active force provide the basis for Darwinian evolution, which, in Nietzsche's view, is a secondary by-product of the activity of force in nature.[33] That Nietzsche

[31] See Wolfgang Müller-Lauter, *Nietzsche: His Philosophy of Contradictions and the Contradictions of His Philosophy*, trans. D. J. Parent (Urbana, IL: University of Illinois Press, 1999), p. 232, for discussion of Lange's influence on Nietzsche's understanding of Darwin.

[32] The issue of whether Nietzsche adheres to a Darwinian or non-Darwinian account of evolutionary development is debated in Nietzsche studies. For non-Darwinian accounts of Nietzsche's appeal to biology, see Dirk R. Johnson, *Nietzsche's Anti-Darwinism* (Cambridge: Cambridge University Press, 2010) and Gregory Moore, *Nietzsche, Biology and Metaphor* (Cambridge: Cambridge University Press, 2002). According to Moore, 'The will to power is essentially a *Bildungstrieb*, and is, as it were, an amalgam of a number of competing Darwinian theories: Nägeli's perfection principle, Roux's concept of an internal struggle, and Rolph's principle of insatiability' (Moore, *Nietzsche, Biology and Metaphor*, p. 55). According to Christian Emden, however, Nietzsche criticizes popular receptions of Darwin rather than Darwin's evolutionary theory itself. Emden acknowledges the influence of Rolph and Roux on Nietzsche's thinking but denies that they rejected Darwin. According to Emden, Roux's overcompensation, which is a precondition of life, operates at a molecular cellular level such that life is not the result of specific properties of cells and molecules but rather is the result of the interaction amongst the cells and molecules. Emden describes this interaction as agential in an entirely relational sense rather than in an intrinsically causal sense. Accordingly, Emden claims that Nietzsche's appropriation of Roux's biology sees him move away from the notion of *Bildungstrieb* and vitalist metaphysics (*Nietzsche's Naturalism*, pp. 94, 77). Still, it remains the case that Nietzsche presented himself and his appropriation of nineteenth-century biology as non-Darwinian (TI, 'Reconnaissance Raids', 14). This presentation is backed up by his description of the will to power in terms of the operation of an inner directive and formative force (GM, II, 12), even though his suggestion in GS, 357, that Hegel anticipates Darwin indicates that he thought of the claims of Darwinism as a secondary off-shoot. Adopting a non-Darwinian or Darwinian interpretation, however, makes for either an essentialist or non-essentialist interpretation of Nietzsche's account of causality. According to Emden's Darwinian interpretation, Nietzsche's engagement with the life sciences, under the influence of the first generation of neo-Kantians, resulted in a non-essentialist, Humean account of causality (ibid.). For a further account of Nietzsche in Darwinian terms, see John Richardson, *Nietzsche's New Darwinism* (Oxford: Oxford University Press, 2004).

[33] Although Nietzsche's appeal to the resources of nineteenth century biology is historically specific, the metaphysics of dispositional powers which he draws from it and which takes the intentional to be the marker of the dispositional is not. For reference to contemporary approaches to these issues, see note 27 in Chapter 4. As will become evident in the remainder of this chapter and further in Chapter

thinks in this way is particularly evident in his praise for Hegel and his claim in GS, 357, that without Hegel there would have been no Darwin.[34] However, even in this passage it is clear that Nietzsche's praise of Hegel's 'philosophy of evolution' (WP, 412, KSA 12: 7 [4]) is intended as a response to Kant. In particular, it is a response to what he thinks is ultimately missing in Kant's account of causality. What is missing in this account, according to Nietzsche, is the appeal to the driving force or causality of the cause, which, for Kant, in Nietzsche's view, is relegated to the unknowable noumenon but which should be properly understood to obtain at the level of empirical relations. Nietzsche's appropriation of evolutionary theory as a response to Kant, then, sees him appeal to active force in intrinsically causal terms.[35] He writes that the Darwinian appeal to self-preservation is only one of the 'indirect and most frequent *consequences*' of life as will to power (BGE, 13). That active force, for Nietzsche, is to be understood in intrinsically causal terms is made evident in BGE, 36, where he describes the will to power as the inner causal nature of all natural events.

Consequently, Nietzsche allows for the possibility of objective knowledge that he thinks is missing in Kant. Drawing on the resources of

---

4, the cogency of his argument here, then, does not rest on the merits or demerits of his use of specific biological accounts or whether they are successful or warranted responses to Darwin.

[34] Gregory Moore, 'Nietzsche and Evolutionary Theory' in Keith Ansell Pearson (ed.), *A Companion to Nietzsche*, pp. 517–531, pp. 519–520. Although Nietzsche speaks of Hegel in approving terms in GS, 357, suggesting perhaps that Nietzsche thinks that Hegel's answer to the relationship between self and world is more satisfactory than Kant's, Nietzsche thinks that neither the Kantian approach nor the Hegelian is ultimately satisfactory. He writes, alluding to Hegel, that '[w]e have become cold, hard, and tough in the realization that the way of the world is anything but divine; even by human standards it is not rational, merciful, or just' (GS, 346). Despite the teleological overtones to Nietzsche's appeal to active force, he denies that it is superfluously teleological (BGE, 13) in a Hegelian sense by rejecting the notion of the Absolute as a final end of the activity of force. Rather, Nietzsche's emphasizes the insatiability and creativity of the will to power (WP, 619 KSA 11: 36 [31]).

[35] That Nietzsche's praise of Hegel in GS, 357, should be understood as a response to Kant should come as no surprise to us given that Nietzsche had intended to write a dissertation on the concept of the organic since Kant (KGW I/4, pp. 548–578). Kevin Hill points out that Lange too had come to see that Kant's account of teleology was central to reconciling mechanism with biology in later versions of his *History of Materialism* but that since Nietzsche read only the first edition of Lange's book, he must have come to the conclusion about the importance of Kant's appeal to teleology independently of Lange (Hill, *Nietzsche's Critiques*, p. 83). Hill's claim that Nietzsche reaches conclusions about Kant independently of Lange indicates that although his interpretation of Kant is mediated by his reading of neo-Kantian authors, his estimation of and response to Kant is intended as a response to Kant himself and not his commentators. However, although Nietzsche's practice of drawing on biology to account for the inner nature of force shares similar aims to Kant's identification of the internal nature of things with biological life in his *Critique of Judgment*, Nietzsche is ultimately critical of what he sees as Kant's bifurcation of empirical and non-empirical explanatory levels as evidenced in his appeal to a supersensible designer to reconcile mechanism and teleology, even if the appeal is made at the level of reflective rather than determinative judgement. For further discussion of Nietzsche's engagement with Kant's arguments on this issue, see my *Nietzsche on Epistemology and Metaphysics: The World in View* (Edinburgh: Edinburgh University Press, 2009), Chapter Five.

nineteenth-century biology, such as the previously mentioned Roux's law of assimilation whereby organisms are driven to increase their intake of nutrition and Rolph's principle of insatiability whereby organisms are driven by a desire for growth rather than self-preservation primarily, he proposes, as we saw in Chapter 2, that we can contentfully conceive the intrinsic causal character of the relational forces that make up nature analogously to our own experiences of willing and desiring (BGE, 36). The latter psychological experiences, in his view, are distinctly grounded in our biological drives that are immersed in and interact with the natural world (BGE, 23). Arguing that a 'force we cannot imagine is an empty word', Nietzsche maintains that the 'victorious concept "force" … still needs to be completed: an inner will must be ascribed to it, which I designate as "will to power"' (WP, 619, KSA 12: 36 [31]). Consequently, he proposes that we can capture the 'intelligible character' (BGE, 36) of the relational powers that make up the empirical world without collapsing into dogmatism.[36]

Nevertheless, given Nietzsche's charge that Kant's synthesis is guilty of the genetic fallacy, one cannot help but wonder whether Nietzsche is similarly guilty. This concern is heightened by the fact that in BGE Nietzsche maintains that psychology is the key to basic issues (BGE, 23).[37] However, his rejection of Kant's and indeed his own earlier impositionist account of mind in favour of an interactionist account of the relation between mind and world indicates that he must be able to differentiate his own appeal to psychology from that of Kant's. By understanding our psychological starting point as 'provisional' (WP, 497, KSA 11: 26 [12]), Nietzsche holds that our interests guide our investigation of nature but he does not attempt to guarantee, contrary to Kant as he sees it, that our interests will be instantiated in the empirical world from the

---

[36] It should be noted that Nietzsche's appeal to an inner will is quite different from Schopenhauer's view that the body can be known both as an object amongst other objects in the empirical world and as will or thing-in-itself. First, Nietzsche rejects Schopenhauer's empirical idealist account of the status of empirical objects when he states that 'I do not mean the material world as a delusion, as "appearance" or "representation" (in the Berkeleian or Schopenhauerian sense)' (BGE, 36). Second, he rejects the Schopenhauerian idea that the will is simple and immediately known (BGE, 16). Third, he rejects what he calls Schopenhauer's 'denial of will as an "efficient cause"' (WP, 95, KSA 12: 9 [178]) when he identifies force with efficient causality in BGE, 36. For further discussion on the latter issue, see my 'The Kantian Background to Nietzsche's Views on Causality'.

[37] Emden would no doubt argue that this problem disappears if we adopt his interpretation of biology first, psychology second (Emden, 'Nietzsche's Will to Power: Biology, Naturalism and Normativity', *Journal of Nietzsche Studies*, 47.1, 2016, pp. 30–60, p. 31). However, making psychology our starting point fits with Nietzsche's claim in BGE, 23, that psychology is the key to basic issues, notwithstanding his view that psychology is physiological. Moreover, a psychological starting point fits with Nietzsche's rejection of a God's Eye View of knowledge (GM, III, 12).

outset. Rather as heuristic maxims for investigating the world, our initial psychological starting point is capable of evolving and refinement over time. Our knowledge has, in Nietzsche's view, an important historical dimension that it lacks in Kant.[38] Moreover, in response to possible objections to Nietzsche's use of analogy and indeed objections that Nietzsche himself levies at illegitimate uses of this method independently of his engagement with Kant (TI, 'Errors', 3), it must be stressed that, in the context of my interpretation of him, Nietzsche is not guilty of pre-supposing the transparency of the mind to itself and then using such supposed psychological 'facts' as a foundation for understanding mind-independent reality. This is because, for him, although our understanding of the world must always be coloured by our specifically human point of view, our proposals must be treated as provisional conjectures that are deemed warranted, or not, through a process of subjecting these conjectures to critical scrutiny. Only those that can be supported by strong reasons in their favour, he contends, can be accepted as rationally justified (GS, 2, 319).[39] But, even assuming that the proposal of the will to power can avoid the charge of the genetic fallacy and that it is justifiable on the grounds outlined previously, what does Nietzsche mean when he appeals to the intelligible character of things, and is it consistent with his other claim that the empirical world is relationally structured?

On my understanding of Nietzsche's proposal, to say that force operates according to an intrinsic nature is not to deny the relationality of force, but rather it is to say that its relationality, contrary to Kant, emanates from its internal nature rather than from mind-imposed relations and that its obtaining is mind-independent. Thus, Nietzsche's argument is that force is metaphysically real and not just relative to us. However, if he is to avoid the charge that Kant levies at Leibniz, Nietzsche must show that the metaphysically real is physical and that the metaphysical reality of causal powers is compatible with their physical instantiation. To be physically instantiated force must be spatially located, and for Nietzsche, such spatial location cannot be constituted by the human mind as it is in Kant.

---

[38] Nietzsche praises the anti-sceptical import of Hegel's notion of the development of species concepts in GS, 357.

[39] Rational thinking, for Nietzsche, entails relations between the multiple drives that constitute the self (GS, 333). Rational justification thus entails, for him, the consideration of multiple perspectives in relation to an issue, that is, reasons for and against considering a particular response to the issue justified (GS, 2, 319). The criteria of rational acceptability for Nietzsche are aesthetic and include frugality and simplicity of explanatory principles (BGE, 13) in addition to comprehensiveness and ease of fit with our other judgements (GM, III, 12).

Unfortunately, Nietzsche does not address this issue explicitly. Moreover, the spatial location of causal powers is a contentious issue, independently of the Kantian-Nietzschean context under discussion here. The contention surrounding the issue impacts on Nietzsche's response to Kant because it implies that spatiality, even if it is not considered to be an imposition of the human mind, nevertheless presupposes a fundamentally un-Nietzschean idea. That is, spatiality presupposes non-relational material substances. According to this argument, causal powers can be considered to be spatially located only if they are grounded in a non-relational substance, which itself has a non-power nature.[40]

However, there is a counter-argument available, which can facilitate the spatial location of powers without committing Nietzsche to the idea that they must be grounded in a power-less substrate. George Molnar provides us with such an argument. He probes what we mean by a substantial object and contends that our common understanding of such objects is that they are bulky or voluminous objects. He argues that although bulky or voluminous objects must have size and shape, it is more correct to say that such objects fill rather than occupy space. On this basis, he contends that only sub-microscopic objects, such as powers, can be properly said to occupy a space, and they do so by being located at mathematical points. Moreover, whilst our common understanding of objects takes them to have an intrinsic nature, he argues, it is not ultimately prescriptive about whether this intrinsic nature must have a non-power character. Consequently, he proposes that we should adopt a position that he calls 'moderate dispositionalism', which holds that objects have extrinsic and intrinsic properties. Its intrinsic properties have a power nature whilst spatial location is an extrinsic property. This means that an object can change its spatial location with its intrinsic, power-full, nature intact.[41] Nietzsche's description of the world as will to power as ' . . . a firm, iron magnitude of force *set in a definite space as a definite force* (*sondern als bestimmte Kraft einem bestimmten Raum eingelegt* [my emphasis]' (WP, 1067, KSA 11: 38 [12]) fits with Molnar's argument.[42]

Still, before we can consider our defence of the will to power thesis properly secure, we must consider a recent objection to interpreting it as a

---

[40] See, for example, John Foster, *The Case for Idealism*, pp. 67–69. See GM, I, 13, for Nietzsche's denial that force is grounded in a property-less substrate.

[41] George Molnar, *Powers: A Study in Metaphysics* (Oxford: Oxford University Press, 2006), pp. 175–179.

[42] See also WP, 545 KSA 11: 36 [25], where Nietzsche describes space as the 'substratum' of force whilst also rejecting the notion of space 'in itself'.

metaphysical thesis about the character of reality. The objection, put forward by Clark and Dudrick, combines both a textual and philosophically substantive argument by contending on the basis of a close reading of BGE, 36, that Nietzsche should not be interpreted as proposing the will to power as a metaphysical thesis. On the basis of this textual argument, Clark and Dudrick draw the philosophically substantive conclusion that the will to power serves as an explanation of human life only in Nietzsche's philosophy, where life is understood in a specifically normative sense and distinguished from the mechanical and biological operations of nature as described by empirical science. Clark and Dudrick's view, if left uncontested, undermines my argument that the will to power is a metaphysical thesis that applies to both human and non-human nature and highlights their fundamental metaphysical unity. As I have interpreted it, Nietzsche's claim, contrary to Kant, is that once the human mind has been translated back into nature (BGE, 230), mind and nature must be understood as metaphysically continuous, such that explanations of the natural world, both biological and physical, must suffice as explanations of the specifically human – psychological and normative – world, and vice versa. In the natural world, the will to power is supported by and supplements Boscovich's rejection of mechanical atomism's account of causality as contact of material bodies in favour of understanding causality as action at a distance. The will to power is also informed by and supports biological theories that appeal to internal formative force as the basis of evolutionary development. And, in the human world, the will to power allows us to reconfigure the self as a non-substantial bundle of drives contrary to the idea that the self is a non-relational substance (BGE, 12).

Clark and Dudrick argue that Nietzsche is not committed to the will to power as a metaphysical thesis about the character of both the human and non-human world on the grounds that he demarcates, in Kantian fashion, the – normative and 'unnatural' – sphere of the human from the – mechanical causal – sphere of the natural sciences. According to them, the will to power applies to human normative life but not to physics or biology. We encountered a version of Clark and Dudrick's argument in brief in Chapter 2 in our discussion of Nietzsche's view of the epistemic status of the natural sciences. However, we meet it again here in the form of a specific textual argument against interpreting the content of BGE, 36, as providing reasons in favour of the metaphysics of the will to power. Since Clark and Dudrick's textual argument also poses a philosophically substantive challenge to my thesis about the metaphysical continuity of mind and nature in Nietzsche, it is important that we address both the textual and philosophical arguments

directly. The philosophically substantive challenge to what I take to be
Nietzsche's non-Kantian metaphysical continuity thesis is grounded in
Clark and Dudrick's two-pronged claim that Nietzsche adheres to a
Kantian demarcation of the normative from the sphere of natural causes
and that causality for Nietzsche should be understood in Humean mechanical
terms. By taking up Clark and Dudrick's challenge, I will argue that BGE, 36,
can justifiably be interpreted as proposing a metaphysical thesis that supports
the metaphysical continuity of the human sphere of values with, rather than
their separation from, the causal sphere of the natural world. Central to this
argument for Nietzsche is the idea that the will to power applies to both
human normative life and the natural world as described by the natural
sciences.

A Textual and Philosophical Challenge

Clark and Dudrick argue that the will to power is to be properly understood as a thesis about the character of normative life and not as a
metaphysical thesis about the character of reality. Normativity, they
argue, is constituted by political relations between the drives that make-
up the Nietzschean soul such that the will to power is a 'doctrine of what
constitutes the human soul, what makes us persons or selves hence what
differentiates humans from other animals'.[43] Consequently, their interpretation relies on the will to power being applicable only above the
dividing line between the normative and the mechanically causal spheres.
On the basis of their view that the sphere of normative reason-giving and
justified evaluative commitments is to be distinguished from the causal
order of mechanical nature, they contend that Nietzsche precludes the
extension of the will to power to physics. However, including biology
under their description of the natural sciences from which they claim the
human capacity for normative reason giving can be demarcated, they also
deny that Nietzsche applies the will to power to biological life. Their
interpretation, however, relies on particular accounts of Nietzsche's stance
in relation to the status of physics and biological life, which I think are
ultimately suspect from both a narrowly textual and broadly philosophical
perspective.

   Clark and Dudrick frame Nietzsche's argument in BGE, 36, into three
segments for the purposes of analysis. Their interpretation of the premises
of the first segment is largely unproblematic. The premises in question are:

---

[43] Clark and Dudrick, *The Soul of Nietzsche's Beyond Good and Evil*, p. 139.

1. Our world of desires and passions is 'given' as real, and nothing else is.
2. Our world of desires and passions is to be understood in terms of the drives and their relationship to one another.
3. The kind of causality that characterizes the drives and their relationship to one another is the causality of the will.
4. Therefore, everything that is 'given' as real is to be understood in terms of the causality of the will (1, 2, 3).

According to Clark and Dudrick, the third premise is implied in Nietzsche's account, although it is not made explicit. The content of this premise pertaining to the causality of the will is the basis upon which the non-observationally 'given' world of desires and passions is 'to be *understood* in terms of the drives, not that the existence of the drives is to be inferred from the "given"'.[44] Clark and Dudrick take Nietzsche to hold that our knowledge of what we feel and desire does not depend on observation in the way that we observe the material world, though our beliefs about what we feel and desire may be subject to correction in light of observation. The interpretation offered here regarding the givenness of the drives and passions is a departure from Clark's earlier view[45] that these premises presupposed the transparency of consciousness to itself, a thesis that Nietzsche rejects.[46]

Clark and Dudrick's interpretation of the second segment of Nietzsche's argument, however, is more problematic, especially with regard to how they understand Nietzsche's position in relation to mechanical causality and the status of physics in premises six to nine. The second segment contains the following premises:

5. We may not posit several kinds of causality until we have attempted to make do with one kind of causality.
6. Acceptance of any kind of causality implies acceptance of the causality of the will.
7. Therefore, we must not assume that a different kind of causality (i.e., mechanical causality) operates in the 'material' world until we have attempted to understand it on the basis of the causality of the will. (5, 6)
8. To attempt to understand the 'material' world on the basis of the causality of the will is to 'venture the hypothesis' that 'all mechanical

[44] Ibid., p. 232.
[45] Maudemarie Clark, *Nietzsche on Truth and Philosophy* (Cambridge: Cambridge University Press, 1990), pp. 213–214.
[46] Clark and Dudrick, *The Soul of Nietzsche's Beyond Good and Evil*, pp. 230–232.

occurrences, insofar as force is active in them, are force of will, effects of will.'

9. Therefore, we must 'venture the hypothesis' that 'all mechanical occur-rences, insofar as force is active in them, are force of will, effects of will.' (7, 8)

Clark and Dudrick contend, correctly I believe, that Nietzsche accepts the parsimony of explanatory principles premise (premise five). And, on the basis of their reading of BGE, 19, they also claim, again correctly, that he accepts the causality of the will (premise six). The causality of the will, which need not be identified with conscious thoughts and feelings, for Nietzsche, they argue, entails the idea that 'the will is the political order of the drives and affects, and that this order is capable of bringing about actions through the "commanding and obeying" of its components'.[47] The political structure of human willing, according to Clark and Dudrick, is normative and not merely causal in the mechanical sense of causality. Mechanical causality, according to their interpretation, entails understand-ing causality in terms of Humean observed regularities of events and does not entail a commitment to the reality of causality *per se*. However, the appeal to the causality of the will involves a commitment to the reality of its causal capacity. The normativity of the causality of the will, they argue, derives from the fact that actions that are willed are based on the evaluative commitment of the actor. Clark and Dudrick explain the latter point as follows:

> Because the notion of causality involves that of commitment, if we are to affirm the reality of causality, we must affirm that of commitments. And if commitments are real, then the will must be causal. For a commitment – in reality, and not 'in name only' – it must be the case that the person who has it usually acts in accordance with it.[48]

Now, Clark and Dudrick contend that Nietzsche defends prioritizing the causality of the will over mechanical causality in premise six because, for him, our belief in causality of the will is 'our belief in causality itself'. Clark and Dudrick take Nietzsche's reference to our belief in causality itself to refer to our belief in unobserved necessary connections between events. The relation between this belief and the causality of the will is that both pertain to the sphere of human valuing. The belief in causality as necessary connection entails appealing to necessary laws of nature, and like Nietzsche's appeal to the causality of the will, it is an interpretation that

[47] Ibid., p. 234.   [48] Ibid., p. 236.

expresses and projects human evaluative commitments that are to be differentiated from the mechanical scientist's explanation of causal relations in terms of non-evaluative observed regularities. Nietzsche prioritizes the causal-normative structure of the human will over the mechanical scientist's appeal to regularities on the grounds that the latter cannot account for or incorporate the former. Mechanical science, Clark and Dudrick argue, cannot explain everything, and what it cannot explain is the phenomenon of human valuing. What Nietzsche calls the causality of the will and which is the structure of normativity cannot be dispensed with.[49] Accordingly, Clark and Dudrick contend that Nietzsche distinguishes between the sphere of mechanical causes and the sphere of normative reasons.

According to Clark and Dudrick, the preceding argument can be defended by offering a particular interpretation of Nietzsche's account of causality in BGE, 21. According to them, Nietzsche's reference to causality itself in BGE, 36, refers to the view of causality discussed in BGE, 21. That is, they argue that Nietzsche is referring to our belief in causality as unobserved necessary connections that obey invariable laws of nature. According to Nietzsche in this passage, as interpreted by Clark and Dudrick, we should employ 'cause' and 'effect', where cause and effect are understood to entail necessary connection 'only as pure *concepts*, that is to say as conventional fictions for the purpose of designation, mutual understanding, *not* explanation'.[50] They contend that Nietzsche emphasizes the interpretive and evaluative character of this view of causality as opposed to the non-interpretive claim of natural science that causality should be understood in terms of observed regularity. The designation of something as a cause in the necessitarian sense, according to Nietzsche, they claim, communicates something 'about ourselves, about our own mental state, in an attempt at "mutual understanding"'.[51] This is the point that Nietzsche wants to make about the causality of the will, they argue, when he describes our belief in the causality of the will as a belief in causality itself. That is, the belief in the causality of the will, being interpretive, also communicates something about ourselves. Moreover, Clark and Dudrick claim that we should understand Nietzsche's point here in Kantian rather than Humean terms. That is, whereas Hume thinks that what we communicate is our expectations, Nietzsche thinks that we communicate our evaluative commitments. Clark and Dudrick write:

---

[49] Ibid., p. 234. [50] Ibid., p. 235. BGE, 21, cited by Clark and Dudrick. [51] Ibid.

Whereas Hume would think that what we communicate to others is our expectations, we take Nietzsche's talk of 'purposes' and 'understanding' as indicative of a more Kantian or normative view that we communicate more than expectations, namely, our commitments. To take oneself to have causal knowledge is not just to be disposed to act and think in certain ways but to regard those ways of thinking and acting as *justified* – it is to be committed to thinking and acting in the ways picked out by these dispositions.[52]

Unsurprisingly, I find Clark and Dudrick's interpretation of BGE, 21, highly speculative. First, it presupposes that Nietzsche thinks that mechanical science captures the world non-evaluatively in terms of a Humean – regularity – account of causality. Second, it sees him appeal to a separate and evaluative sphere of normativity, which they take to be Kantian in character. However, I don't see that Nietzsche is making the claims that they attribute to him here. In relation to the second issue, he says nothing about Kantian-style normative constraints in the passage in question (BGE, 21). If anything, his explicit criticism of what he takes to be the dualism involved in Kant's distinction between the spheres of causal determinism and freedom counts against it. For example, he claims that Kant's distinction between the two spheres is merely a disingenuous and philosophically illegitimate attempt to combine 'the best scientific decorum' with the dogmatic theological ideals of God, immaterial soul, freedom and immortality (GM, III, 25; GS, 335). Moreover, to interpret the distinction between causes and reasons along Kantian lines, as Clark and Dudrick suggest, runs counter to Nietzsche's naturalism by construing the sphere of normativity as *sui generis*, contrary to their criticism of this idea in McDowell elsewhere.[53] Indeed, rather than suggesting that Nietzsche distinguishes between mechanical causality and demarcates it from the sphere of human willing or normativity, Nietzsche suggests, as I argued earlier, that we should replace the mechanist account with a more refined account of causality understood as the will to power. For him, 'in real life it is only a matter of *strong* and *weak* wills' (BGE, 21). Clark and Dudrick will surely respond to this objection, however, and on the basis of their interpretation of BGE, 22, argue that Nietzsche proposes the will to power as an alternative interpretation to causality understood in terms of necessary connection rather than as a claim that he proposes to be true and that challenges the mechanical account of nature as observed regularities. They argue that in section 22 he claims that the appeal to the lawfulness of nature and necessary connection is a case of bad

---

[52] Ibid., pp. 235–236.
[53] Maudemarie Clark and David Dudrick, 'Nietzsche and Moral Objectivity: The Development of Nietzsche's Metaethics' in Brian Leiter and Neil Sinhababu (eds.), *Nietzsche and Morality* (Oxford: Oxford University Press, 2007), pp. 192–226, p. 215.

interpretive practice and that the appeal to the will to power is merely an alternative interpretation rather than a non-evaluative scientific explanation. However, it is not clear that Nietzsche distinguishes between the appeal to necessary laws of nature and regularity views of causal connection in BGE, 21 and 22, as Clark and Dudrick take him to do. Rather, whilst claiming that all appeals to laws of nature are suspect and a projection of human interests and concerns (BGE, 21), he seems to take it that the appeal to causal necessity is derived from observed regularities. The appeal to necessary causal laws of nature are projected on the basis of the physicist's observed correlations of events and the physicist is guilty of appealing to such laws of nature. Consequently, when Nietzsche criticizes the appeal to laws of nature, he criticizes the physicist directly in BGE, 22. This means that if the appeal to necessary laws of nature is evaluative and interpretive, then physics is also evaluative and interpretive, contrary to Clark and Dudrick's claim that physics is value-free. Clark and Dudrick deny that Nietzsche thinks that physics is ultimately an interpretation and argue that Nietzsche's point in BGE, 22, is to present the will to power not as an alternative to physics[54] but rather as an alternative to a particular interpretation of physics. For them, Nietzsche thinks that there are 'facts' or a 'text' to be discovered by physics, which is not ultimately an interpretation and expression of our values.[55] The will to power and the appeal to law-like necessity as opposed to generalized Humean regularities, they take Nietzsche to say (BGE, 22), are mere interpretations that are coloured by our values. In response to the possible objection that Nietzsche explicitly describes physics as an interpretation in BGE, 14, Clark and Dudrick respond that physics is an interpretation in this passage only if we accept the standard of 'eternal popular sensualism' (BGE, 14), which takes the view that that which is real is that which can be seen and touched. Nietzsche rejects sensualism and, therefore, is not committed to the idea that physics is an interpretation. According to Clark and Dudrick, Nietzsche thinks 'that physics and psychology differ in an important respect: he holds that while psychology rationalizes its object in order to explain it, sciences like physics do not – it is for this reason that psychology, unlike physics, is an "unnatural" or interpretive science'.[56] However, Clark and Dudrick's view here doesn't fit with Nietzsche's view that there are no facts, only interpretations. He writes the following in the *Nachlass*:

> Against positivism, which halts at phenomena – 'There are only *facts*' – I would say: No, facts is precisely what there is not, only interpretations . . . In

[54] Clark and Dudrick, *The Soul of Nietzsche's Beyond Good and Evil*, p. 224.   [55] Ibid., p. 226.
[56] Ibid., p. 229.

so far as the word 'knowledge' has any meaning, the world is knowable; but it is *interpretable* otherwise, it has no meaning behind it, but countless meanings. – 'Perspectivism'. (WP, 481, KSA, 12: 7 [60])

It cannot be objected that this passage is an isolated passage from the *Nachlass* because Nietzsche reiterates the claim made here in GS, 344, GM, III, 24 and 25. In GS, 344, he calls into question the will to truth as it is embodied in science and argues instead that science is always informed by presuppositions. In GM, III, 24, he criticizes the appeal to non-interpretive scientific facts, what he calls 'that stoicism of the intellect that finally forbids itself a "no" just as strictly as a "yes"; that wanting to halt before the factual, the *factum brutum*' and argues that the appeal to such facts represent a disingenuous attempt at renouncing 'interpretation'. Moreover, in GM, III, 25, he stresses that scientific investigation is evaluative, although it is never, of itself, value creating. He writes: 'Science is far from standing enough on its own for this, in every respect it first needs a value-ideal, a value-creating power in whose *service* it *may believe* in itself – it is itself never value-creating' (GM, III, 25). These passages should count against Clark and Dudrick's view even though they are not taken from BGE because Nietzsche tells us on the inside cover of GM that he wrote the latter book as a 'supplement and clarification' of BGE. Moreover, it is not clear to me that Clark and Dudrick are right when they claim that Nietzsche's prioritization of the causality of the will entails an acceptance of the distinction between mechanical causes and normativity. Rather, on the basis of the passages just cited and indeed my argument in Chapter 2, Nietzsche's argument is that our account of causality is always informed by our values. According to Clark and Dudrick, when we seek to explain things solely in mechanistic terms, we leave out of the picture what makes us characteristically human, that is, our values and sense-making abilities. But I don't think that this is Nietzsche's point. Rather, it is that we cannot give a non-interpretive account of causes or anything else simply because we cannot leave ourselves out of the picture in order to provide a value-neutral explanation. This brings us to premise ten in Nietzsche's argument, which, according to Clark and Dudrick, asserts the truth of premise nine:

10. All mechanical occurrences, insofar as force is active in them, are force of will, effects of will.

Whether we accept my interpretation or that of Clark and Dudrick has implications for how we respond to the pivotal claim in premises nine and ten. If we accept my reading, then Nietzsche must be seen as replacing the mechanist account of causality in the world with the causality of the will. Accordingly, Nietzsche accepts premise ten. However, Clark and Dudrick will, no doubt, object that my view takes Nietzsche's account of mechanism too literally and that an 'esoteric' reading suggests that we should understand Nietzsche's claim in premise ten as one about the character of willed actions where willed actions are ones that reflect our values and to which we are, accordingly, committed.[57] An esoteric reading, for Clark and Dudrick, entails a denial 'that the form and unity of the work [i.e. *Beyond Good and Evil*], and therefore its philosophical content, can be adequately appreciated without recognizing that its surface meaning differs substantially from what Nietzsche actually argues in it'.[58] They contend that an esoteric reading of BGE, 36, yields the conclusion, contra premise ten, that not all actions are willed actions and consequently that Nietzsche rejects the conclusion that all mechanical occurrences are the effects of will.[59] The success of Clark and Dudrick's argument here rests on the success of their account of Nietzsche's description of 'all mechanical events' as will to power. According to them, Nietzsche should be taken as referring to 'bodily movements that are willed' rather than to all mechanical events unqualifiedly. If he means the latter, they contend, the result would be philosophically troubling and 'laughable'. They write:

> If the phrase 'all mechanical events' is read in a completely unqualified way, so that it includes, for instance, events such as rocks rolling down hills, the hypothesis in premise 9 is clearly a nonstarter for Nietzsche. This is troubling: Nietzsche claims that we *must* undertake this experiment concerning causality, and yet it appears that the hypothesis it puts forward is laughable.[60]

However, the reason for rejecting the unqualified extension of the will to power to mechanical events as a plausible possibility betrays a certain prejudice on the part of the authors. The claim that rocks rolling down the hill are instances of the will to power is not laughable if we take it that the will to power entails that objects in the world have dispositional tendencies to manifest their powerful natures under facilitating circumstances. Understood thus, we would say that rocks have the power or natural capacity to roll down hills by virtue of their primary qualities. That is, rocks are possessed of the powerful property to roll because of their shape. Understood thus we have a case for understanding mind-independent reality as constitutively dispositional. As mind-independent and empirically instantiated, these dispositions are real, but as dispositions, they are not

---

[57] Ibid., p. 240.   [58] Ibid., p. 9.   [59] Ibid., p. 244.   [60] Ibid., p. 237.

always occurrently manifested and exist as potentials or possibilities for manifestation. Now, it might be asked what the description of rocks in terms of powerful properties has to do with Nietzsche's account of the causality of the will. My answer is that powerful properties can be understood on the model of the causality of the will because the causality of the will as Nietzsche describes it in BGE, 19, is dispositional. This is clear from his claim that the will does not necessitate its effect. This is a characteristic of the modality of dispositions in the sense that dispositions tend towards their outcomes but do not necessitate them due to the influence of preventive conditions. Rocks tend to roll down hills but won't do so necessarily if there is some other object obstructing their path, for example. In BGE, 19, Nietzsche tells us that although a dominant will may command a particular action, the action may not ensue due to a lack of cooperation or obstruction on the part of the other wills under its command. This – dispositional – account of causality accounts for the phenomenon of akrasia or weakness of will in human agents. However, to point to a structural similarity between them is not to say that the dispositional character of rocks must be identical in every particular to the dispositional character of the human will. Nietzsche's criticism of mythological thinking in BGE, 22, tells against such identity and it makes sense that we should expect that there are some differences in that the human will, for example, has a certain phenomenological quality that presumably rolling rocks do not. We will address this particular issue in Chapter 5. For our present purposes, however, it is enough that Nietzsche thinks that the two instances of dispositional causality – that of rolling rocks and human willing – are structurally and modally similar to warrant describing the modality of rocks in terms of the causality of the will and hence for understanding the two phenomena as metaphysically continuous. Metaphysical continuity allows that things may share a common nature and yet be differentiated from one another by metaphysical degrees, ruling out the need for a sharp dividing line between the causal and the normative. Clark and Dudrick must agree to my appeal to structural similarity as grounds for licensing a non-literal appeal to the causality of the will because they too appeal to an argument based on structural similarity in their account of the premises that make up the final segment of Nietzsche's argument in BGE, 36. The final segment contains the following premises:

11. 'The life of the drives' – that is, the drives and their relationship to one another – can be understood as the 'development and ramification of *one* basic form of will – as will to power.'

12. The causality of the will can be understood as the 'development and ramification of *one* basic form of the will – as will to power.' (2, 3, 11)
13. We can trace all organic functions back to this will to power.
14. All efficient force may be defined as will to power. (10, 12, 13)
15. Therefore, 'the world seen from within, the world described and defined according to its "intelligible character" is "will to power" and nothing else.' (14)

According to Clark and Dudrick, Nietzsche takes life to denote normative life and his reference to organic functions to denote not organisms in a literal sense but rather the organic-like structure of the normative ordering of the drives that constitute the human soul. They write that '. . .when premise 13 states "all organic functions" are ultimately due to the will to power, we should take it to mean that all aspects of normative life can be traced back to the development of the will to power: if there were no will to power among the drives, the drives would not form a normative order, and thus there would be no "organic functions" in this sense'.[61] Clark and Dudrick rest this argument on their taking Nietzsche's reference to 'organic' to mean 'having to do with organization'. They write that '[t]o say of things that they form an "organic" whole is to say that they are organized in such a way as to constitute a unified individual, as opposed to a disparate collection of elements. Biological organisms are, of course, "organic" in this sense, but the term is also used to characterize things that *do not* have life in the biological sense, for instance, social structures, by likening them to things that do.'[62] However, if it is the case that 'life' means any organic-like structure composed of parts and wholes, then 'life' clearly extends beyond the sphere of the normative and includes any object, such as physical objects, whether natural or artificial, that share a similar structure. One might even go further and maintain that reality in its entirety can be likened to an organic whole and is, accordingly, alive in Clark and Dudrick's sense. I can see no reason why when organic is used in the sense suggested by Clark and Dudrick that it need be restricted to the normative-evaluative sphere as they define it. Rather, their argument at this point seems to license the unqualified extension of the will to power to all things, that is, to human life and non-human organisms in addition to organically structured physical objects, including reality as a whole, that are not alive in a biological sense. Now, Clark and Dudrick may respond that Nietzsche considers the unqualified extension of the will to power as 'nonsense' on the grounds that in BGE, 36,

---

[61] Ibid., p. 240. [62] Ibid., p. 217.

he invites us to consider the applicability of the will to power to the point of nonsense (*bis zum Unsinn*). It is curious that Clark and Dudrick are happy to interpret the reference to nonsense here literally given their emphasis on an esoteric reading. However, if we interpret it non-literally as intending to mean that we should extend the experiment of BGE, 36, to its furthest limits, then there is no reason for arguing that Nietzsche rejects the unqualified extended and metaphysical version of the will to power in this passage.

Still, Clark and Dudrick might respond further that there are no other passages apart from BGE, 13, 22 and 36, in Nietzsche's published writings where he holds that both biological life and the world of the physicist can be described as will to power.[63] They claim that Nietzsche's reference to will to power applies only to life in the other published passages and that, on the basis of their argument here, life means normative rather than biological life. However, I beg to differ on this issue. Take, GM, II, 12, for instance, where, as in BGE, 186, Nietzsche describes the will to power as the 'essence' of life. One might adopt Clark and Dudrick's view and take his reference to life in this passage to mean normative life on the grounds that the discussion in GM, II, 12, takes place in the context of a larger discussion about the socialization of the human being through punishment. However, this restricted application of the will to power is cast into doubt when we consider Nietzsche's claim in the passage that he intends the will to power to apply to the supposedly most 'objective sciences', by which I take him to include physics in addition to psychology and biology on the grounds that he claims that the will to power applies to all happenings (*in allem Geschehn*). That he intends his description of life as will to power in this passage to refer to biological life generally is suggested by his application of the will to power to the demonstrative behaviour of the bird of prey and the lamb in GM, I, 13. Moreover, in GS, 349, as we saw in Chapter 2, Nietzsche claims that the will to power is the 'will of life' in the context of a discussion of 'our modern natural sciences (*unsre modernen Naturwissenschaften*)'. He writes that 'a natural scientist should come out of his human nook; and in nature it is not conditions of distress that are *dominant* but overflow and squandering, even to the point of absurdity'. His discussion in this passage also casts doubt on Clark and Dudrick's esoteric reading of BGE, 13. A literal reading of the passage has Nietzsche reject the idea that the will to self-preservation is the dominant drive of organic life in favour of the claim that life is the will to power. According to Clark and Dudrick's reading of this passage, we should not take

---

[63] Ibid., p. 212.

Nietzsche's claim that life is will to power in a biological sense, but rather they argue that we should take him to mean life in the normative sense where the will to power is understood as a 'cardinal drive' by virtue of which normative and reason-giving persons are structured.[64] But it is difficult to square this esoteric reading with the obviously literal intention on Nietzsche's part in GS, 349, when he writes in the context of a discussion of the natural sciences that '[t]he wish to preserve oneself is the symptom of a condition of distress, of a limitation of the really fundamental instinct of life which aims at the *expansion of power. . .*' (GS, 349).[65] Although it might be argued that Nietzsche precludes physics from his extended version of the will to power on the grounds that he mentions physiology in particular in GM, II, 12, for example, his reference to physiology in that passage is meant to indicate that the will to power is already evident in physiology and that it needs to be extended more widely than is currently the case or currently considered to be obvious. That Nietzsche intends the will to power thesis to be extended to physics can also be further discerned from his interest in the character of causality more generally. In GS, 112, for example, he suggests that when the natural scientist ceases to 'humanize' the world, in the specific sense of taking the senses at face value without subjecting them to interpretation, it will be seen that causality can be understood on the model of a continuum rather than as a relation between discrete and successive events.[66] Moreover, that Nietzsche understands this alternative model to entail causal powers is evident from his description of causality in terms of the powerful properties of explosive powder in GS, 360. His comments in these passages are commensurate with his criticism of materialistic atomism in BGE, 12, and his criticism of the 'physicist's' appeal to nomological necessity on the grounds of observed regularities (*'aber jene "Gesetzmässigkeit der Natur", von der ihr Physiker so stolz redet'*) in favour of a power model

---

[64] Ibid., p. 221.

[65] Clark and Dudrick deny that the will to power applies to biology on the grounds that the will to power is a cardinal or second-order drive by virtue of which the drives form a political order or soul, which constitutes human personhood and normativity (ibid.). However, the identification of the dominant drive with the will to power seems incorrect to me. This is because the dominant drive is distinguished from its subordinate counterparts by their strength, which, for Nietzsche, is a degree of the will to power. All drives are will to power and the competitive relations between them contribute to and constitute the social structure that is the Nietzschean self. Accordingly, Nietzsche describes the drives as weak or strong (GM, I, 13), where these degrees of strength are will to power and the essence of life (GM, II, 12). As I will argue in Chapter 4, normativity is constituted by the degree of power of a drive.

[66] In TI, 'Reason', 3 Nietzsche tells us that although the senses are 'fine instruments of observation', we must nonetheless 'think them through to the end'.

in BGE, 22. Obviously, this interpretation does not fit with Clark and Dudrick's view that Nietzsche thinks physics is non-evaluative and non-interpretive. But, as I argued earlier, I cannot see that this is Nietzsche's view of physics. Rather, it seems to me that Nietzsche thinks that all epistemic claims, including those of physics, are interpretations of the world. This is not to say that there isn't a world that serves to constrain our interpretations and what Clark and Dudrick take Nietzsche to be referring to as the 'text' in BGE, 22. But it is to say that we always and by necessity come to the world from a particular interpretive point of view. In the absence of the possibility of a God's Eye View, we must distinguish from within between better and worse interpretations, what Nietzsche refers to as lighter and darker shades of appearances in BGE, 34.

If my previous arguments are cogent, then Clark and Dudrick's claim that Nietzsche restricts the will to power to above the line normative relations and does not extend it to below the line causality, is open to question. This is because the normative and the causal, for Nietzsche, are more closely intertwined than Clark and Dudrick's interpretation allows. Although they contend that Nietzsche's account of causality of the will is informed by Kant's distinction between the normative and the causal, this separation, for Kant, presupposes a distinction between the empirical sphere of deterministic mechanical causes and the noumenal sphere of freedom and normativity. My argument in this chapter as a whole has been that Nietzsche's engagement with Kant on the issue of causality and the noumenal sees Nietzsche bring the intrinsic character of the noumenal, what we have seen Kant calls the 'causality of their cause', to bear at the level of empirical causal relations such that causes operate according to an internal intrinsic and powerful nature. As a result, it seems to me that we need to take Nietzsche seriously when he proposes that we translate the human being *back into* nature (*zurückübersetzen in die Natur*) and that such a translation entails appealing to the will to power (BGE, 230). This is not to suggest, however, that Nietzsche thinks that human beings and their evaluative activities are reducible to nature. In this, I think Clark and Dudrick are correct. But, it is to indicate, contrary to them, that any differentiation between human beings and the rest of nature must be made from the point of view of the internal – metaphysical – continuity of the human being within nature and not from a stance where a division is already in place or presupposed.

However, although we have rehearsed the reasons why Nietzsche would reject Clark and Dudrick's claim that he operates within a distinction between causes and reasons that is Kantian in character, it might still be argued, contrary to my appeal to the metaphysical continuity of our values with the causal nature of reality, that if Nietzsche doesn't distinguish between causes and normativity in the Kantian sense, perhaps we should understand him as committed to the Humean version of the distinction between facts and values. After all, it might be contested, Hume is a naturalist and any objection that Nietzsche might have to the Kantian distinction does not necessarily apply to the Humean version. We already have the first step of a rebuttal of this proposal in place. That is, part and parcel of our efforts to justify the metaphysics of the will to power in this chapter has been to argue that Nietzsche adopts a specifically non-Humean account of causality. However, clearly more needs to be said about the non-Humean character of Nietzsche's account of the metaphysical continuity of our values with the causal fabric of reality. Consequently, my argumentative strategy in the next chapter will be to focus on how Nietzsche's alignment of value with the will to power poses a further challenge to Hume in the guise of the fact-value distinction. My investigation of this challenge will entail examining values as psychological dispositions, which, owing to their causal-dispositional nature, are also normative in character. However, although Nietzsche does not distinguish between reality and our values in the Humean sense of separating facts from values and although he does not appeal to a Kantian distinction between mechanical nature and normative life, he still thinks that human minds can be demarcated from the rest of nature as a result of their capacity to offer justifications and reasons for their values. However, it will be seen, contrary to the Humean and Kantian views, that this distinctively human capacity is not a projection on our part onto reality but rather is metaphysically continuous with the causal fabric of reality by virtue of having a dispositional ground.

CHAPTER 4

Value and the Will to Power

This chapter will examine Nietzsche's account of the metaphysical status of human values in the context of his will to power thesis. In so doing, it continues and adds a further ingredient to the arguments proffered in the previous two chapters. In Chapter 2, we established that our values can be objective by virtue of being necessary conditions of our experience of the world in addition to being constrained by it and that Nietzsche's conception of objectivity is not metaphysically neutral but implies the particular metaphysics of the will to power. Having examined Nietzsche's justification of the will to power as offering a non-Humean account of causality in Chapter 3, we now turn to ask what a value *is*. It will be argued that by aligning value with power, Nietzsche offers a dispositional account of value that renders value metaphysically continuous with but irreducible to the causal fabric of mind-independent reality. Specifically, this entails that values and norms can be differentiated from the causal fabric of reality but that they are nonetheless metaphysically continuous with it by virtue of being grounded dispositionally and causally. Although the predominant view is that Nietzsche is a Humean of some variety when it comes to considering the metaphysical status of value and that this commits him to the metaphysical dissociation of values from the world in the form of the fact-value distinction, I argue that Nietzsche's alignment of value with power ultimately challenges Hume's distinction between facts and values in addition to the more Kantian take on the distinction, which holds that causes and reasons, or mechanical nature and normative life, are radically different in kind. Despite sharing Hume's naturalist credentials in addition to appealing to the role of the affects, Nietzsche is critical of Hume's standing as a philosopher, describing him as having issued in 'a century-long degradation and devaluation of the concept "philosopher"' (BGE, 252). Since the primary task of the genuine philosopher, for Nietzsche, is to be concerned with questions of value (BGE, 211), we can take it that

Nietzsche's criticism of Hume is targeted at his account of value, central to which is his distinction between facts and values.[1]

However, it cannot be denied that Nietzsche sometimes appears to adopt a Humean position with regard to the metaphysical status of value. This is especially suggested on those occasions when he employs the analogy of colour in his discussion of the metaphysical status of values as mind-dependent projections onto non-evaluative reality (HAH, I, 16; WP, 12 KSA 13: 11 [99]; D, 210). Nevertheless, there is an alternative account of value available in Nietzsche, which stems from his alignment of value with the will to power. This alignment sees him offering a more robustly causal account of nature and the human being's immersion in it than is available in Hume, and it plays an important role in facilitating a rejection of Hume's projectionism and fact-value distinction.

Consequently, although Hume, like Nietzsche, is a naturalist and considers the human being to be part of nature, there are some important dissimilarities between the two thinkers. One important point of disagreement resides in the character of their respective naturalist approaches. That is, in his 'attempt to introduce the experimental method into moral subjects',[2] Hume restricts our knowledge, founded on observation, to that of effects where the 'causes' of those effects are events that merely precede the effect in time rather than causal powers that bring about the effect. With regard to the issue of causal powers, Hume writes that '[n]othing is more requisite for a true philosopher than to restrain the intemperate desire of searching into causes'.[3] Our knowledge of the human being's immersion in nature, according to this account, is not based on knowledge of inner essential natures but is, rather, restricted to that knowledge afforded from the 'outside' by observation. However, contrary to what he calls the 'doltish mechanistic English ideas about the world' (BGE, 252), Nietzsche's naturalism and his project of translating the human being back into nature, contrary to supernaturalist accounts of

---

[1] Peter Kail investigates the relation between Hume and Nietzsche in 'Nietzsche and Hume: Naturalism and Explanation', *Journal of Nietzsche Studies*, 37, 2009, pp. 5–22. Kail focuses on methodological issues pertaining to Hume's and Nietzsche's naturalism whilst I focus primarily on substantive metaphysical issues in relation to value. He contends that whilst there is nothing antinaturalistic in investigating the will to power as an alternative paradigm of causality to the dominant paradigm, Nietzsche's will to power thesis does not condition his naturalism. In contrast, I argue that Nietzsche's metaphysics of the will to power gives rise to a specifically non-Humean metaphysical-cum-naturalistic account of value.

[2] This is the subtitle that Hume gives to his *A Treatise of Human Nature*.

[3] David Hume, *A Treatise of Human Nature*, L. A. Selby-Bigge and P. H. Nidditch (eds.) (Oxford: Clarendon Press, 1989), pp. 12–13. Hereafter abbreviated as T.

the self, entails acknowledging a 'fundamental will of the spirit' (BGE, 230) that he calls will to power.[4] As we argued in the previous chapter, the will to power is a causal essentialist thesis, which operates at the level of human, non-human, organic and inorganic nature, and is, for Nietzsche, an explanatory account of the metaphysical continuity of the self with nature. Human psychology, for Nietzsche, is metaphysically continuous with non-human nature as will to power and provides, in his view, the key to 'fundamental issues' (BGE, 23). Writing that 'Mechanistic theory can – only *describe* processes, not explain them' (WP, 660 KSA 12: 2 [76]; BGE, 36), Nietzsche's appeals to explanations 'from the inside' (BGE, 36) rather than descriptions from the outside, which results in a different account of value to that of Hume.

I argue that Nietzsche formulates his challenge to Hume in three ways. First, he rejects Hume's spectator point of view with regard to values by denying Hume's view that values must be identified with affective responses of observers. In so doing, Nietzsche identifies values with genuine causal powers rather than effects that are merely observed to follow a preceding event. Second, by making values causal-dispositional properties that are metaphysically continuous with the causal fabric of reality, Nietzsche rejects Hume's projection thesis that holds that the affective-evaluative responses of observers are projections onto the world. Third, Nietzsche puts the final nail in the coffin of the fact-value distinction when he argues that despite their continuity with the causal processes of nature, values understood dispositionally are normative in character.[5]

---

[4] By mechanism here, I take Nietzsche to be referring to empiricism generally. This is suggested by the fact that he references Hobbes, Locke and Hume together in BGE, 252.

[5] There are contemporary – Humean – dispositional accounts of value such as the one put forward by David Lewis, for example. Despite being a Humean, Lewis rejects the idea of an ideal observer as the determiner of value. Instead, he replaces such ideal observations with full imaginative acquaintance. And, he abandons the identification of values with secondary or phenomenal qualities, arguing against the 'longstanding attempt to make dispositional theories of value and of colour run parallel' (Lewis 'Dispositional Theories of Value' in Michael Smith, David Lewis and Mark Johnston, 'Dispositional Theories of Value', *Proceedings of the Aristotelian Society, Supplementary Volumes*, Volume 63, 1989, pp. 89–111, 113–137, 139–174, p. 123). Nevertheless, the 'Humean' flavour to his argument is expressed in his identification of a value with that which we desire to desire. According to Lewis, X is a value iff we are disposed to value it under ideal conditions of imaginative acquaintance, that is, iff under ideal conditions of imaginative acquaintance we desire to desire X. Imaginative acquaintance, he argues, plays a causal role in the sense that it causes us to value X such that we respond to X by desiring to desire it (ibid., p. 112). Although Nietzsche, according to my account, offers a dispositional account of value, it differs considerably from response-dependent accounts such as that of Lewis's. Whereas, value, for Nietzsche, is a psychic disposition, Lewis offers a dispositional analysis of value but does not identify values as dispositions. He argues that the disposition to respond to X resides in the responder but that the value itself is not a disposition. He writes 'Being a value comes out as a dispositionally analysed property, but not as a disposition of the things that have

Nietzsche meets the first challenge by making values causal-dispositional properties of intentionally directed human drives. I focus on the evaluative character of human drives as they function in the context of the hierarchically structured unit that, for Nietzsche, constitutes the self. I use the term 'self' here to denote a bundle of drives ruled by a dominating drive (BGE, 12) without prejudice as to whether this self must be conscious or self-conscious to be considered a self. Furthermore, I take the evaluating agent to be the self even though Nietzsche often writes of the individual drives that compose the self as evaluative and as agents in their own right.[6] This is because, as will become apparent later, the subordinate drives of the self must express their evaluative point of view through the perspectival and evaluative lens of the dominating drive.

The second challenge is addressed by arguing that Nietzsche's alignment of value with power extends beyond the powerful self to include worldly power.[7] That is, value entails power, for Nietzsche, not just because values reflect the point of view of powerful agents but because they must overcome resistances to the manifestation of their natures exerted by the powerful capacities of reality. It is the exertion of such resistance that results in the manifestation of the value property as feelings of strength in the case of veridical values and feelings of weakness in the case of

---

it. Values themselves are not disposed to do anything' (ibid., p. 124n16). In contrast, according to my argument, Nietzsche runs together evaluation and value and identifies values with psychic causal-dispositions. Moreover, Nietzsche's account is neither a counterfactual nor conditional analysis of value. Rather, it is a metaphysical account of what value is and cannot be reduced to a conceptual formula. To reduce dispositions to such formulae, according to Nietzsche, is to fail to capture their real causal efficacy. He articulates such a view in his criticism of the attempt to explain physical force in terms of a mathematical formula (WP, 628 KSA 12: 2 [89]).

[6] See, for example, BGE, 6; WP, 481 KSA 12: 7 [60]; WP, 567 KSA 13: 14 [184]. For discussion of this issue in the literature, see Leslie Paul Thiele, *Friedrich Nietzsche and the Politics of the Soul* (Princeton, NJ: Princeton University Press, 1990); Maudemarie Clark and David Dudrick, 'Nietzsche's Philosophical Psychology' in Maudemarie Clark, *Nietzsche on Ethics and Politics* (Oxford: Oxford University Press, 2015), pp. 260–286; Peter Poellner, *Nietzsche and Metaphysics* (Oxford: Oxford University Press, 1995). For an argument against the coherency of Nietzsche's description of the drives as homunculi, see Paul Katsafanas, 'Nietzsche's Philosophical Psychology' in Ken Gemes and John Richardson (eds.), *The Oxford Handbook of Nietzsche* (Oxford: Oxford University Press, 2013), pp. 727–755.

[7] I argue in this way contrary to the dominant view in the secondary literature that power in Nietzsche should be interpreted primarily in psychological terms. For example, Nadeem Hussain writes that power, for Nietzsche, is a 'property of agents' (Nadeem J. Z. Hussain, 'Honest Illusion: Valuing for Nietzsche's Free Spirits' in Brian Leiter and Neil Sinhababu (eds.), *Nietzsche and Morality* (Oxford: Oxford University Press, 2007), pp. 157–191, p. 177). Bernard Reginster also interprets power psychologically, arguing that the will to power should be understood as a desire for the overcoming of resistance in the pursuit of some determinate first-order desire ('The Will to Power and the Ethics of Creativity' in Leiter and Sinhababu (eds.), *Nietzsche and Morality*, pp. 32–56, p. 41). See also Richardson's interpretation of the will to power as a form of power egoism and self-mastery: *Nietzsche's System* (Oxford: Oxford University Press, 1996), pp. 154–155.

non-veridical ones.[8] In the case of veridical values, I argue that resistance takes the form of cooperation of values with the natural capacities of reality such that the realization of such values entails the mutual manifestation of the natural capacities of mind and world. This is a specifically non-Humean thesis because it holds that although values reflect human beings and their perspectival interests, veridical values are not projections onto the world but rather manifest their natures in cooperation with the powerful character of the world. Consequently, it will be argued that although all values, for Nietzsche, are normative by virtue of expressing the interests of the most powerful drive of the evaluating agent, only some value-norms are objective by virtue of being powerful enough to cooperate with the dispositional fabric of reality. Still, it will be further argued that the normativity and objectivity of a value are distinguished in terms of degrees of power only, such that the evaluating agent's engagement with the world is normative through and through. Accordingly, human values are not reducibly ideal or dualistically separate from the metaphysical character of the world.

Finally, the normative character of Nietzsche's dispositional account of value will be demonstrated in two ways. The first involves an independent and anti-Humean argument about the modality of dispositions. This examination will show that rather than cutting values off from the world, norms operate according to the same dispositional modality as the causal processes of nature. The second entails an examination of Nietzsche's own argument that claims that our capacity to formulate explicit value judgements supported by reasons is metaphysically continuous with nature's causes.

Nietzsche's Dispositional Account of Value

In this section I argue that by aligning value with power Nietzsche identifies values with dispositional properties of psychic drives rather than with the affective responses of outside observers and that in so doing he puts in place the first step to overcoming Hume's fact-value distinction. I rehearse Hume's position in brief followed by Nietzsche's alternative account of value. For Nietzsche's appeal to an agent and causal

---

[8] It might be argued that feelings of strength cannot be the marker of veridical values on account of the fact that slave values give rise to such feelings. But, as we shall see, the slave's feelings of power are brought about by the slave's turning against the world rather than acting successfully in it through the overcoming of external resistance. Accordingly, the slave's feelings are of a weaker form than the noble's.

point of view in his alignment of value with power is in marked contrast with the particulars of Hume's argument.

According to Hume, value is to be demarcated from questions of fact, questions about what there is, non-evaluatively, in the world. The idea informing the fact-value distinction is that natural science affords us an evaluatively neutral description of the world in its – objective – quantitative aspects. But it offers us no account of value or normativity. Modern philosophy, according to Hume, describes the world non-evaluatively in terms of quantifiable inert matter in motion, devoid of phenomenal qualities. In contrast, values are reducible to feelings or emotions that we project onto the world but are not found in the world itself.[9]

Since the emotions/passions, for Hume, are identified by a particular and irreducible phenomenal quality, he likens values to secondary qualities, which, he contends are 'in' the mind rather than in objects.[10] In so doing, he adopts a particularly Malebranchian understanding of the metaphysical status of secondary qualities, which denies the Lockean view that such qualities are in fact dispositions or powers in the object.[11] Since human minds, for Hume, are inextricable parts of nature and subject to the same explanations as other natural phenomena, he is unable to identify the value property of an action or character with causal powers of those objects to induce emotional responses in us. This is because Hume denies that we are entitled to attribute causal powers to nature generally on the basis that if there were such powers they must be necessary and that their necessary causal influence could not be prevented.[12] He argues that were causal powers to obtain, they would necessitate their effects such that if we were acquainted with powers we could predict a priori what effects *must* follow from them.[13] However, he claims that cause and effect, understood

[9] Hume, T, pp. 468–469; David Hume, *Enquiries Concerning Human Understanding and Concerning the Principles of Morals* (Oxford: Clarendon Press, 1987), p. 294. Hereafter cited as EHU and EPM.

[10] Hume, T, p. 469.

[11] Peter Kail, *Projection and Realism in Hume's Philosophy* (Oxford: Oxford University Press, 2007), p. 153. Sometimes Hume writes as if he identifies values with powers or dispositions in the object. For example, he writes that 'since the power of producing pain and pleasure make in this manner the essence of beauty and deformity, all the effects of these qualities must be deriv'd from the sensation' (T, p. 299). However, although he appears to identify beauty and deformity with powers of the object to induce sensations, he nevertheless, on the very same page, identifies beauty and deformity with the sensation itself when he writes that 'Pleasure and pain, therefore, are not only necessary attendants of beauty and deformity, but constitute their very essence' (T, p. 299).

[12] In this and in the explanation of dispositional modality that follows later, I draw heavily on the argument of Rani Lill Anjum, Svein Anders Noer Lie and Stephen Mumford in 'Dispositions and Ethics' in Ruth Groff and John Greco (eds.), *Powers and Capacities in Philosophy: The New Aristotelianism* (London: Routledge, 2013), pp. 231–247, pp. 234–235.

[13] Hume, T, p. 90; EPM, p. 63.

in terms of spatial contiguity and temporal succession, are conceivably separable from one another, which allows that preventive conditions may obtain that interfere with the production of an effect by its cause. According to Hume, '[a]ll events seem entirely loose and separate; but we never can observe any tie between them. They seem *conjoined* but never *connected*'.[14] Consequently, for him, ''tis impossible to admit of any medium betwixt chance and necessity'.[15] Rather, questions of necessity in nature, just like questions about values, are reduced to sentiments or feelings in us. It follows that Hume cannot identify values with causal properties of agents or objects. Instead, he identifies values with emotional responses of observers or outside perceivers. These responses might be to character traits of individuals and their actions in the case of moral value. In the case of aesthetic value, they are responses to works of art. According to Hume, the value or moral quality of an action or character trait, or the aesthetic quality of the art object, resides in the emotional response of the observer of these agents or objects. What makes the character trait or action morally good or the features of an art object aesthetically beautiful is the – ideal – spectator's emotional response rather than value qualities in the moral agent or art object itself.[16] For example, he writes that '[b]eauty is not a quality of the circle. It lies not in any part of the line whose parts are all equally distant from a common center. It is only the effect, which that figure produces upon a mind, whose particular fabric or structure renders it susceptible of such sentiments.'[17]

There is no ambiguity involved in the identification of values with effects in Hume despite his denial of causal powers. Although it is the case that if he allows that there are effects then he must also allow that there are causes, the causes that he allows are those features of objects with which our affective responses are constantly conjoined. This is because Hume continues to refer to causes and effects in terms of constant conjunctions of events. It is in this specific sense that value feelings are effects. Hume argues that although our evaluative sentiments are irreducibly phenomenal experiences and not to be discovered mind-independently in the world, the sentiments themselves are correlated with non-evaluative features of the object which are 'fitted by nature to produce these particular feelings'.[18] Nevertheless, the features of objects with which our value feelings are correlated are not causal powers that necessitate those effects, according

---

[14] Hume, EHU, p. 74.   [15] Hume, T, p. 171.   [16] Ibid., p. 475.
[17] David Hume, 'The Sceptic' in David Hume, *Essays: Moral, Political and Literary*, Eugene F. Miller (ed.) (Indianapolis, IN: Liberty Fund, 1987), pp. 159–180, p. 165.
[18] Hume, EPM, p. 235.

to Hume. And, although he sometimes describes evaluative sentiments themselves as action motivating desires or passions, these feelings cause actions only to the extent that there is an observed correlation between desires and actions. Hume denies that we are introspectively aware of any causal power that connects necessarily our impression of willing and subsequent actions.[19] As such, moral feelings do not cause actions in the stronger sense of attributing to these moral feelings a causal power to bring about the subsequent action. Rather, our claim that moral feelings cause subsequent actions is a claim made from the outside on the basis of observation rather than by appealing to the essential causal nature of the will. Whilst Hume thinks that this outside account of causal connection is sufficient for attributing causality to the will,[20] it remains the case that by causality he means observed constant conjunctions of events rather than causal power. Moreover, his concern with the causal connection between sentiments and action pertains to contexts where those sentiments are objects of evaluative appraisal rather than evaluative responses *per se.* Thus, when he talks about the causality (in the sense of constant conjunction) of the will, he does so with a view to a moral spectator attributing praise or blame to an agent's intentions, motives and actions. The moral value of the agent's intentions, motives and actions is determined by and resides in the spectator's response to them, even though the response may be caused (again, in the sense of constant conjunction) by the agent's character traits.[21] The value of something, according to Hume, whether that something be an action, a person's intentions or a thing, resides in the spectator's response. It is in this spectator sense that I claim that values, for Hume, are effects rather than causes. Consequently, values, in his view, are not causal or genuinely creative but rather are irreducibly phenomenal and correlated responses to actually existing objects. That these objects must be actually existent is determined by the fact that our feelings are responses to them.[22] When Hume describes values as 'new creations',[23] we must

---

[19] Hume, T, p. 402.   [20] Ibid., p. 405.

[21] Ibid., pp. 468–469. Although Hume sometimes writes as if virtue is a property of agents themselves (T, p. 591), it is *really* a projection of the spectator's response onto the agent as the object of evaluative appraisal (T, pp. 468–469; EPM, p. 290).

[22] According to Hume, there are only two circumstances in which passions, as non-representational original existences, can be deemed unreasonable. The first, which concerns us here, arises when 'a passion – is founded on the supposition of the existence of objects, which do not really exist' (Hume, T, p. 416). That is, for Hume, the passion is a response to the actual or supposed actual existence of the object and would not itself exist were it not for the actual existence of the object or the mistaken judgement about the actual existence of the object.

[23] Hume, EPM, p. 294.

understand them to be creations only in the sense that the phenomenal-feeling character of our responses to objects does not correspond to feeling properties in the objects themselves.

Like Hume, Nietzsche denies that values reside mind-independently in objects. Nevertheless, he identifies values with powerful psychic dispositions that are continuous with the causal fabric of reality itself rather than with Humean responses to actually existent objects. Although Nietzsche allows that we can formulate evaluative appraisals of currently existing objects and although such appraisals attend to qualities of these objects, such appraisals are nonetheless formulated in the context of the actually existing object's contribution to or detraction from the realization of some further object, which, for Nietzsche, is the proper intentional object of our evaluations and which may not currently exist. It will be noticed that Nietzsche runs together values and evaluations in the sense that values are dispositional properties of psychic drives and evaluation is the process whereby the drive endeavours to overcome resistances to manifest its dispositional nature. External objects of our evaluative appraisal are such because overcoming or cooperating with them forms part of the process of evaluation in the sense of realizing the dispositional capacities of psychic drives. Whilst the disposition is currently actual, its manifestation and proper intentional object are inexistent. The futuristic direction of Nietzsche's thought regarding value indicates that, for him, values or evaluative activity may be intentionally directed to currently inexistent objects. Moreover, as we shall see a little later in section two, to the extent that our value-dispositions fit the world, in Nietzsche's view, they do so in the sense of collaborating with powerful capacities in the world to bring about some jointly produced effect rather than tracking some inert and non-evaluative features of objects with which our responses are correlated. And whereas, for Hume, our responses play no causal role in generating their intentional objects, in Nietzsche's account of value, psychic dispositions, like the dispositional fabric of reality itself, are genuinely causal and can, under suitable conditions, bring about or realize their intentional objects, which need not be an actually existent object to which we respond, as it is in Hume, but rather the manifestation of the psychic disposition's nature. Since the psychic disposition may be currently unmanifested, the power of the disposition to manifest itself brings about something not already there and can be considered to be genuinely causal and creative rather than response-dependent.

These conclusions follow from Nietzsche's alignment of value with the will to power. For example, in AC, he writes:

What is good? – All that heightens the feeling of power, the will to power, *power itself in man*. (my italics)
   What is bad? – All that proceeds from weakness.
   What is happiness? – The feeling that power *increases* – that a resistance is overcome. (AC, 2)[24]

His reference to 'power – in man' in the preceding passage indicates that Nietzsche's account of power as a measure of value is concerned with power on the part of the human valuer.[25] He tells us that that which is good results in heightened feelings of power on the part of the valuer and that such feelings arise from the overcoming of resistance. One might worry, however, that if Nietzsche reduces value to feelings of power on the part of the valuer, then he has not travelled very far beyond Hume for whom values are irreducibly phenomenal and not part of the world as depicted by natural – mechanical – science. Nietzsche's description of the will to power as entailing a conception of 'a world with the same level of reality that our emotion (*Affeckt*) has' (BGE, 36) suggests, on a first glance, that by extending phenomenal experience to reality itself, he can avoid the Humean dichotomy between facts and values. No such distinction obtains if both human and non-human reality are phenomenal or affective in character. This might offer us a solution to Nietzsche's trouble with

---

[24] Nietzsche also takes power to be an objective measure of value when he writes:

> The attempt should be made, whether a scientific order of values could be constructed simply in a numerical mensural scale of *force* – All other 'values' are prejudices, naiveties, misunderstandings – They are everywhere *reducible* to this numerical and mensural scale of force – The upwards on this scale means every growth in value. (WP, 710 KSA 13: 14 [105])

He contends: 'What is the objective measure of value? Solely the quantum of enhanced and organized power' (WP, 674 KSA 13: 11 [83]; Cf. WP, 858 KSA 13: 11 [36]).

[25] Richardson also argues that Nietzsche identifies valuings with the drives but stresses that all organic life operates according to drives (John Richardson, *Nietzsche's New Darwinism* (Oxford: Oxford University Press, 2004), p. 25). This means that animals and plants, for example, are valuers. However, given the organisms that we are, it is entirely conceivable that the manifestation of a drive in the case of human beings is different from the operation of drives in other organisms. Notice that in GS, 301, Nietzsche distinguishes between non-human animals and human animals in terms of degree rather than kind. He contends that we evaluating thinking-feelings ones see more than non-human animals. This difference in degree, according to Nietzsche, amounts to the idea that we are valuers in a way that non-human animals are not. Whilst Nietzsche writes in BGE, 19, that willing entails feeling or affect, it is clear in this passage from his reference to 'the person willing' and by the fact that the discussion in the passage centers round that of free will that it is human willing he has in mind. Nietzsche also warns against extending value beyond the human sphere when he writes that 'all our sensations of value (i.e., simply our sensations) adhere precisely to qualities . . . Qualities are an idiosyncrasy peculiar to man' (WP, 565 KSA 12: 6 [14]). However, even if we were to extend values to non-human animals capable of affect, it is clear that these values would be for basic needs such as those required for the preservation of the organism, which are far removed from the realization of the 'higher' values that Nietzsche seeks.

Hume, but the cost of achieving the solution is a gross anthropomorphization of non-human reality, which is inconsistent with Nietzsche's denial
that man is 'the measure of all things' (BGE, 3; GS, 109). However, closer
examination shows that Nietzsche does not intend to suggest that non-
human reality is identical to human emotional experience. He writes that
although the world has 'the same level of reality that our emotion (*Affekt*)
has', the world itself is composed of a 'more rudimentary form of the world
of emotions (*als seine primitivere Form der Welt der Affekte*)'. These metaphysically basic constituents are intentionally directed causal powers,
which Nietzsche describes as will to power and which explain 'from the
inside' the operations of both 'mechanical' and organic nature. Whilst he is
unclear about how these basic constituents are more primitive or rudimentary than the emotions, we might say, perhaps a little charitably, that the
fundamental constituents of reality, which are metaphysically continuous
with phenomenal feelings, are themselves non-phenomenal in character.
Interpreted in this way, as was argued in Chapters 2 and 3, we would say
that Nietzsche arrives at the will to power thesis as a comprehensive
metaphysical explanation by analogy with the structure of human psychology. Such an argument makes human psychology the unavoidable starting
point of our inquiry but does not make humankind the measure of all
things by prescribing that non-human inorganic reality must be identical
to human psychology. Instead, Nietzsche concludes that human and non-
human organic and inorganic reality are metaphysically continuous with
and structurally similar to one another. According to Nietzsche, metaphysical continuity entails appealing to how things are from the inside, that is,
to how they are essentially. The structure of things emanates from what
they are like essentially. Since his essentialism is of the causal variety,
Nietzsche refers to intentionally directed (from the inside) causal powers
and psychic drives rather than mere correlations of events detected and
described from the outside.

Nonetheless, Nietzsche clearly wants to allow for a role for phenomenal
affect in relation to human value. However, phenomenal affect, for him,
cannot be of the spectatorial or merely responsive kind as it is in Hume. At
the same time, he wants to argue for the metaphysical continuity of human
value with the causal fabric of reality but without extending the phenomenal affective aspect of human valuing to the world. He accommodates
these requirements by arguing that human values are non-phenomenal
dispositional properties of psychic drives that are manifested through the
directive role of the affects but are nonetheless irreducible to them.
According to Nietzsche, although values have an affective dimension,

they are ultimately dispositional and metaphysically continuous with the causal-dispositional character of the world.[26] Both physical powers and psychic dispositions, in his view, are causal in nature and intentionally directed to bringing about particular effects. These effects are the manifestation of a power's irreducibly particular nature. Human drives, which can operate beneath the level of explicit conscious awareness, are, according to Nietzsche, continuous with worldly forces. The nature of the continuity between human drives and worldly forces lies in Nietzsche's view that both can be explained as will to power.

As wills to power, worldly forces and human drives are dispositional tendencies towards certain types of behaviour (BGE, 36). However, despite their structural similarity, the human drives are directed towards species-specific forms of behaviour. Accordingly, of the human drives Nietzsche writes that '[i]t is *our needs* that interpret the world; *our drives* and their for and against. Every drive is a kind of lust to rule; each has its perspective that it would like to compel all the other drives to accept as a norm' (WP, 481 KSA 13: 14 [22]) [my italics]. This account differs from Hume because neither the drives nor the affects, for Nietzsche, are primarily responding to external pre-existing objects. That our evaluative drives are not primarily responses to actually existent objects can be discerned from Nietzsche's claim that such objects should be understood as either facilitators or obstacles to the drive's aim to manifest its irreducibly particular quantum of power optimally. He writes that every animal strives for the 'most powerful doing' by striving for 'an optimum of favourable conditions under which it can vent its power completely and attain its maximum in the feeling of power; just as instinctively, and with a keenness of scent that "surpasses all understanding", every animal abhors troublemakers and obstacles of every kind that could do or could lay themselves across its path to the optimum' (GM, III, 7; GM, I, 13). Running together evaluation and value, the human drives, as dispositional tendencies, are intentionally directed to the manifestation of their perspectival and, for Nietzsche, particularly human evaluative point of view. He writes that 'Every "drive" is the drive to "something good", seen from some standpoint' (KSA 11: 26 [72]).[27] These evaluations, for Nietzsche, are directed

---

[26] For other dispositional accounts of the drives in Nietzsche see Christoph Cox, *Nietzsche: Naturalism and Interpretation* (Berkeley, CA: University of California Press, 1999), pp. 126–127; Richard Schacht, *Nietzsche* (London: Routledge, 1983,) pp. 279–280; Steven D. Hales and Rex Welshon, *Nietzsche's Perspectivism* (Urbana, IL: University of Illinois Press, 2000), p. 159; Richardson, *Nietzsche's New Darwinism*, p. 75.

[27] However, one might object that if drives are perspectival, interpretive, evaluative and intentional, then they are not really dispositions but rather conscious agents. That is, it might be argued that the drives must be conscious if they are to be intentionally directed to one another, interpret one

to the realization of some end such that the intentional object of a drive is the manifestation of its particular point of view. As an aim, the drive's intentional object may be currently unmanifested but exist as an aspiration or disposition to be realized. Since human agents are biological and sensate creatures, human drives can also be expected to have an affective phenomenal component that causal powers in nature lack. But to the extent that human value entails phenomenal affect, for Nietzsche, it signals and results from the activity of the specifically human drive and is not reducible to a response in a spectator or outside perceiver. That these feelings are not of the Humean spectatorial kind is already evident in the fact that, for Nietzsche, the proper intentional object of our evaluative activity is not an external object to which we passively respond but rather the manifestation of the drive's causal nature.

another and indeed negotiate with one another and that dispositions, by virtue of being dispositions, are not conscious. The worry here also is that if the drives are individually conscious then Nietzsche is committed, implausibly, to the idea of multiple selves within the self and to a form of panpsychism that understands the operation of nature in similarly conscious-psychological terms. In response, however, we can say that intentionality, despite the common view, need not be conscious. That Nietzsche agrees can be discerned from his denial that consciousness is the mark of the mental (GS, 354). Still, it might be objected that even if this is the case, surely conscious intentionality is required to facilitate the negotiation between drives that Nietzsche envisages. But, even to this, we can respond that the type of negotiation between drives that Nietzsche envisages at its most basic level is not of the deliberative kind but rather operates more closely to the dynamics of attraction and repulsion that Boscovich had attributed to force. According to Nietzsche, 'We cannot think of an attraction divorced from an intention' (WP, 626 KSA 11: 24 [10]). That intentionality need not be conscious can also be discerned from George Molnar's claim that physical – non-conscious – powers in the world operate intentionally. According to Molnar, physical powers such as solubility or electromagnetic charge have a direction towards something outside themselves. He writes that 'a physical power is essentially an *executable* property' where 'the intentional object of a physical power is its proper manifestation' (George Molnar, *Powers: A Study in Metaphysics* (Oxford: Oxford University Press, 2003), p. 63). For the reasons just rehearsed, I agree with John Richardson who contends that dispositionality and intentionality are compatible because the intentionality of drives, for Nietzsche, is non-conscious. Richardson writes that 'when [Nietzsche] says that a drive "aims" at certain ends, "views" the world in a consequent way, and "experiences" certain values within it, none of this is supposed to entail that the drive is conscious' (Richardson, *Nietzsche's System*, p. 38).

It is the close relation between causes and intentionality that has led some to explain dispositions in terms of intentionality. They argue that dispositions are intentionally directed towards manifesting their natures and hence to the intentionally inexistent (see U. T. Place, 'Dispositions as Intentional States' in Tim Crane (ed.), *Dispositions: A Debate* (London: Routledge, 2002), pp. 19–32, and Molnar, *Powers: A Study in Metaphysics*, Chapter Three). For them, intentionality is the criterion of the dispositional rather than the mental. Anjum, Lie and Mumford, however, argue that dispositions explain intentionality rather than the other way around. They follow Armstrong in arguing that intentionality should be explained in causal dispositional terms. According to them, this strategy is the most conducive to naturalizing intentionality (Anjum et al., 'Dispositions and Ethics', p. 240). It seems to me, however, that Nietzsche's strategy is closer to that of Molnar's on account of his taking human psychology as his investigative starting-point and his use of an argument from analogy in his proposal of the will to power thesis.

However, it might be argued that Nietzsche could combine attributing a phenomenally affective component to human valuing with the metaphysical continuity of this valuing with the causal fabric of reality by identifying evaluative drives with affects and by construing the affects as genuinely causal. However, there are a number of reasons why Nietzsche should not adopt this argumentative strategy. First, despite the fact that he often seems to use the terms 'drive' and 'affect' interchangeably, Nietzsche indicates that they are nonetheless logically and metaphysically, even if not phenomenologically, distinct for us.[28] For example, in BT the Dionysiac art drive induces feelings of intoxication, which Nietzsche later describes as feelings of power (WP, 48 KSA 13: 14 [68]; WP, 800 KSA 13: 14 [117]). That the drives are distinct from feelings of intoxication can be discerned from Nietzsche's description of the Dionysiac, along with the Apolline drive, as 'artistic drives of nature (*Kunsttriebe der Natur*)' (BT, 2) and his

---

[28] This would account for Nietzsche's description of the will in BGE, 19, in terms of feeling, commanding thoughts and conscious emotions. That is, he describes the phenomenon of willing in this passage from the perspective of our phenomenal consciousness of it and argues that we tend to conflate its various components with one another. However, Nietzsche does not always clearly distinguish between the drives and the affects, so much so that at times he uses the two terms interchangeably. Similarly to his description of the drives, he also describes affects as interpretive, perspectival, intentional and evaluative. For example, in TI, 'Reconnaissance Raids', 8, he describes the affective mental state of intoxication as a capacity to 'idealize' objects or bring to attention its essential or principal features. Affects, so understood, are interpretive and evaluative, an idea that is supported by Nietzsche's statements about the evaluative and interpretive influence of the affects in GM, III, 12. Equally, and similarly to drives, the affects can operate unconsciously (GS, 354).

Although we have focused on those passages where Nietzsche asserts a connection between values and drives, there are also a number of passages in which he draws tight connections between values and affects. Consider the following examples: 'It is clear that moral feelings are transmitted in this way: children observe in adults inclinations for and aversions to certain actions and, as born apes, imitate these inclinations and aversions; in later life they find themselves full of these acquired and well-exercised affects and consider it only decent to try to account for and justify them. . .' (D, 34) and 'You still carry around the valuations of things that originate in the passions and loves of former centuries!' (GS, 57). In these passages, Nietzsche claims that there is a relationship between affects and values. Unfortunately, it is not clear what sort of relationship he has in mind. In GS, 57, he claims that valuations 'originate in' affects whereas in D, 34, he seems to claim that evaluations are constituted by affects that we consider warranted. Katsafanas remarks that it is difficult to see how Nietzsche can identify values with affects-as-justified because affects are fleeting. A value that is similarly fleeting cannot properly be considered a value (Paul Katsafanas, *Agency and the Foundations of Ethics: Nietzschean Constitutivism* (Oxford: Oxford University Press, 2013), p. 14). Similarly Gemes argues that drives have a temporal spread that the affects do not. (See Ken Gemes, 'Life's Perspectives' in Gemes and Richardson (eds.), *The Oxford Handbook of Nietzsche*, pp. 553–575 n25.) However, as I suggest in the main text, Nietzsche's tendency to use the language of drives and affects interchangeably can be accounted for by considering his account of causality. Moreover, although the affect in isolation cannot be considered as justified, later in the chapter I will reflect on how, in their relations with other affective points of view, they may be considered so. However, values should still not be identified with the affects. Rather, the process of affectively focussing on the world in order to direct the drives can support the activity of the drives with reasons rather than constituting value as such.

description of the mental state of intoxication as the result of 'nature playing with human beings' (DWW, p. 121). Furthermore, in BGE, 187, he describes the affects as a 'sign language' of our values suggesting that values are irreducible to affects but manifested through affect. Second, drives are more stable and less fleeting than the affects. Given that we associate the holding of a value as something at least relatively stable rather than momentary, we should expect values to be identified with dispositional drives rather than with momentary and fleeting affects. Whilst affects come and go, values arguably represent a more stable perspective or point of view. Understanding the difference between drives and affects in this way fits with Nietzsche's description of their respective roles.

As noted by Paul Katsafanas, Nietzsche tends to employ the language of affects to explain particular types of action, whilst he describes the drives in terms of more general behavioural tendencies.[29] For example, I may have a disposition to engage in sport, but that disposition can be manifested in a variety of sporting activities, such as playing football, skiing or surfing, to name just a few possible activities. The sporting tendency drives me to engage in one of these activities, which are themselves very particular ways of manifesting the sporting drive. The affects direct action specifically by colouring the world according to the interests and perspective of the drive. This colouring of the world highlights, by selectively focussing on aspects of the world, the particular and specific ways in which the world affords opportunities for the manifestation of the drive. Thus, if I live by the sea with suitably high tides, then these features of my local environment are highlighted as opportunities for the manifestation of the sporting drive through, say, surfing rather than skiing.

Distinguishing between the drives and affects in this way also precludes Nietzsche from holding the affects to be the primary motive force informing an action. That is, employing a distinction that Nietzsche makes but which, he claims, is often conflated, we might say that drives are the 'driving force' whilst affects are the 'directing force' of an action. Nietzsche warns us against conflating the steam with the helmsman and argues that we must distinguish the 'cause of acting' generally from the 'cause of acting in a particular way', more specifically (GS, 360). Comparing driving and directive forces to the relationship between explosive powder and a match, he contends that whilst the match influences the manner in which the powder manifests its explosive nature it is not to be conflated with the motive power of the driving force

[29] GS, 1; BGE, 23; GM, III, 20. Paul Katsafanas, 'Nietzsche on Agency and Self-Ignorance', *The Journal of Nietzsche Studies*, 43.1, 2012, pp. 5–17, p. 7.

itself. The primary cause of the explosion of the powder is the causal power of the powder itself and not the directing role of the match. The match simply influences the particular manner in which the causal power of the powder is manifested. Similarly, for Nietzsche, although the affects direct action, they are not its primary motive cause. Rather, the primary motive force of the action is the drive itself. Understood thus, the affects are assigned a directive rather than executive role. A further key to explaining how he can describe drives and affects as sharing some features whilst still differentiating them in the way that he does without inconsistency or conflation, then, resides in his account of causal connection. It follows from our conclusions in the previous chapter that Nietzsche's power metaphysics offers us an alternative account of causal connection to that of the Humean event model that treats cause and effect as successive events in time.[30] Rather, according to Nietzsche, causal relations involve the activity of force rather than spatial contiguity and temporal succession. Understanding causality in terms of the activity of force allows that cause and effect can be simultaneous, such that it is impossible to distinguish the doer and the deed in terms of contiguous and successive events (GM, I, 13). To interpret drives as causes of affects and the causal influence of the drive as simultaneous with the affects would account for Nietzsche's practice of employing the two terms – drive and affect – interchangeably. This model of causality allows us to understand how and why Nietzsche sometimes conflates the affects with the drives but also why we should distinguish between their roles more clearly than Nietzsche obviously does. Consequently, we can agree with Katsafanas that the drives, for Nietzsche, are 'explanatorily prior to affects'.[31]

However, the drives are not just explanatorily basic, they are also metaphysically basic such that we can say that the value feeling or affect signals the degree to which the dispositional capacity of the drive is realized or manifested. That is, feelings of increased power denote the successful realization of a drive's end through the affect's direction of successful action, whilst feelings of weakness or diminished power signal the frustration of the drive's endeavour through the affect's direction of unsuccessful action. The affects direct action and become heightened as a result of successful action and diminished as a result of action that proves unsuccessful. The activity of the drives and the successful realization of their evaluative points of view are mediated by directive affects, where the

---

[30] See my 'The Kantian Background to Nietzsche's Views on Causality', *Journal of Nietzsche Studies*, 43.1, 2012, pp. 44–56 for further discussion of this issue.
[31] Katsafanas, 'Nietzsche on Agency and Self-Ignorance', pp. 7–8.

affect's ultimate measure of power signals either the successful or unsuccessful activity of the drive.

Accordingly, for Nietzsche, 'happiness' entails the 'feeling that power increases – that a resistance is overcome' (AC, 2). In the case of our example of the sporting drive, resistance is overcome when the natural features of the environment can be brought to facilitate the manifestation of the drive through surfing or whatever. We can say, then, on the basis of AC, 2, that that which is good is that which heightens feelings of power by overcoming resistances to our drive's intentional evaluative activity.[32] Since the motive cause is the drive rather than the affect, the value property – the good, for example – is identified with the dispositional capacity of the drive. Understood in this way, we can account for Nietzsche's appeal to affect in value experience without drawing Humean conclusions about the metaphysical discontinuity of facts and values. That is, the value exists as a dispositional capacity of a drive or psychic force to bring about its aim and is, accordingly, irreducible to Hume's spectatorial affective responses.

However, it might be thought that my argument that values, for Nietzsche, are not affective responses or propensities to affectively respond to pre-existent objects but rather that they are intentionally directed dispositions to manifest their causal natures, rests on a misidentification of the aim of a drive and its object. Katsafanas, for example, stresses the need to distinguish between objects and aims. He writes:

> The drive's *aim* is the relatively constant end of the drive, in terms of which it is distinguished from other drives. Drives *aim* at their characteristic forms of activity: the aggressive drive aims at manifesting aggressive activity, the sexual drive aims at manifesting sexual activity, and so on. In order to express this activity, the drive needs to find some *object:* the aggressive drive might vent itself on another drive, or a cashier, or a participant in an athletic game. In other words, we can distinguish between what the drive seeks (i.e., the manifestation of some characteristic form of activity) and how the drive expresses this aim (i.e., by finding some object upon which to vent its form of activity).[33]

According to Katsafanas's aim-object distinction, the intentional object of a desire must be an actually existing object. This is evident in his view that

---

[32] Note that, according to Ken Gemes, 'feelings', for Nietzsche, 'seem – to be largely a product of the drives and their interactions with reality – e.g., it is the conflict between the slave's drive to dominate and his lowly and impotent position in the world that gives rise to his feeling of resentment. So talk of affects speaking can be read as a reflection of the interpretive drives' interactions with the world' (Ken Gemes, 'Life's Perspectives', p. 567n25)

[33] Katsafanas, *Agency and the Foundations of Ethics*, p. 168.

these objects are opportunities for the expression of the drive. But, contrary to Katsafanas, these objects are not the drive's proper intentional object. Intentionality is characterized by the fact that the intentional object does not have to exist occurrently and can be an aim or aspiration to be realized.[34] The futuristic direction of Nietzsche's thought suggests that it is precisely such inexistent intentional objects that he has in mind.[35] Consequently, the proper intentional object of a drive, for him, is its aim or the manifestation of its nature, which may or may not exist occurrently. But, as mentioned earlier, this is not to say that Nietzsche denies that we form evaluative appraisals of actually existing objects. However, it is to say that such evaluative appraisals are determined and coloured by the extent to which currently existent objects facilitate or obstruct the realization of the psychic disposition's nature. Moreover, the consideration of actually existent objects as facilitators or obstructions is not to suggest that our evaluative appraisal is unconcerned with the actual character or nature of the existent object. On the contrary, to view an object as a facilitator or obstruction is to attentively focus on the character of the object that merits, or not, the drive's evaluative appraisal of it as a facilitator or obstruction. We recall from our discussion of the affects that the affects play a directive role in selectively focussing on features of the environment as potential facilitators or obstructions to the manifestation of a drive's nature. The affects, then, are responsible for paying attention to and evaluatively appraising actually existent objects in relation to a drive's aim and object to manifest its own nature. Now, it might be contested that there must be cases where the object of a drive has been realized such that its object actually exists. Whilst this is true, it is true only momentarily. According to Nietzsche, drives seek to increase their power continuously (WP, 689 KSA 13: 14 [81]). Individual drives increase their power not by becoming other than they are essentially but by conspiring with other drives and powers to increase their sphere of influence.

Still, Katsafanas will argue that my identification of value with a disposition is, nonetheless, misguided. To make this argument, he gives the example of the Ascetic who possesses both a disposition to celibacy and a disposition to having sex. In the case of the Ascetic, we would say that he

---

[34] See J. N. Findlay, *Values and Intentions* (London: George Allen and Unwin Ltd. and New York: The Macmillan Company, 1961). For an application of this idea to naturalistic causal powers, see George Molnar, *Powers: A Study in Metaphysics*, p. 62.

[35] According to Nietzsche, our evaluative ideals are directed towards, what he calls, 'an as yet undiscovered country' (GS, 382). He describes these ideals as ones that need to be created rather than being 'already available' (WP, 585A KSA 12: 9 [60]).

values celibacy but does not value having sex, which rules out the identification of value with a disposition. However, whilst Katsafanas is arguably correct that the Ascetic values celibacy whilst not valuing having sex despite having a disposition to engage in the latter activity, the reason for this is not because value cannot be identified with a disposition but rather that, for Nietzsche, values are to be identified with dominating or strong dispositions. In the case of the Ascetic, the disposition to celibacy is stronger and overrules the disposition to engage in sexual activity. This view is fully commensurate with Nietzsche's view of the self as a hierarchical organization of drives (BGE, 12). One's values are identified, then, with one's ruling drives and dispositions. Nietzsche writes that 'interpretations of the world are symptoms of a ruling drive' (WP, 677 KSA 12: 7 [3]). According to him, 'the ruling drives want to be viewed as highest courts of value in general, indeed as creative and ruling powers' (WP, 677 KSA 12: 7 [3]). The measure of the ruling drive is determined by its capacity to overcome resistances to the successful execution of its aim. In the case of the Ascetic, the power of the disposition to celibacy is measured by its capacity to manifest itself in a celibate life in spite of both internal and external sources of resistance. The internal source of resistance comes in the form of the disposition to having sex whilst the source of external resistance comes in the form of various stimuli that the world presents.[36]

Nevertheless, one might worry that the identification of values with powerful dispositions that are intentionally directed to manifesting their natures commits Nietzsche to the idea that values are projections of the interests of human drives onto the world. Concomitantly, it might be worried further that by understanding values as projections, Nietzsche also places our values beyond criticism or correction in light of a constraint by mind-independent reality. However, in the next section, I will show how Nietzsche's understanding of human values as psychic dispositions avoids Hume's projection thesis by holding that the veridicality or objectivity of

---

[36] These resistances can be overcome, according to Nietzsche, through the act of disciplining rather than extirpating the drive. The act of disciplining the drive entails incorporating the drive and bringing it to function cooperatively with the other drives under the dominating guidance of the ruling drive (D, 109). Such incorporation is evident, according to Nietzsche, in the case of the philosophical rather than the religious Ascetic. The religious celibate, according to Nietzsche, values celibacy out of weakness and a hatred of the senses and aims to extirpate sensual desires. The philosophical celibate, however, should be understood similarly to the sports person who must channel their energy creatively to bring about a particular end. The sex drive, for the philosophical celibate, is re-channelled to give birth to creations other than children. With such self-discipline, Nietzsche concludes that there is no need to shun women or torture one's body in an attempt to extirpate the sex drive and give expression to the dominant drive to celibacy (GM, III, 8).

human values is determined by their capacity to cooperate with the powerful capacities of nature generally. This will be seen to entail that rather than placing values beyond criticism, Nietzsche distinguishes – even if only implicitly – between the normativity and the veridicality of our values. However, although all values are not objective, for Nietzsche, the distinction between objective and non-objective value is one of degree rather than kind such that our values should not be understood to be either reducibly ideal and dualistically separate from the world, on the one hand, or projected onto the world, on the other.

Anti-Projectionism

It might be argued that it is not quite enough to say that psychological dispositions are irreducible to phenomenal feelings to warrant considering Nietzsche's dispositional account of value as an alternative to Hume's fact-value distinction. Rather, it might be objected, there is nothing in the identification of value with psychic dispositions to constrain or prevent the illegitimate projection of these specifically human values onto non-human reality. The overcoming of resistance of which Nietzsche writes might in fact entail precisely such a projection. Because they are concerned with the manifestation of their own natures or points of view, value dispositions, it might be thought, have little regard for the character of reality and are instead divorced from reality.

However, the explanation of value in terms of psychic dispositions does not capture the full story of how Nietzsche understands the metaphysical and epistemic status of our values. Rather, Nietzsche considers the relationship between psychic dispositions and the world significant to his account of value on both counts. That he does so can be made evident by qualifying and examining further his description of value in terms of a drive's capacity to overcome resistance to the realization of its aim. Whilst it is clear from the preceding discussion that Nietzsche identifies values in terms of the dispositional capacities or powers of the self to overcome resistances to its wants and needs, what he means by power extends further than just the power of the self. That is, his notion of resistance indicates that the powerful is extended to include the power of those objects that resist the self's wants and needs.

The human self, as a bundle of dispositional and intentionally directed drives, in Nietzsche's view, interprets the world evaluatively, that is, aspectually according to its own interests and needs. These interests and needs are those of the dominating drive for without such hierarchy there can be no unity and consequently, for Nietzsche, no self. Yet the self in the guise of the dominating drive meets with resistance to its efforts. As indicated in our earlier discussion of the Ascetic celibate, these resistances can be internal or external.[37] Internal resistances are those of other real dispositions or drives that constitute the self and that compete with the dominating drive for expression. External resistances to the hierarchical but collective activity that constitutes the self come in the guise of other selves and objects in the world with natural capacities to resist the self's dominating drive. The power to overcome internal and external resistances are intimately related for Nietzsche, and despite the language of internality and externality here, the power to overcome both forms of resistance is ultimately gauged by the manner in which the evaluating agent engages with the world. However, in order to see that this is the case, we first need to show that what constitutes a high degree of power or strength in Nietzsche does not entail coercion. That it does not is evident in his account of overcoming resistance generally, regardless of whether that resistance is of the internal or external variety.

According to Nietzsche, overcoming resistance, whether it be of the internal or external variety, need not involve the vanquishing or extirpation of competing drives or powers but, rather, can take the form of cooperation or an 'arrangement' (WP, 636 KSA 13: 14 [186]) between competing powers to manifest their respective natures. He writes:

> My idea is that every specific body strives to become master over all space and to extend its force (– its will to power) and to thrust back all that resists its extension (*und Alles das zurückzustoßen, was seiner Ausdehnung wide-rstrebt*). But it continually encounters similar efforts on the part of other bodies and ends by coming to an arrangement ('union') with those of them that are sufficiently related to it: thus they then conspire together for power. And the process goes on … (WP, 636 KSA 13: 14 [186])

For Nietzsche, even when other power-wills in the guise of the subordinate drives of the self or indeed other selves, or the mind-independent world, comply with our wants and demands and where such demands are

---

[37] One might argue that talk of internal and external is made redundant in Nietzsche to the extent that, for him, there is no self, only a multiplicity of drives and forces. Whilst it is true that Nietzsche treats both human drives and non-human forces as components of the real and as equally real (BGE, 36), he nonetheless preserves a distinction between the self and world. Nietzsche makes it clear that although he rejects the traditional account of the self as a substance, he does not abandon the intelligibility of the notion of the self altogether (BGE, 12, 230). Rather, the self is firmly rooted in the natural world and is redefined as a hierarchical bundle of drives where the dominating drive represents the evaluative perspective of the self.

determined by the dominant drive of the self, such compliance must be understood as resistance. By this I take Nietzsche to mean that compliance on the part of an obedient will or disposition does not entail a relinquishing of its intrinsic-dispositional nature but rather a realization of it. It is compliant or obedient, then, only to the extent that there is a certain mutuality between the commanding and obedient will. He writes:

> To what extent resistance is present even in obedience; individual power is by no means surrendered. In the same way, there is in commanding an admission that the absolute power of the opponent has not been vanquished, incorporated, disintegrated. (WP, 642 KSA 11: 36 [22])

A high degree of power or strength as a measure of value for Nietzsche, then, entails cooperation rather than coercion.

This cooperative form of resistance is evident in Nietzsche's account of self-formation or giving style to one's character, his account of the formation of healthy political communities, such as he envisages for a new unified Europe, and his account of culture as second nature. In the case of self-formation, unruly drives should not be extirpated, as is the case with religious forms of asceticism, in Nietzsche's view, but rather brought into cooperative behaviour through the perspective of the dominating drive (GS, 290). According to Nietzsche, this stylization of the self involves highlighting the role of some drives whilst constraining the role of others. By constraint here is meant that the subordinated drives will express their natures through the perspective of the dominating drive. He writes: 'To "give style" to one's character – is practiced by those who survey all the strengths and weaknesses of their nature and then fit them into an artistic plan until every one of them appears as art and reason and even weaknesses delight the eye' (GS, 290). All of this is achieved, he argues, through the 'constraint of a single taste' that governs and forms 'everything large and small' (GS, 290). Nietzsche also describes the emergence of a healthy and unified Europe in terms of a hierarchical 'synthesis' (BGE, 256) of the constitutive members of the community. However, such communities will not be formed on the basis of a coercive principle of custom (HAH, I, 475; HAH, II, 'The Wanderer and His Shadow', 215) that prescribes a single identity for all. That is, although the new Europe will be hierarchically structured and must be so if it is to be a unified community, the hierarchy will facilitate the expression of the constituent members, a factor that contributed to Nietzsche's popularity amongst national independence movements of Eastern Europe in the nineteenth and twentieth centuries

(BGE, 242).[38] The formation of culture, more generally, for Nietzsche, entails resistance through cooperation of the dispositional capacities of nature with our evaluative attempts to mould it. That is, this moulding does not take the form of a projection of alien features onto nature but rather the ultimate realization of the dispositional capacities of nature itself similarly to the artistic activity of 'rounding off something and, as it were, finishing the poem' (GS, 107). In his discussion of how one gives style to one's character, Nietzsche describes the stylized product in terms of 'second nature'. Second nature, he tells us, involves concealment rather than extirpation such that '[m]uch that is vague and resisted shaping has been saved and exploited for distant views' (GS, 290). In SE he describes culture as a 'transfigured physis' (SE, 3), writing that '[i]t is the fundamental idea of *culture*, insofar as it sets for each one of us but one task . . . *to work at the perfecting of nature*' (SE, 5).[39] Of course, there is something fundamentally 'unnatural' (GS, 355; GM, III, 25) about the final products that are stylized selves, political communities undefined by geography and culture more generally, but such unnaturalness, if it is genuinely powerful, for Nietzsche, is ultimately continuous with what the dispositional capacities of first nature allow.

Yet it might be objected that Nietzsche's account of the role of Christianity speaks against my interpretation of resistance as cooperation. That is, it might be pointed out that Nietzsche thinks that Christianity has played a strong hand in giving rise to and shaping Western culture and that Christianity has been powerful in doing so but that its power is of the coercive and extirpative rather than cooperative kind. However, we must remember that although Nietzsche acknowledges these factors and makes much of them in his account of the genealogy of morality and society, for example, he nonetheless thinks that Christianity is a reactive and, therefore, weak philosophy that is responsible for what he considers to be the current weakness of modern Western culture (BGE, 62). The evaluative perspective of Christianity, for Nietzsche, is a weak form of power. His aim is to overcome this form of culture founded on principles of equality and sameness and to instigate an aristocratic culture founded on the hierarchical principles of nature. In Christianity, principles of sameness and equality are tools of coercion and extirpation. Natural hierarchy and

---

[38] See Diane Morgan, 'Nietzsche and National Identity' in Keith Ansell Pearson (ed.), *A Companion to Nietzsche* (Oxford: Blackwell, 2006), pp. 455–474.

[39] Note that Nietzsche defines 'creation' in terms of a 'selection and finishing of the thing selected' (WP, 662 KSA 10: 24 [5]). He also defines 'perfection' as 'greater power' (WP, 660 KSA 12: 2 [76]).

genuine strength, in contrast, allow for the expression of intrinsic natures.[40]

From his account of self-formation, the formation of political communities, and culture more generally, then, we see that overcoming resistance has two aspects for Nietzsche. It involves a relation between powers or capacities on the part of the ruling and subordinate drives of valuers in addition to relations between those valuing selves and external objects (constituent members of the political community and non-human nature itself). Our ruling drives, for Nietzsche, are dispositionally and intentionally structured such that they seek to express and manifest their own intrinsic wants and demands. Yet they must seek the cooperation of internal and external resistances in so doing. It is because power-wills require such cooperation from other power-wills to satisfy their aim of 'shaping' (WP, 656 KSA 12: 9 [151]) things according to their evaluative point of view that Nietzsche claims that power-wills must seek resistance. He writes:

> The will to power can manifest itself only against resistances; therefore it seeks that which resists it – this is the primeval tendency of the protoplasm when it extends pseudopodia and feels about. Appropriation and assimilation are above all a desire to overwhelm, a forming and reshaping, until at length that which has been overwhelmed has entirely gone over into the power domain of the aggressor and has increased the same. (WP, 656 KSA 12: 9 [151])

According to Nietzsche's view here, power-wills seek out resistance not as an end in itself but rather to facilitate the optimal manifestation of their own natures. However, the seeking out of cooperative partners is not simply instrumental in facilitating the manifestation of a power's nature. Rather, the highest degree of power, for Nietzsche, is measured by the level of reciprocal cooperation between powers.[41]

---

[40] In BGE, Nietzsche writes:

> Let's just say there is always the question of who *he* is, and who the *other* person is – we have to force morals to bow down before *hierarchy*, until they all finally come to a clear understanding that it is *immoral* to say, 'What's good for the goose is good for the gander.' (BGE, 221)

[41] For further discussion of the issue of whether drives seek out resistance as an end in itself or instrumentally, see Bernard Reginster, *The Affirmation of Life: Nietzsche on Overcoming Nihilism* (Cambridge, MA: Harvard University Press, 2006), pp. 131–135 and John Richardson, *Nietzsche's System*, p. 34. Reginster adopts the former view in response to Richardson's adoption of the latter. The idea of seeking out resistances as an end in itself arguably lends itself to a more aggressive account of power than I have offered here. Sometimes Nietzsche is ambiguous about how he views the role of seeking resistance, which leads to occasional inconsistencies on his part between viewing

We have seen that Nietzsche's notion of overcoming resistance through cooperation comes in two guises in that he appeals to both internal and external resistance to a drive. What needs to be made clear, however, is that the distinction between the ability to overcome internal resistance only and the ability to overcome both forms of resistance gives rise to a further distinction in Nietzsche between the normativity and the objectivity of our values. The latter distinction is important for Nietzsche in terms of responding to the charge that his alignment of value with the will to power makes him vulnerable to a Humean form of projectionism. The capacity of a drive to overcome internal resistance and dominate the bundle of drives that constitutes the self, for Nietzsche, acts as a measure of the normativity of a value. However, a self that rules through cooperation, in Nietzsche's view, is more powerful than one that rules through acts of extirpation, and these forms of power are ultimately characterized by the self's capacity to overcome external resistance to the manifestation of its nature outwardly. The highest degree of power, for Nietzsche, entails the capacity of a dominant drive to overcome external resistance in order to manifest its nature and serves as a marker of the value's objectivity.

Nietzsche clearly takes noble values to be more objective or better than those values – for example, Christian values – that he describes as slavish. Moreover, what constitutes Nietzsche's characterization of these agent types as noble or slavish is determined by their respective degrees of power in engaging with the world and external forms of resistance. The slave is a slave because the world resists its aims. The dominant drive of the Ascetic, for example, represents that particular agent's typical form of engagement with the world. One might argue that the Ascetic type is such because the world affords more stimuli than this particular agent type can cope with. The Ascetic's particular form of engagement with the world is, therefore, reactive. As a result, the only form of resistance that this agent type can overcome is internal to itself, such that its reaction to the power of the world is to retreat inwards and force the drives that make up the self to

power in terms of cooperation and power as aggressive assimilation of subordinate drives. For the latter, see, for example, WP, 656 KSA 12: 9 [151]. Richardson's account of power as mastery is a less aggressive account than Reginster's. Mastery, in Richardson's view, does not involve the tyranny of denying subordinate drives and desires their own determinate ends. Rather, according to Richardson, the dominant drive incorporates these ends into the pursuit of its own end such that mastery involves the development of the master drive. Although my account of power is closer to that of Richardson's, I stress power as cooperation rather than incorporation in order to draw out the manner in which the powerful constitution of reality, for Nietzsche, both facilitates and constrains our values.

express themselves inwardly rather than outwardly. What makes a drive dominant, then, is its degree of strength in relation to the other drives whilst what determines whether this dominancy is of the coercive or cooperative kind is its capacity to overcome resistance that it meets in the world. Although Nietzsche considers the inward form of dominancy to be weaker than one that is achieved cooperatively, he still considers the perspective of the dominant drive of the reactive agent to be normative. By virtue of being the dominant drive of the agent self, however reactive that self is, the Ascetic's values are normative even if they are not objective. Values that Nietzsche considers to be normative but not objective are ultimately less powerful than those that have the requisite capacity to manifest their natures externally in cooperation with reality. Compared to actions that stem from the direction of the most powerful affect, the actions that emanate from non-objective value-norms are guided by reactive feelings of weakness.[42]

That Nietzsche runs together values and norms is evident from the fact that he uses the term 'value' in two ways. That is, he uses the term 'value' to describe some*thing* that he values (for example, rank, egoism, hierarchy) whilst also using the term to describe something that he doesn't find valuable (*ressentiment*, pity, equality). This dual use of the term is captured in the fact that, for Nietzsche, all values, as expressions of the dominant drive of an agent, are normative. The values dominant in the Christian tradition are normative but only for those who espouse them, that is, only for particular psycho-physical types. By dismantling the distinction between values and norms, then, Nietzsche offers an account of norms that is essentially plural. Moreover, he distinguishes between the two senses of value (something that he values and values that he does not find valuable) by appealing to the notion of objectivity as cooperation with the world. To distinguish between values that Nietzsche approves of and those that he does not, we can say that he considers that those values he approves of can manifest themselves outwardly or actively. The ability to manifest its nature outwardly and cooperatively with the world is the process that I have described in terms of overcoming external resistance.

However, lest the preceding talk of overcoming internal and external resistance, normativity and objectivity, evaluating selves and the world that constrains values be interpreted dualistically, we must stress that, for Nietzsche, all value-norms are metaphysically continuous with the dispositional fabric of reality. All value-norms are expressions of the dominant

---

[42] For Nietzsche on the reactivity of the slave's relation to the world, see GM, I, 10.

drives of the agents that espouse them and are, in this specific sense, metaphysically continuous with the world as will to power. But this is not to say that all value-norms are objective in epistemic terms. That is, some values are epistemically subjective. I use the term 'epistemic' here not to depict a drive's level of success in representing the world from a viewpoint outside of the world but rather to denote the degree to which some drives fit better with what the world affords than others, where 'fit' is to be understood in terms of a reciprocal cooperation between values and the world. To the extent that a drive fits the world in this sense it is epistemically objective whereas a drive that fails to fit is epistemically subjective. This distinction between epistemically subjective and objective value-norms captures the manner in which value-norms are irreducible to, and subject to constraint by, the world for Nietzsche. Though *some* value-norms are merely subjective by failing to complement the world, some are objective by virtue of their capacity to cooperate with the dispositional fabric of reality. Still, it is important to recognize that the epistemic distinction that is being drawn here between the subjectivity and objectivity of values is made possible by the extent to which Nietzsche thinks that what we traditionally and dualistically think of as the 'subject' or evaluator and the 'object' or world that constrains our evaluations through the exertion of external resistance, share a metaphysical unity as the will to power and are defined by this fundamental metaphysical unity.

The non-dualistic implications of Nietzsche's view here can be highlighted by comparing and contrasting it to what Joseph Rouse in a contemporary context describes as the intra-action of an organism with its environment, a position that he presents as a development of Nietzsche's 'commitment to philosophical naturalism'.[43] Rouse describes the relationship between an organism and its environment as one of *intra*-rather than *inter*-action in order to highlight that our evaluative perspectives are not 'subject positions, external to the situations upon which they provide a perspective' but, rather, they are 'configurations of an agent's situation'.[44] Drawing on and modifying Robert Brandom's view that 'differences in bodies and desires' is the 'ground for differences in conceptual perspective',[45] Rouse contends that our evaluative perspectives are embodied intra-actions with the world rather than mere responses to it.[46] Moreover, he contends that bodies are distinguished and differentiated as such through these intra-actions with their surroundings.

[43] Joseph Rouse, *How Scientific Practices Matter: Reclaiming Philosophical Naturalism* (Chicago, IL: University of Chicago Press, 2002), pp. 3–4, 95, 303, 359–360.
[44] Ibid., p. 235.   [45] Ibid.   [46] Ibid., p. 248.

Correlatively, these surroundings are 'configured as significant through their responsiveness to bodily activity'.[47] As a result, for Rouse, embodied perspectives are patterns of intra-action and mutual configurations of the environment as meaningful for us. The very distinction between self and world, then, is made possible by and emerges from their fundamental intra-action. Thus, the evaluative perspectives of the self are perspectives *in* rather than *on* the world and emerge through intra-action with the world rather than indicating a 'standpoint outside of what it discloses'.[48] Rouse appeals to Karen Barad's account of intra-action, according to whom 'nature's lack of a fixed essence is essential to what it is – nature is an intra-active becoming (where "intra-action" is not the classical comforting concept of interaction but rather entails the very disruption of the metaphysics of individualism that holds that there are discrete objects with inherent characteristics)'.[49] Instead of metaphysically discrete subjects and objects, Barad appeals to 'phenomena', which denote ontological relations without pre-existing relata through which relata emerge.

Although Rouse's argument is formulated as a response to particular issues in contemporary debates about naturalism and normativity, in particular to a residual dualism that he detects in these contemporary debates, Nietzsche shares a similar motivation to Rouse in wanting to establish that our evaluative perspectives are *in* rather than *on* the world. However, Nietzsche articulates his argument in more psychological and causally essentialist terms than Rouse when he claims that psychology is the key to fundamental issues (BGE, 23) and when he describes the 'essence' of different psychological evaluative types in terms of strength or weakness (GM, I, 13).[50] We cannot ignore the fact that Nietzsche identifies values with dispositional properties of psychological drives and that these drives are intentionally directed to manifesting their essential or intrinsically powerful natures.[51] However, we can show how Nietzsche thinks that psychological drives or dispositions are immersed in the world and are not

---

[47] Ibid., p. 253.   [48] Ibid.

[49] Karen Barad, *Meeting the Universe Halfway: Quantum Physics and the Entanglement of Matter and Meaning* (Durham, NC: Duke University Press, 2007), p. 422n15.

[50] For a non-essentialist interpretation of Nietzsche that shares Rouse's point of view, see Christian J. Emden, 'Nietzsche's Will to Power: Biology, Naturalism and Normativity', *Journal of Nietzsche Studies*, 47.1, 2016, pp. 30–60. However, my non-dualist argument still stands despite its difference from Rouse. Moreover, non-essentialist accounts of Nietzsche's metaphysics are vulnerable to the problem of an infinite regress of existential dependency. See my *Nietzsche on Epistemology and Metaphysics: The World in View* (Edinburgh: Edinburgh University Press, 2009), Chapter Six, for further discussion and for a response to a tension between essentialism and non-essentialism that is sometimes evident in Nietzsche's writings.

[51] Emden argues that this can be avoided by putting biology first and psychology second in 'Nietzsche's Will to Power: Biology, Naturalism and Normativity', p. 31. For the differences between my interpretation and that of Emden, see my discussion in the notes in Chapter 3.

dualistically apart from it. The non-dualism becomes evident when we consider that the powerful essence of a psychological or evaluative type, for
Nietzsche, is characterized by its immersion in and metaphysical continuity
with the world as will to power. The distinction between self and world only
makes sense, in Nietzsche's view, against this particular metaphysical backdrop. That is, self and world should be understood in terms of the interplay of
causal agencies or wills to power rather than metaphysically discrete substances. Moreover, Nietzsche also distinguishes in this context between different types of evaluating agencies, which he describes as slave and noble types.
Slave and noble types, differentiated in terms of degrees of power (GM, I, 13),
share the same world although it manifests as meaningful in different ways for
them. For the slave, the world manifests as something that is recalcitrant to its
particular degree of power or capacity for acting, whereas for the noble the
world manifests as something that facilitates its capacity for acting.
Accordingly, when Nietzsche describes the essence of slave and noble evaluating types in terms of weakness or strength, this essence is to be understood
agentially as degrees of power. Power, for Nietzsche, is something that an
agent *is* rather than something that it *possesses* and what the agent *is*, is not
metaphysically distinct from what it *does* (GM, I, 13).[52] Despite the more
psychological and essentialist flavour to Nietzsche's argument, it is not worlds
apart from that of Rouse's. However, since Nietzsche describes the essence of
self and world in causal terms as will to power, it is probably more appropriate
to describe the distinction between them as emerging from *action in* the world
rather than from their intra-action. *Action in* the world better captures
Nietzsche's view that self and world share a fundamental metaphysical unity
as will to power and that any differentiation between them takes place from
within the world and presupposes their metaphysical continuity. According to
Nietzsche, the self is individuated by the power-led activity of forces and drives
of similar natures forming hierarchical bundles/spheres of activity and experiencing 'external' resistance from other such bundles or spheres of activity
(WP, 636 KSA 13: 14 [186]; BGE, 12; AC, 2). It is on the basis of these
resistances that self and world can be said, for Nietzsche, to interact and value
dispositions realized or curtailed.[53] Interaction best captures his view that

---

[52] Nietzsche writes: 'A quantum of power *is* [my emphasis] just such a quantum of drive, will effect –
more precisely, it is nothing other than this very driving, willing, effecting–'. He describes 'the very
weakness of the weak' as 'his *essence*, his effecting, his whole unique, unavoidable, undetachable
reality' (GM, I, 13).

[53] Nietzsche's account of dispositions is not that of contemporary conditional analyses that render
dispositions passive and dependent on an external stimulus to manifest. Accordingly, there is no
discrepancy in my description of values as dispositions and forms of action. Values, for Nietzsche,
are dispositions that, by virtue of being intentionally structured, are always seeking to act, although

although the evaluating self is immersed *in* the world, the evaluative perspectives of the self are nonetheless constrained by the world.

It remains the case, however, that Rouse and Nietzsche share a similar motivation that is of both historical and contemporary philosophical significance and that aspects of Rouse's attempt to articulate a non-dualist position in relation to the question of naturalism and normativity can be usefully deployed to shed light on aspects of Nietzsche's arguments. The metaphysical basis of Nietzsche's distinction between epistemically subjective and objective, or better and worse, value-norms overlaps fruitfully with Rouse's argument that intra-action is power-ful, where power, in his view, is not something that an agent possesses or has imposed on them but rather reflects the success, or lack thereof, of the realization of an agent's goal.[54] Although the two positions are not identical, Rouse's alignment of power with the realization of an agent's goal is nonetheless similar to my description of objective value-norms in Nietzsche as the most powerful value-norms on account of their ability to complement the causal capacities of the world. We recall that Nietzsche describes both epistemically subjective and objective value-norms in terms of degrees of power such that an epistemically subjective value-norm is powerful because it is the dominant perspective of the evaluating self even though objective value-norms are ultimately more powerful still because they complement better what the dispositional capacities of reality afford. Rouse's account of power-inflected value-norms is instructive for our purposes, then, because it indicates how the ultimate power of an objective value-norm in Nietzsche's sense is indexed to its ability to realize its goal through acting in the world. However, since all value-norms, for Nietzsche, reflect their powerful capacities to act in and interact with the world, the distinction between epistemically subjective and objective value-norms should not be understood dualistically. Rather, the

---

they are, in some circumstances, prevented from manifesting their natures. To the extent that they seek to manifest but are prevented from doing so, they exhibit a dispositional modality that is neither contingent nor necessary, as will be explained in the final section of this chapter. But by virtue of being will to power, dispositions are essentially active even when their form of activity manifests as passivity. Contrary to the possible objection to my identification of dispositions and powers on the grounds that the latter are active whilst the former are passive, activity and passivity, in Nietzsche's view, should be understood as continuous. He defines passivity in terms of being 'hindered from moving forward: thus an act of resistance and reaction', whilst he defines activity as a 'reaching out for power' (WP, 657 KSA 12: 5 [64]). However, resistance and reaction are acts. Rather than being binary opposites, activity and passivity, for Nietzsche, are 'degrees of power' (WP, 55 KSA 12: 5 [64]; GM, I, 10). Unlike the contemporary conditional analysis, Nietzsche's dispositions are causally powerful. For further discussion of how Nietzsche differs from contemporary analyses, see my *Nietzsche on Epistemology and Metaphysics: The World in View*, Chapter Six.

[54] Rouse, *How Scientific Practices Matter*, p. 260.

characterization of objective value-norms in terms of their ability to overcome external resistance is made on the understanding that the distinction between inner and outer is grounded in a fundamental metaphysical unity.

That such a metaphysical unity is presupposed here highlights that the overcoming of external resistance, in the cooperative sense discussed earlier and which distinguishes between subjective and objective values in an epistemic sense, precludes Humean projectionism. That it does so is evident from the fact that the world, for Nietzsche, contrary to Hume, is also one of powerful capacities that are not evaluatively inert. By this we mean that these capacities do not merely constrain in a negative sense, but they also act as positive facilitators of the realization of some, that is, objective, values. Consequently, the manifestation of objective dispositional value properties of a drive and its relation to the constraint of the dispositional capacities of other drives and forces in the world should be understood in terms of what C. B. Martin calls, in a different and non-Nietzschean context, mutual manifestation partners.[55] According to Martin, dispositions manifest when in the company of an 'appropriate partner for their mutual manifestation'.[56] For example, a soluble substance and water can be considered mutual manifestation partners whose mutual manifestation produces dissolving. According to this account, 'the mutual manifestation partners are – both active and genuinely productive of their effects'.[57] Martin highlights the reciprocity of manifesting partners when he argues that the partnering of the dispositions *is* the manifestation rather than the cause of the manifestation. He writes:

> You should not think of disposition partners jointly *causing* the manifestation. Instead, the coming together of the disposition partners *is* the mutual

---

[55] C. B. Martin, *The Mind in Nature* (Oxford: Oxford University Press, 2007), pp. 48–51.

[56] Anjum et al., 'Dispositions and Ethics', p. 245.

[57] Ibid., p. 245. As indicated, I am drawing on Rouse's argument only to the extent that it helps us make sense of Nietzsche's non-dualism. However, Rouse might object to the development of my argument here on the grounds that we shouldn't think of dispositions as awaiting appropriate circumstances for their useful deployment (Rouse, *How Scientific Practices Matter*, p. 253). But this objection applies only if Nietzsche understands dispositions similarly to that of contemporary conditional analyses. Rather, we saw in an earlier note that, for Nietzsche, values, understood as dispositions, are always actively *seeking* to manifest their natures (GM, III, 7). As a result, passivity and activity are degrees of power (WP, 55 KSA 12: 5 [64]; GM, I, 10). Rouse might also object to the reference to manifestation partners in my use of Martin's illustration as dualistic. But the appeal to such partners, such as the partnering of self and world in Nietzsche's case, is made against the backdrop of the metaphysics of the will to power. Dualism follows only if we consider the relation between self and world from 'the outside' rather than from the inside perspective of their metaphysical continuity as will to power. Moreover, Martin's example of mutual manifestation partners shows that reciprocity still stands despite my causal essentialist interpretation of Nietzsche. Reciprocity is not necessarily tied to non-essentialism.

manifestation; the partnering and the manifestation are identical. This partnering-manifestation identity is seen most clearly with cases such as the following. You have two triangle-shaped slips of paper that, when placed together appropriately, form a square. It is not that the partnering of the triangle *causes* the manifestation of the square, but rather that the partnering *is* the manifestation.[58]

For Nietzsche, such mutual manifestation partners are evident not just in naturalistic events but also in cases of value. Instead of understanding values as Humean projections onto the world, objective value dispositions and the dispositional fabric of reality are mutually manifesting and, therefore, reciprocal. In this sense, objective value-norms are neither projections of our interests nor simply 'found'. That is, the manner in which dispositions manifest is reciprocally dependent on their manifestation partners. The reciprocity and mutual manifestation are evident from the fact that as Martin relates, for example, '[a] piece of gold is capable of being melted at a certain temperature or dissolved in *aqua regia*, but both together cannot be manifested'.[59] Reality as constituted dispositionally for Nietzsche is, in Rouse's terms, 'a field of possible activity, which in turn shape the active, responsive integrity' of the active bodies that intra-act with it.[60] Yet Martin's example, when extended and applied to Nietzsche and the issue of value, indicates how although reality is a field of possible configurations or evaluative manifestations, it cannot facilitate the realization of all evaluative goals. Rather, it must, in addition to facilitating the realization of some goals preclude the realization of others even though those others are forms of action in the world. As a result, what is precluded for Nietzsche is not the simultaneous multiple manifestations of the natural capacities of gold, as it is for Martin, but rather the cooperation of reactive values with the dispositional character of the world. Understood along these lines, we can say that the objectivity of value does not involve just powerful selves but also the mutually manifesting power of reality to cooperate with the self's appraisal. It follows that the most powerful value-norms are also epistemically objective. Although slave values engage with reality, their reactive character indicates that these values are out of synch with reality in the specific sense that reality negatively resists rather than facilitates the realization of slave goals and aims. This lack of cooperation is evident, in Nietzsche's view, from the fact that slave values result in the internalization of the drives and the postulation of an alternative metaphysical world to

---

[58] Martin, *The Mind in Nature*, p. 51.   [59] Ibid.
[60] Rouse, *How Scientific Practices Matter*, p. 253.

accommodate its values. Slave values, then, are normative for the particular psycho-physical types that espouse them without being objective.

Still, despite distinguishing between the normativity and subjectivity/objectivity of our values, questions of normativity and subjectivity/objectivity, according to Nietzsche, differ in only degree rather than kind. This is because the normativity of our values and their objective standing, or not, for him, are metaphysically continuous with one another and are measured by their degree of power. To reiterate, value-norms, as expressions of the dominant drive of the evaluating agent, reflect the agent's particular degree of power or capacity to act in the world. This degree of power, in turn, determines the epistemic subjectivity or objectivity of a value-norm. It follows from this that our very interaction with the world is normative and that the distinction between the epistemic subjectivity and objectivity of our value-norms must be made from within our normative interaction with the world. And since the distinction between the normativity and objectivity of our value-norms is measured by degrees of power, the causal fabric of reality cannot be understood to be dualistically external to our normative practices. Rather, these practices interact with the world and are resisted by it such that the causal fabric of reality can be said to be normatively ert. It is by stressing the normative ertness rather than inertness of the world that Nietzsche can avoid subjectivism and idealism, in a metaphysical sense, in relation to value.[61] As Rouse argues, 'In a normatively inert world of indifferent and senseless objects, significance could only come from the commitments or desires of subjects.'[62] Despite his identification of values with dispositional properties of psychological drives, it is nonetheless the case that, for Nietzsche, values, whether they are of the subjective or objective epistemic variety, cannot be *reducibly* ideal but rather reflect an agent's particular way of acting in and interacting with the world. Value-norms are in the world and reflect the metaphysical continuity of mind and world rather than their dualistic separation.

---

[61] The distinction between subjective and objective, as I use it here, is an epistemic rather than a metaphysical distinction. Now, whilst the interpretation I propose has certain affinities with meta-ethical subjectivism and must do so if it is not to be a reductive realism, it is nonetheless the case that, metaphysically speaking, values reflect an agent's particular form of acting in and interacting with the world such that they have both psychological and worldly aspects even when those values are reactive and do not fit with or complement the dispositional fabric of reality. That this is the case becomes evident only when we consider Nietzsche's meta-ethics in the context of his metaphysics and not just the psychology of the will to power. The preceding account fits with Nietzsche's view that mind and world are metaphysically continuous such that the mental and the non-mental are two sides of the one metaphysical coin. The latter view will be discussed in more detail in Chapter 5.

[62] Rouse, *How Scientific Practices Matter*, p. 257.

What I have described in terms of external resistance in Nietzsche, then, is to be understood as resistance exerted from within our normative engagement with the dispositional fabric of reality and not in terms of resistance exerted by a standard dualistically external to those practices. Moreover, as we have just seen, it is precisely from within those patterns of interaction that we can deem some value-norms better than others. What makes them better is their power-ful ability to realize their goals through interaction with what the dispositional fabric of reality affords. And, importantly, it is by virtue of being understood in terms of power that values and their measurement, for Nietzsche, must be understood dispositionally and non-projectionally. Rather than being projected onto an inert and evaluatively indifferent world, our value-norms are metaphysically continuous with the world as will to power and reflect types of powerful engagement with the world. However, by securing Nietzsche's anti-Humean and anti-projection thesis, we come to our third aim of this chapter, which is to show that a dispositional account, such as the one that I have attributed to Nietzsche, is compatible with the normative and potentially objective character that Nietzsche attributes to value in the first place.

Dispositions and Normativity

There is a general view that holds that dispositional accounts of value cannot provide an adequate ground for the normativity of our values as Nietzsche understands them. This is because it is argued that norms must function differently to the causal processes of nature.[63] Informing this objection is the idea that our values must be different in kind from physical and psychic dispositions. There are two issues here. One is the claim that normativity is metaphysically discontinuous with natural causal processes. The second is that our capacity to form value judgements and justify those judgements with reasons presupposes such discontinuity. Although these claims are not identical in every particular to Hume's fact-value distinction, they are nonetheless informed by a similar rationale to the extent that they presuppose that the sphere of values must be distinguished from the world of facts. According to Hume, values cannot be observed to be amongst spatially contiguous and temporally prior empirical causes, but rather, as mentalistic projections, they must be metaphysically demarcated from them. In what follows, however, it will be seen, contrary to Hume,

---

[63] John McDowell, *Mind and World* (Cambridge, MA: Harvard University Press, 1996), p. xv.

that normativity and the causal processes of nature are metaphysically continuous by virtue of sharing the same modal structure. Secondly, I will show how Nietzsche thinks that our capacity to formulate value judgements is grounded dispositionally in the drives and affects.

The first point can be made by drawing on an argument offered by Anjum, Lie and Mumford in a non-Nietzschean context and applying it to Nietzsche's account of value. The argument holds that the modality of dispositions entails natural tendencies that are neither necessary nor contingent and is to be sharply demarcated from the modality that we saw earlier informs Hume's distinction between facts and values. Hume is unable to recognize the dispositional modality that renders facts and values metaphysically continuous because he misunderstands the modality of natural causal processes, which leads to his denial both that there are causal powers in nature and that values are metaphysically continuous with them. The modality informing Hume's distinction is dualistic and holds that natural causal processes are either completely necessary or completely contingent. However, contrary to Hume, the modality of natural causal processes is dispositional and best captured by describing them as tending towards their outcomes but where the outcomes or manifestations are not necessitated. The modality of dispositions is such that dispositional properties are more than purely contingent but less than necessary. For example, gunpowder tends to explode if ignited by a spark. But it doesn't always explode, and its exploding cannot be guaranteed. In cases where exploding occurs, we can still say that had some preventive condition obtained, such as high humidity, it need not have exploded. Nevertheless, despite not necessitating its outcome or manifestation, the power or disposition is a power to do a delimited range of things, and so its outcomes are not purely contingent but stem from the nature of the thing and its capacities to do a certain range of things in different circumstances. That is, to say that a thing is disposed to do something, such that the gunpowder is explosive and disposed to exploding if ignited, is to say that the dispositional property of explosivity is more than a merely contingent one. There is a delimited range of things that the gunpowder is disposed to do. Its disposition to explode, if ignited, is intimately tied in with its nature. Given this nature, we can say that it is disposed to explode but not disposed to turn into a cat.[64]

---

[64] Anjum et al., 'Dispositions and Ethics', p. 235. It might be counter-argued that causality is not dispositionally structured on the grounds that we can determine the necessity of the gunpowder exploding by outlining necessary and sufficient conditions under which it must explode. But to do this would be to reduce the disposition to a counterfactual rather than a real feature of the world.

That value-norms have a dispositional nature can be discerned from the fact that they exhibit a 'structurally parallel' modality to the modality of natural causal processes.[65] That normativity entails neither absolute necessity nor complete contingency is evident from, for example, the phenomena of moral ennui and moral frailty, cases where a particular course of action is demanded and where I nonetheless fail to act as required. Value-norms are dispositional because they prescribe certain situations or objects as calling for a particular form of action and yet that action may fail to ensue. For example, an object may be beautiful and disposed to induce commendatory responses in appropriately situated perceivers, and yet I may fail to respond in the prescribed fashion due to the influence of depressed spirits. In Nietzsche's case, the object is the aim of the intentional drive, which requires a particular form of activity to realize its aim. The point is, however, that whether the prescribed response or activity is actualized, according to the dispositional account, depends on other – potentially interfering – factors. Yet, although normativity does not necessitate an outcome, it is not mere contingency. This is because the normative fact delimits what ought to be done and demarcates it from the non-selective range of things that *could* be done but which lack genuine prescriptiveness. In the case of the Ascetic discussed earlier, the dominancy of the drive to celibacy commanded sexual restraint and was demarcated from the weaker subordinate drive to engage in sexual activity. In this instance, the drive to celibacy represents, by virtue of being dominant, for Nietzsche, what ought to be the case for such individuals, whilst the disposition to engage in sexual activity represents what could be the case merely.[66] To say that I ought to do something is to say more than that it is merely possible for me to do it. That is, whilst there are many things that I *could* do, only a selective range of these things are things that I *ought* to do.[67] The structural parallel between the modality of

That is, it would be to understand dispositions along the lines of contemporary conditional analyses that threaten the metaphysical reality of dispositional causal powers by making their obtaining dependent on a stimulus, which has the effect of making them vulnerable to the problem of finkish dispositions as diagnosed by C. B. Martin, 'Dispositionals and Conditionals', *The Philosophical Quarterly*, 44.174, 1994, pp. 1–8. For further discussion of the issue, see George Molnar, *Powers: A Study in Metaphysics*, Chapter Four.

[65] Anjum et al., 'Dispositions and Ethics', p. 242.

[66] The disposition to engage in sexual activity represents what could be the case merely because it is actively prevented from manifesting its nature by the dominant drive to celibacy. Clearly, though, the disposition to engage in sexual activity has the same modal structure as its stronger-normative counterpart by virtue of being dispositional. But this is the point. Norms and causes are metaphysically continuous. The difference between the dispositions to sexual restraint and sexual activity resides in their respective degrees of power only.

[67] Anjum et al., 'Dispositions and Ethics', p. 242.

dispositions such as explosivity and that of normativity allows us to place normativity on the fact side of Hume's fact-value dichotomy, thus dispelling the very basis of the dichotomy.

That Nietzsche understands values dispositionally is evident from his account of the will in BGE, 19. According to him, all actions result from a normative relationship between commanding and obeying wills. However, it sometimes happens that the commanding will directs a course of action but the obeying will fails to execute it. Here we have a case of willing where the corresponding action fails to ensue. In the following passage, Nietzsche makes it clear that to will something is to be disposed to bring about an action but that merely willing the effect does not necessitate it:

> . . . a whole series of erroneous conclusions and therefore of false assessments of the will itself has been appended to willing in such a way that the person who wills now believes in complete faith that willing is *enough* for action. Because in the vast majority of cases, willing has only occurred when there is also the *expectation* that the effect of the command – that is obedience, action – will follow, this *impression* has been translated into the feeling that there is a *necessary effect*; suffice it to say, the person willing thinks with some degree of certainty that will and action are somehow one . . . (BGE, 19).

Although this passage has previously been interpreted as a statement on Nietzsche's part against believing in the causal efficacy of the will, it would be more correct to interpret it as a warning that willing is a more complicated phenomenon than others, for example, Schopenhauer, have acknowledged (BGE, 19).[68] However, although he allows for the causal efficacy of the will, Nietzsche holds that willing does not necessitate its effect. Nevertheless, as it contains a commanding component to its complicated structure, it is not contingent either. The will, even in cases where its effect does not manifest itself, is nonetheless directed to bring some particular, rather than just any, effect about.[69] The will, Nietzsche has just demonstrated, has a dispositional structure.[70] It must be so structured, moreover, if

---

[68] Although Clark previously interpreted the passage as articulating the view that 'the causality of the will is an illusion', we saw in the previous chapter that she has since revised her position to accept that Nietzsche allows for the causality of the will. (Maudemarie Clark and David Dudrick, *The Soul of Nietzsche's Beyond Good and Evil* (Cambridge: Cambridge University Press), p. 234.) It should be noted that even in cases where the commanded course of action fails to ensue, value dispositions are still forms of activity in the world. See note 53 for discussion.

[69] The particular effect to be brought about here is that commanded by the commanding will, which, however, does not necessitate the effect.

[70] In GS, 360, Nietzsche warns against taking purposes to be driving causes of actions and events. This claim is not problematic for my interpretation that dispositions are non-contingent, however, because despite rejecting purposes as driving causes, Nietzsche claims that power operates in the way that it does 'because it – must' (GS, 360), that is, according to its nature. According to Nietzsche,

we are to make sense of the phenomenon of *akrasia* or weakness of will. Nietzsche is clearly concerned to make sense of this phenomenon, as testified by his interest in typology of persons according to whether they typify weak or strong wills.

Normativity, as Nietzsche describes it in his account of the will, has a dispositional and causal ground.[71] Whilst his account of willing here is not necessarily of the explicitly conscious type (BGE, 3) and although he contends that the normative character of values is not constituted by explicitly conscious value judgements on the grounds that thinking can operate beneath the level of explicit conscious awareness (BGE, 3; GS, 354), he nonetheless acknowledges the importance of the specifically human capacity to formulate reflective value judgements. But now our question is: how can Nietzsche account for the practice of giving reasons and justifications from within the context of the dispositional and causal account of value? With this we return to the objection that such an account cannot be had and that the practice of explicitly formulating value judgements presupposes, contrary to Nietzsche, that values are different in kind from the causal processes of nature. However, Nietzsche disagrees and argues that our capacity for formulating value judgements, although differentiating us from the rest of nature, is nonetheless metaphysically continuous with it.[72]

Nietzsche demonstrates this continuity by arguing that conscious evaluative judgements have their ultimate grounding in more basic but evaluative drives. For him, the sphere of conscious evaluative judgement is not different in kind from the dispositionality of the drives. Rather, our reason giving capacities, such as those evidenced in evaluative judgements, according to Nietzsche, have a dispositional ground. He tells us that although fundamental

power operates 'accidentally' because it does not follow a plan extrinsic to its nature, but 'necessarily' because it operates according to its nature. Nietzsche's account of causality is dispositional and operates independently of the traditional notions of necessity and contingency.

[71] According to R. Kevin Hill, power should be understood in terms of abilities rather than causal propensities. What demarcates the former from the latter, for Hill, is that '[a]bilities, unlike causal propensities, can succeed or fail in their exercise' (R. Kevin Hill, *Nietzsche: A Guide for the Perplexed* (London: Continuum, 2007), p. 69). However, Hill's claim here presupposes a very particular account of causality. That is, Hill presupposes that causes necessitate their effects. But this conception of causality runs counter to Hill's description of it as dispositional or as entailing propensities. As we have seen, dispositions tend towards their outcomes but do not necessitate them. Dispositions, then, can succeed or fail. Abilities and dispositions are, contrary to Hill, modally identical. Moreover, we have also shown, in contradistinction to Hill, that dispositions have a normative ground.

[72] In 1872 in 'Homer's Contest', Nietzsche denies that human beings can be separated from nature despite having capacities that differentiate us from nature. He writes: 'But in reality there is no such separation: "natural" characteristics and those specifically "human" have grown together inextricably' (HC, 95).

dispositions are not in themselves reasons but rather 'instinct (*Instinct*), drive (*Trieb*), folly, lack of reasons' (GS, 1), they nonetheless provide the dispositional base for the manifestation of the drives as 'reason and passion of the mind (*als Vernunft und Leidenschaft des Geistes*)' (GS, 1; BGE, 3). He accounts for how the drives ground value judgements in the following way. Affective evaluative experience or the 'passion of the mind' (GS, 1) that directs the drive's negotiation of external resistance has the consequence of colouring the world or presenting the world evaluatively in line with a drive's aim. However, this act of colouring not only makes things in the world appear to us as valuable or non-valuable, good or bad, but, in so doing, generates reasons for our considering it good or bad insofar as the world is amenable, or not, to the realization of our goals. The slavish evaluation of the world, as we saw in the previous section, is characterized precisely by its – negative and reactionary – engagement with the world. However, we also saw that Nietzsche's account of agential engagement with the world reciprocally informs his account of the objectivity of our values and his distinction between those values that are normative and those values that are both normative and objective. We witness this distinction once again in his view that although slave values can be articulated in terms of reasons, we can nonetheless distinguish between good, 'objective', and bad, merely 'subjective', reasons. Indeed, for Nietzsche, the articulation of good reasons in support of a particular evaluation demarcates the higher from the lower slavish types and values. He writes of the need for 'intellectual conscience' and argues that the quest for good reasons 'separates the higher human beings from the lower' (GS, 2; cf. 301, 319). According to Nietzsche, the process of selectively and aspectually focussing on the world in order to realize some aim initiates the process of generating reasons in favour of or against considering that aim to be objective. Although the intentional object of a drive is its aim or realization of its point of view, the objectivity, or not, of this particular point of view is determined by the level of positive cooperative or negative uncooperative resistance that the powerful nature of objects in the world exert to a drive's aim. I use the term 'object' here not to denote substances in the world but rather to acknowledge that whilst, for Nietzsche, reality ultimately comprises individual quanta of force (GM, I, 13; WP, 635 KSA 13: 14 [79]), these quanta group together in hierarchical structures and according to commonality of purpose to manifest their natures (WP, 636 KSA 13: 14 [186]).[73] By appealing to the power of such objects,

---

[73] According to Deleuze, 'Every relationship of forces constitutes a body – whether it is chemical, biological, social or political' (Gilles Deleuze, *Nietzsche and Philosophy*, trans. Hugh Tomlinson (London: Athlone Press, 1992), p. 40).

Nietzsche draws a close connection between the nature of objective reasons and the level of resistance that objects in the world exert and which are experienced by us as feelings of either strength or weakness, value or disvalue. By virtue of having to prove their worth by confronting external resistances to their particular points of view, the affects or passions contain what Nietzsche calls 'its quantum of reason' (WP, 387 KSA 13: 11 [310]). But whether these affects denote objective or subjective reasons can be made explicit only when they are brought into relation with and considered in the context of other affectively informed points of view.[74] This reflects Nietzsche's view, more generally, that normativity and objectivity entail relations of power at both the level of explicit conscious awareness and beneath that level. He writes of 'the capacity to have one's pro and contra *in one's power* – so that one knows how to make precisely the *difference* in perspective and affective interpretations useful for knowledge' (GM, III, 12). Feelings of power that mark out our evaluative engagement with the world, for Nietzsche, are not irreducibly phenomenal feelings, such as Hume's appeal to feelings of pain and pleasure as the markers of value and disvalue.[75] Rather, Nietzsche derides what he calls the 'proof from pleasure' (TI, 'Errors', 5; WP, 171 KSA 13: 14 [57]) and contends that our value feelings interact with the world and can be deemed objective or non-objective (GM, III, 12) when they are suitably constrained by the powerful character of the world itself and justified through the consideration of other affectively informed perspectives. Nietzsche's value feelings are constrained by the world by virtue of their powerful interaction with it rather than being merely correlated responses of an – ideal – spectator of the object as in Hume. Since the process of determining the objectivity of our values is made possible for Nietzsche by the evaluating agent's normative engagement with the world as described in the previous section, and since both the normativity and objectivity of our values involves power relations that mirror those that constitute the causal fabric of reality itself, Nietzsche warns against the mistake of taking evaluative judgements, whether they be objective or not, to be metaphysically discontinuous with the powerful character of non-human reality. For him, the affects and judgements arise from and are metaphysically continuous with the dispositional capacities of our drives and the causal powers of mind-independent reality. Values and their

---

[74] The ability to consider things from multiple points of view is arguably what Nietzsche means by 'seeing more' (GS, 301), and it distinguishes human valuers and reason-givers from non-human sensate animals. These capacities, presumably, enable us to consider some of our affective points of view as justified or 'objective' (GM, III, 12) rather than as merely fleeting and momentary feelings.

[75] Hume, T, p. 299.

measurement, for Nietzsche, are not divorced from the causal processes of nature but are metaphysically continuous with them.

As we noted in Chapter 2, the relations between the affects as they perspectivally focus on and are, in turn, constrained by the world lends a certain cognitive character to our dispositional and affective engagement with the world. However, for Nietzsche, the contemporary distinction between cognitivism and non-cognitivism does not really apply here. This is because the ability to consciously reflect on and consider multiple points of view is a distinctively human capacity and power. The fact that the human being has capacities that distinguish it from the rest of nature does not mean that our cognitive capacities are different in kind from the rest of nature. Nietzsche claims that the human being *in toto* rather than in part should be translated back into nature, including those aspects, such as our capacity for conscious reflective thought, that were previously considered to raise us beyond nature (BGE, 230). When Nietzsche describes these capacities as 'unnatural' (GS, 355; GM, III, 25), he seems only to mean that they can be differentiated from some aspects of nature from within nature but not that they are themselves beyond nature. Consequently, any grounds for claiming that our capacity for formulating intellectual and value judgements is metaphysically discontinuous with physical causes is made redundant. Better to admit, according to Nietzsche, that the difference is one of degree and allow oneself the conceptual and metaphysical resources of a power ontology that is a necessary prerequisite for all intellectual and evaluative activity. As capacities, evaluative judgements are conceptually distinct from physical causes but they are not metaphysically different in kind by virtue of their shared dispositional ground. On the basis of this argument, we can conclude that value judgements, for Nietzsche, are not divorced from the causal sphere of nature but are, rather, subject to the same metaphysical explanations and modus operandi as physical causes. This conclusion follows directly from his commitment to a metaphysics of causal powers and to a dispositional account of value, as articulated in the will to power thesis.

Nietzsche's alignment of value with power thus succeeds in putting in place the three requisite steps to overcome Hume's distinction between facts and values. Rather than reduce values to affective responses of observers, Nietzsche makes values dispositional and causal properties of valuing agents that act in and interact with the world. Consequently, these dispositional properties should not be understood as unconstrained projections, but, rather, they manifest their natures and execute their intentional aims through overcoming resistance exerted by the world, which, for

Nietzsche, is not external to our normative practices but is itself normatively ert. And, finally, the normativity and possible objectivity of our values is secured by virtue of the fact that both physical causes and values have a dispositional ground. According to Nietzsche, contrary to Hume, values are metaphysically continuous with the causal-dispositional fabric of reality. That which ought to be, he concludes, is rooted dispositionally in what is.

However, although Nietzsche argues that values are metaphysically continuous with the causal fabric of reality, we should not gloss over his view that human beings can also be differentiated from the rest of nature by their capacity for reflective conscious thought. Neither should we downplay the suggestion that it is our capacity for conscious thought that enables us to recognize and differentiate between 'higher' and 'lower' human values, where higher values denote those objective value-norms that manifest themselves outwardly in cooperation with the dispositional fabric of reality. Moreover, Nietzsche writes of the education of the drives, which arguably presupposes both the conscious awareness of drives and the ability to consciously influence them. Now, it has recently been argued by Paul Katsafanas that agential activity and autonomy, for Nietzsche, do not presuppose the causal efficacy of consciousness. According to Katsafanas, consciousness is necessary for reflective choice, which he argues entails the reflective approval of actions that are determined by motives that may operate unconsciously. Katsafanas calls this 'equilibrium', and it is, for him, the constitutive aim of agential activity, characterizing the conditions under which an agent is said to be 'in control' of her actions.[76] Katsafanas writes that '[e]quilibrium is an analysis of what it is for an agent to determine her actions through choice'.[77] Motives determine one's actions, but choice involves the reflective approval of one's actions. Actions that are determined by motives that one would reflectively disavow were one to be aware of them are not actions based on choice. According to this account, conscious reflection is necessary for choice but does not cause action. Accordingly, conscious reflection need not be causally efficacious for agential activity. One might ask whether causally efficacious conscious reflection is necessary for autonomous agency, but Katsafanas answers this question negatively. He contends, contrary to Kant and Kantian-inspired accounts of autonomy such as those of Korsgaard and Velleman, that 'autonomy is interpreted in terms of agential activity rather than as being subject to the Categorical Imperative'.[78] Katsafanas writes that

---

[76] Katsafanas, *Agency and the Foundations of Ethics*, p. 140.   [77] Ibid., p. 143.   [78] Ibid., p. 241.

'[p]ower is an aim that arises not from our nature as *reflective* agents, but merely from our nature as *agents*. It is shared, Nietzsche claims, by all creatures that act: it is the one aim that is intrinsic to action as such.'[79] However, it seems to me that although Nietzsche sees the human being as metaphysically continuous with nature, he nevertheless differentiates between human and non-human nature. He accredits a higher human culture – existing only potentially at the time he writes – with the perfection of nature (SE, 5). And he defines such perfection in terms of 'greater power' (WP, 660 KSA 12: 2 [76]). Despite Nietzsche's argument in GM, II, that civilization and culture arise through acts of coercion that result in the internalization of the drives and where conscious thought emerges to compensate for their internalization, he never suggests that we can return to a pre-civilized state and the unfettered expression of the drives along the lines of the Roman barbarians of GM, I. Rather, Nietzsche points to the possibility of a higher culture shaped by the higher values of the nobles of the future (BGE, 'What Is Noble?'). Employing imagery of animal husbandry he suggests that the emergence of such nobles and culture of the future will entail educating the drives. Presumably, this education will involve facilitating the expression of the drives through the cooperative stylization of the self that we discussed earlier. Such stylization amounts to the disciplining of the drives along the lines that Nietzsche outlines in D, 109. There he argues that we can discipline the drives by associating wayward drives with a painful thought, for example, or by avoiding stimuli to the drive. However, such efforts at discipline presuppose the causal efficacy of conscious thought, which, accordingly, becomes a necessary condition of the emergence of the noble of the future and a revitalized culture.[80] All of this suggests, despite the imagery of animal husbandry, that Nietzsche thinks that *human* autonomy specifically can be differentiated from non-human agential activity and that what differentiates it is that human autonomy is *more powerful* than its non-human counterparts. If we take power as a criterion of autonomy, it is no great leap to think that the causal efficacy of consciousness would make us more powerful and, consequently, more autonomous. As Anjum, Lie and Mumford argue, autonomy entails empowerment. The more abilities one has the more autonomous one, accordingly, is.[81] Nietzsche seems to argue in this vein when he suggests that our actions are not irrevocably determined by

---

[79] Ibid., pp. 241–242.
[80] Although Nietzsche seems to presuppose the causal efficacy of consciousness in D, 109, he argues in D, 129, that most of our motives for action are unconscious.
[81] Anjum et al., 'Dispositions and Ethics', p. 241.

non-conscious motives but that they can be consciously trained. Such conscious training presupposes the causal efficacy of conscious reflective thought as a component of human autonomy specifically. The problem with this, though, is that Nietzsche often argues that conscious thought is epiphenomenal (WP, 478 KSA 13: 14 [152]). As these issues are significant to Nietzsche's account of human value and to how he understands the relation between mind and world, they will be taken up in the next chapter, where it will be argued that the will to power thesis provides us with the necessary resources to resolve the issue.

CHAPTER 5

The Capacities of the Conscious Mind

In the previous chapter, we argued that Nietzsche's dispositional account of value sees the human being as part of yet irreducible to nature and that one of the factors that demarcates the human being from nature is its capacity for conscious thought and consciously induced action. That is, Nietzsche presupposes a non-eliminativist and causally efficacious account of the human mind's immersion in nature. However, the issue of the causal capacity of consciousness is a matter of considerable tension in Nietzsche's writings, which stems from his inconsistent claims with regard to human agency: Nietzsche both denies free will and the possibility of something like Kantian self-legislation whilst at the same time expressing admiration for individuals who exhibit self-mastery and who are capable of consciously committing themselves to a course of action without indiscriminately responding to stimuli (GM, II, I). Consequently, discord rages between interpreters who, emphasizing Nietzsche's fatalism,[1] contend that he denies a necessary condition for autonomous action and those others who, emphasizing his appeal to the sovereign individual, argue that freedom is a 'substantive' and realizable ideal.[2] Nietzsche's fatalistic position holds that an individual's thoughts and behaviour are causally determined by psycho-physiological facts over which they have no conscious control or necessary awareness.[3] We have been misled into thinking that our conscious thoughts exercise causal influence over our behaviour, he argues, on the basis of the temporal contiguity of conscious thoughts to subsequent

---

[1] Brian Leiter, *Nietzsche on Morality* (London: Routledge, 2002), pp. 81–83.
[2] Peter Poellner, 'Nietzschean Freedom' in Ken Gemes and Simon May (eds.), *Nietzsche on Freedom and Autonomy* (Oxford: Oxford University Press, 2009), pp. 151–180. See also John Richardson, 'Nietzsche's Freedoms', and Ken Gemes, 'Nietzsche on Free Will, Autonomy and the Sovereign Individual' in the same volume, pp. 217–250 and pp. 33–50, respectively.
[3] See Brian Leiter, 'Nietzsche's Theory of the Will' in Gemes and May, *Nietzsche on Freedom and Autonomy*, pp. 107–126. See also Mattia Riccardi, 'Inner Opacity. Nietzsche on Introspection and Agency', *Inquiry*, 58.3, 2015, pp. 221–243, for his interpretation that 'self-conscious' mental states, for Nietzsche, are epiphenomenal.

actions (TI, 'Errors', 3). Despite this argument, however, Nietzsche pre-supposes the causal efficacy of conscious thought throughout his writings. For example, his argument that '*ressentiment* becomes creative and gives birth to values' in the guise of the manipulative priest (GM, I, 10), his argument that nihilism can be consciously overcome[4] and his claim that the conscious thought of eternal recurrence can practically impact on our disposition towards life (GS, 341) all presuppose the causal efficacy of conscious thought. Although the terms of the debate have focussed on agency, attention to Nietzsche's account of the mind, and in particular the relationship between mind and nature, can shed significant light on this confusion. This is because central to the debate in question is the issue of Nietzsche's views on the primacy and causal efficacy of conscious mental states. If we are to consider ourselves autonomous agents, then we must also lay claim to meaningful self-knowledge in addition to thinking that our reflective conscious mental states are causally efficacious when it comes to human behaviour. Nietzsche thinks that we can only understand the issues of self-knowledge and the causal efficacy of consciousness by con-sidering how the mind fits non-eliminatively into nature.

Throughout his writings Nietzsche rejects what he sees as the philoso-phical attempt to raise the human mind above nature, to see it as separate and exempt from nature's laws. The supernaturalist account of the human mind, according to Nietzsche, was essentially a Cartesian one that took our capacity for conscious thought and the transparency of consciousness to itself as the factor that separated the human being from nature rather than just distinguishing us within it. Dismissing what he calls 'the seductive melodies of the old metaphysical birdcatchers who have too long been piping at him "You are more! You are greater! You are of a different origin!" as 'the mendacious trash and gold dust of unconscious human vanity', Nietzsche rejects this metaphysics of opposites in favour of what he describes as a naturalist view of the human mind (BGE, 230). Despite this, however, he criticizes what he sees as the naturalist elimination of the human mind altogether, arguing that 'we do not need to get rid of "the soul" itself nor do without one of our oldest, most venerable hypotheses, which the bungling naturalists tend to do, losing "the soul" as soon as they've touched on it' (BGE, 12). Writing that '[s]ince Descartes (and more in defiance of him than because of his example) all philosophers have attempted to assassinate the old concept of the soul' (BGE, 54), he con-tends that such eliminativism results from the materialist attempt to undo

---

[4] In GS, 276, for example, Nietzsche self-consciously declares his wish to be a Yes-sayer.

the specifically Cartesian account of the mind. However, he argues that materialists did not succeed in overcoming Cartesianism but rather perpetuated its presuppositions, including that of substance (BGE, 12; WP, 552 KSA 12: 9 [91]) and the view that the mental and the material are metaphysically opposed as evidenced in the view that the mental is not ultimately real.

In what follows I examine Nietzsche's arguments in favour of a non-Cartesian but non-eliminativist account of the mind, which have been presupposed but not overtly addressed in previous chapters. However, as Nietzsche's arguments in favour of such a position are not always explicitly articulated, my presentation of them here will by necessity entail an element of assembling in order to highlight the intelligible structure of his thought. This assembling will involve a combination of historical contextualization and conceptual analysis. Paying heed to Nietzsche's view that philosophical arguments can be fully appreciated only when understood against the climate and soil from which they emerge (BGE, 20), the examination combines attention to the historical backdrop to Nietzsche's argument with due consideration of the substantive philosophical issues at stake. Thus, despite initial appearances to the contrary, I show, in a series of three steps, that Nietzsche's naturalistic account of the mind stems from his engagement with both Leibniz and Kant.[5] First, by appropriating Leibniz, Nietzsche initiates an anti-Cartesian but non-eliminativist account of mind by endorsing Leibniz's use of the principle of continuity to dissociate the mental from consciousness. Although the claim that consciousness is not the mark of the mental is, for Nietzsche, a step on the path to naturalizing the mind, this step can only be fully realized by dissociating it from the non-naturalistic foundations of Leibniz's arguments. This dissociation is made possible by Nietzsche's appropriation of Kant's argument against rational psychology, which, he contends, does away with the idea of the mind as a substance and, contrary to Kant's aims, naturalizes Leibniz's account of the relation between mind and world. Second, I argue that Nietzsche's adherence to the principle of continuity sees him oscillating, without due acknowledgement, between two non-eliminativist accounts of the mental; the first, which for convenience I shall call the 'containment thesis', sacrifices the extrinsicality of consciousness but secures the causal efficacy of conscious mental states whilst the second secures the extrinsicality of consciousness but sacrifices its causal efficacy.

[5] Whilst Nietzsche's naturalism is influenced by neo-Kantianism, he utilizes Leibniz (GS, 354, 357) and Kant (BGE, 54) in his response to Descartes.

Third, I contend that whilst this oscillation is responsible for Nietzsche's notorious confusion about the causal efficacy of conscious mental states, it is nonetheless possible to reconstruct his arguments in a way that suitably combines elements of the conflicting accounts and which successfully holds together his anti-Cartesian and non-eliminativist account of mind with the possibility of autonomous human action. Finally and in conclusion, I consider whether the proposed reconstruction, despite its promise to combine an anti-Cartesian and non-eliminativist account of the mind with the causal efficacy of consciousness, commits him to the ubiquity of the intentional and hence to panpsychism.

The Leibnizean and Kantian Background to Nietzsche's Account of the Conscious Mind

In this section, I examine Nietzsche's critical engagement with both Leibniz and Kant with a view to demonstrating how Nietzsche arrives at his naturalistic, non-Cartesian but non-eliminativist account of the mind. The non-eliminativism arises from his engagement with Leibniz, whilst his naturalism is secured by his critical engagement with Kant's response to Leibniz's arguments. Having demonstrated the character of Nietzsche's naturalistic non-eliminativism, we proceed to examine the implications of his arguments for the causal efficacy of conscious thought.

Nietzsche initiates his argument in favour of a non-Cartesian but non-eliminativist account of mind when, despite his criticism of Leibniz's substantialist metaphysics and monadic account of the mind, he applauds Leibniz's appeal to the principle of continuity and his consequent denial that consciousness is the mark of the mental:

> *On the 'genius of the species'.* – The problem of consciousness (more precisely, of becoming conscious of something), confronts us only when we begin to comprehend how we could dispense with it; and now physiology and the history of animals place us at the beginning of such comprehension (it took them two centuries to catch up with *Leibniz's* suspicion which soared ahead). For we could think, feel, will, and remember, and we could also 'act' in every sense of that word, and yet none of all this would have to 'enter our consciousness' (as one says metaphorically). The whole of life would be possible without, as it were, seeing itself in a mirror. (GS, 354)

In this passage, Nietzsche uses the term 'consciousness' as 'consciousness of something', designating mental states of which we are currently unaware as unconscious. Of particular interest to Nietzsche here is how Leibniz's appeal to unconscious mental states, when abstracted from his substantialist metaphysics, sheds significant light on how we might understand the status of the human mind as non-eliminatively immersed in nature. According to Nietzsche, the initial instruction stems from Leibniz's denial, contrary to Descartes, that conscious thought is an intrinsic property of human minds. Leibniz writes (in response to Pierre Bayle) that:

> I have already shown more than once that the soul does many things without knowing how it does them – when it does them by means of confused perceptions and unconscious inclinations or appetites, of which there are always an extremely large number, so that it is impossible for the soul to be conscious of them, or to distinguish them clearly.[6]

In the *New Essays on Human Understanding*, Leibniz offers phenomenological arguments in favour of the intelligibility of unconscious mental states. He gives the example of the experience of background noise of which we are unaware but then, as a result of something drawing our attention to it, we realize that we have been hearing the noise all along. That is, we heard the noise in the background earlier without noticing it.[7] The move from not noticing to noticing is described by Leibniz as a move from perception to apperception. Nietzsche praises this aspect of Leibniz's thought, writing of '*Leibniz's* incomparable insight that has been vindicated not only against Descartes but against everybody who had philosophized before him – that consciousness is merely an *accidens* of experience and *not* its necessary and essential attribute' (GS, 357). According to Nietzsche, this amounts to an explanation of the human mind in terms compatible with 'physiology and the history of animals', which, if considered independently of Leibniz's metaphysics, indicates the direction that he must take in reconciling human minds with nature. Whereas Descartes argues that consciousness is the mark of mental substance, which is distinct from unthinking and unconscious material substance, Leibniz denies that human minds can be demarcated so sharply from non-human minds. Central to Leibniz's achievement in this regard, in Nietzsche's view, is his appeal to the principle of continuity.

Leibniz understands the principle of continuity, which holds that '[n]othing takes place suddenly' as '*nature never makes leaps*'[8] in a similar sense to Aristotle's account of the structural continuity of a quantity with

---

[6] G. W. Leibniz, *G. W. Leibniz Philosophical Texts*, R. S. Woolhouse and Richard Francks (eds.) (Oxford: Oxford University Press, 1998), p. 238 (Leibniz's Comments on Bayle Note L). Hereafter cited as PT.

[7] G. W. Leibniz, *New Essays on Human Understanding*, Peter Remnant and Jonathan Bennett (eds.) (Cambridge: Cambridge University Press, 1996), section 54. Hereafter cited as NE.

[8] Ibid., section 56.

respect to its parts. According to this view two things are structurally continuous if they share a boundary. Aristotle contrasts such continuity with contiguity and succession. He writes:

> Now if the terms 'continuous', 'in contact', and 'in succession' are understood as defined above – things being continuous if their extremities are one, in contact if their extremities are together, and in succession if there is nothing of their own kind intermediate between them – nothing that is continuous can be composed of indivisibles . . .[9]

Leibniz endorses this definition in his early writings on matter and motion, acknowledging Aristotle when he writes that 'things whose extrema are one – are continuous or cohering, by Aristotle's definition also'.[10] Leibniz's appeal to this principle informs both his metaphysically grounded physics and psychology. Contrary to the Cartesian account of motion as spatial transfer of solid material bodies, which gives rise to a discontinuous change in the motion of an object, Leibniz argues that all change must take place gradually due to the motive power of physical force underlying all motion.[11] Such physical force, however, as relational and divisible must be grounded in a fundamental unity as only non-aggregates or things which have no parts can be considered metaphysically real.[12] Therefore physical forces must be understood as metaphysically derivative and grounded in intrinsic and inherent immaterial forces, which he describes as the entelechy or substantial form of fundamental substances. These substances, according to Leibniz, must be unities, and if the empirical world is to be grounded in them, they must also allow for diversity and variety. We can appreciate how the notion of substance can accommodate these two features, Leibniz argues, by appealing to the identity of indiscernibles and by drawing on an analogy between substance and the unity of consciousness. The first accounts for empirical diversity by holding that two things cannot be exactly alike,[13] whilst the second accounts for the fundamental unity of substance. That is, according to Leibniz, we can appreciate how the perceptions or appetitions of substances can be at once diverse and unified analogously to the manner in

---

[9] Aristotle *Physics*, VI, 1 p. 231a, cited by Timothy Crockett, 'Continuity in Leibniz's Mature Metaphysics', *Philosophical Studies: An International Journal for Philosophy in the Analytic Tradition*, 94.1/2, 1999, pp. 119–138, p. 126.

[10] G. W. Leibniz, *Sämtliche Schriften und Briefe. Philosophische Schriften* (Berlin: Akademie-Verlag, 1923), p. 266, cited by Crockett, 'Continuity in Leibniz's Mature Metaphysics', p. 126.

[11] Leibniz, PT, pp. 157, 169–172 (Specimen Dynamicum).

[12] Ibid., p. 124 (Correspondence with Arnauld).   [13] Ibid., p. 269 (Monadology).

which consciousness unifies multiple perceptions in one experience or mind.[14]

Although Nietzsche is critical of Leibniz's appeal to immaterial substances, he is nonetheless interested in how Leibniz understands, on the basis of the principle of continuity, that consciousness is an extrinsic property of the mental contents of these substances. That Nietzsche endorses the principle of continuity is evident in his general rejection of the metaphysics of opposites (BGE, 1; HAH, I, 2) and in his rejection of the mechanical model of causal connection between spatially contiguous and temporally successive substance atoms in favour of understanding causality as a continuum (GS, 112). The latter precludes, he argues, sudden changes and the metaphysical discreteness of components of the causal continuum from one another[15] and instead entails that causes and effects must be contemporaneous in addition to relational and interdependent (GS, 112).[16] Nietzsche contends that adherence to this principle allows Leibniz to put forward a distinctive non-Cartesian account of the mind, arguing that consciousness is not the mark of the mental on the basis of the intelligibility of unconscious mental activity and the continuity of a substance's conscious thoughts with both its unconscious perceptions and the perceptions of other substances.[17]

---

[14] G. W. Leibniz, *Philosophical Essays*, trans. Roger Ariew and Daniel Garber (eds.) (Indianapolis, IN: Hackett, 1989), pp. 285–289 (Letters to Thomas Burnett). Hereafter cited as PE.

[15] Although it was argued in Chapter 3 that forces can be spatially differentiated from one another, their spatial differentiation is extrinsic to the intrinsically powerful nature of force and so cannot impact on their metaphysical continuity. Nietzsche sees forces as metaphysically continuous by virtue of sharing a common nature – will to power – and although he describes forces as quanta of power, the difference in quantity, for him, is a qualitative difference in degree of power (WP, 563 KSA 12: 5 [36]). Nietzsche's account here fits with Aristotle's definition of continuity as entailing that 'intermediate between' forces is a shared metaphysical kind or nature. He also satisfies Leibniz's view that continuous things are relational and empirical. Nietzsche's powers are relational by virtue of being intentional and empirical by virtue of being spatially located. For an account of how powers can be both intrinsically powerful and relational, see my *Nietzsche on Epistemology and Metaphysics* (Edinburgh: Edinburgh University Press, 2009), Chapter Six.

[16] Nietzsche's account differs somewhat from Leibniz here. Although Leibniz contends that Cartesian atomism is incompatible with the principle of continuity, he still holds that motion entails collision and contact. Therefore he continues to describe physical motion as mechanical (Leibniz, PT, p. 170 (Specimen Dynamicum)). Bertrand Russell has argued that Leibniz is simply confused on this issue and that his appeal to force should have committed him unequivocally, as it did Boscovich, to action at a distance. Russell suggests that Leibniz's refusal to accept this can be accounted for by his antipathy towards Newton (Bertrand Russell, *The Philosophy of Leibniz* (London: Routledge, 1992), p. 90) Nonetheless, it is clear that Nietzsche accepts the Boscovichean rather than Leibnizean conclusion (BGE, 12).

[17] Larry M. Jorgensen, 'The Principle of Continuity and Leibniz's Theory of Consciousness', *Journal of the History of Philosophy*, 47, 2, 2009, pp. 223–248.

This interpretive angle, with its emphasis on continuity and as stressed by both Kant and Nietzsche, represents a contested, although not unfounded, interpretation of Leibniz's project. It sees Leibniz identifying indistinct sensory perceptions with 'confused' or unconscious thoughts and distinct perceptions with conscious thoughts or thoughts of which we are aware. Leibniz proposes, according to this interpretation, that both the unconscious and conscious mental states of discrete metaphysical substances called monads can be understood on the model of a continuum whereby unconscious thoughts or 'minute' perceptions are distinguishable from conscious thoughts by degrees of clarity and distinctness. Writing that 'every substance is like a complete world and like a mirror of God or the whole universe',[18] Leibniz contends that each substance expresses an infinite perception, arguing, however, that confused or minute perceptions are too faint to be recognized or attended to individually whilst conscious thoughts are those perceptions that are sufficiently strong to be noticed or apperceived.[19]

Furthermore, Leibniz contends not just that the perceptual states of any particular monad are continuous with one another but also that the perceptual states of individual monads are continuous with the perceptual states of other monads. He argues, on the basis of his appeal to the principle of continuity, that rational minds must be understood as continuous with the rest of created substances. Arguing that mentality goes all the way down and appealing to degrees or gradations of perfection of created perceiving substances, Leibniz contends that the least perfect of these, or what we ordinarily refer to as inanimate nature, exist in a 'stupor' whilst the most perfect of created beings enjoy the capacity for conscious thought. According to Leibniz, although the fundamental simple substances of reality consist of perceptions, not all monads are conscious. Distinguishing between simple monads, souls and spirits, Leibniz contends that inert objects and plants occupy the lowest level of perfection, whilst animal souls with their capacity for sensation, memory and imagination, 'which mimics reason but is distinct from it',[20] occupy a higher level. Human spirits, however, operate at the highest level of created perfection,[21] and, in addition to sensory awareness of

---

[18] Leibniz, PT, pp. 60–61 (Discourse on Metaphysics).
[19] Ibid., p. 260 (Principles of Nature and Grace).   [20] Ibid., p. 271 (Monadology).
[21] Kulstadt argues that Leibniz entertains two levels of apperception: one entails distinct sensory awareness of external objects and is a feature of animal souls; the second entails self-awareness or awareness of our mental states and is a feature of rational human minds (Mark A. Kulstadt, *Leibniz on Apperception, Consciousness and Reflection* (Munich: Philosophia Verlag, 1991), p. 165). See Donald Rutherford, *Leibniz and the Rational Order of Nature* (Cambridge: Cambridge University Press, 1998), p. 79, for a discussion of and alternative response to the Kantian one on this issue.

objects, are capable of rational insight into the necessary nature of things. Arguing that we are three-quarters like beasts whilst differentiated from them by a distinctively human form of apperception characterized by our capacity for conscious rational thought facilitated by the use of language,[22] Leibniz writes of what he calls human '*rational animals*' that '[t]hese souls are capable of acts of reflection, and of considering what we call myself, substance, soul, or mind: in a word, things and truths which are immaterial'.[23] Thus Leibniz argues that the principle of continuity applies to our understanding of the mind in two ways: the continuity of conscious with unconscious mental states and the continuity of the human mind with nature. For Leibniz the former leads to the latter. The argument is that if consciousness is not the mark of the mental and if everything is mental then there is no fundamental division, other than that of degree, to be drawn between conscious human minds and other non-human minds. Kant takes up this issue and argues, contrary to Leibniz, that our conscious and unconscious mental contents are not continuous with one another and that they cannot be known to be continuous with nature. Kant's criticisms of Leibniz are of particular interest to us because Nietzsche's engagement with Leibniz is mediated by his critical reflections on Kant's arguments, reflections which secure the naturalistic implications of Leibniz's appeal to continuity, contrary to both Leibniz and Kant.

Kant contests Leibniz's claim that every substance has the world in view to varying degrees of clarity, with human apperception the most distinct of all points of view. Leibniz's appeal, as interpreted by Kant, to only one faculty of the mind results in the view that sensations are confused thoughts,[24] the proper denial of which disallows the further Leibnizean thesis that we can have knowledge of the necessary nature of things, including ourselves as quality-less substances and the mind of God.[25] Kant argues that human apperceptive acts of consciousness cannot be known by us to be the acts of a substantial mind, nor can they be

---

[22] Leibniz, NE, section 275.

[23] Leibniz, PT, p. 261 (Principles of Nature and Grace). See also pp. 60–61 (Discourse on Metaphysics), 270–272 (Monadology).

[24] Immanuel Kant, *Critique of Pure Reason*, trans. Norman Kemp Smith (London: Macmillan, 1929), A271/B327, A262/B320, A270/B326. Hereafter cited as CPR. Kant's interpretation of Leibniz has been challenged by Robert McRae, *Leibniz: Perception, Apperception, and Thought* (Toronto: University of Toronto Press, 1976), p. 126; G. H. R. Parkinson, 'The Intellectualization of Appearances: Aspects of Leibniz's Theory of Sensation and Thought' in Michael Hooker (ed.), *Leibniz: Critical and Interpretive Essays* (Minneapolis, MN: University of Minnesota Press, 1982), pp. 3–20 and Margaret Wilson, 'Confused Ideas', *Rice University Studies*, 63, 4, 1977, pp. 123–137.

[25] Leibniz, PT, p. 253 (Reply to Bayle Note L).

adequately accounted for by the principle of continuity. According to Kant, to the extent that Leibniz stresses the principle of continuity in his philosophy of mind he cannot account for the possibility of higher-order thought. Additionally, he contends that adherence to the principle commits one to the ubiquity of the mental and thus the enchantment of nature.

Leibniz fails to properly distinguish between sensation and intellect because Leibniz, Kant claims, views the distinction as a formal or logical one rather than a distinction in kind.[26] Kant distinguishes, contrary to Leibniz as he sees it, between first-order and second-order awareness, between what he refers to as judgements of perception and judgements of experience. The latter presuppose synthetic a priori judgements whilst the former presuppose only the association of ideas in the imagination or what Kant also refers to as first-order empirical consciousness.[27] Furthermore, second-order consciousness, which entails conceptual awareness of an object as an object, Kant argues, also entails self-consciousness.[28] According to Kant, my second-order awareness of objects or the process whereby objects are thought entails an awareness of myself as the source of unity of the object. However, Kant contends that the self of which we are conscious, what he calls the apperceiving 'I', is a formal condition of unified experience that cannot be known by us to be a simple and persisting substance in the manner of Leibniz's perceiving monads. Leibniz appeals to consciousness as a model for understanding the manner in which simple monadic substances unify the diversity of perceptions, arguing that despite the multiplicity of these perceptions they are experienced as 'mine'. As an experience of unity, consciousness for Leibniz acts as both the source and model of the idea of substance.[29] However, distinguishing between the logical and real use of a concept, Kant argues that we cannot infer that the self is a substance from the logical or grammatical point that the 'I' that thinks can only be a subject of judging and not a predicate.[30] Kant argues, contrary to Leibniz, that in addition to our inability to know that the apperceptive self is a substance, consciousness (in the specifically Kantian sense that aligns consciousness of objects with self-consciousness) must be understood not in terms of perceptual distinctness but rather as the result of thinking sensory intuitions through a process that he calls synthesis. Demarcating sensory from intellectual conditions, whereby the former act as a constraint on the latter, Kant concludes that our knowledge is restricted to appearances rather than extending to things-in-themselves. Thus, central to Kant's transcendental

---

[26] Kant, CPR, A44/B61-2.   [27] Ibid., B133.   [28] Ibid., B132.
[29] Leibniz, PE, pp. 285–289 (Letter to Thomas Burnett).   [30] Kant, CPR, B410-11.

idealism is the argument that we cannot know the intrinsic nature of things but only their mind-imposed spatial properties. Rejecting what he sees as Leibniz's view that appearances are confused representations of things-in-themselves,[31] Kant argues, contrary to Leibniz's appeal to '*substantiae noumena*'[32] that our knowledge is restricted to substantia phaenomena constituted by spatial relations.[33] Moreover, lacking insight into the inner nature of things, Kant argues we must reject the principle of continuity as an objective principle of knowledge. Empirical knowledge, he claims, 'cannot justify us in the objective assertion' of the 'law of the *continuous gradation* of created beings'.[34] Thus, in opposition to Leibniz's prioritization of metaphysics over epistemology, and clearly demarcating animate from inanimate nature, Kant abandons the principle of continuity as a constitutive principle, arguing that it is justified only as a heuristic maxim of research.[35]

Nietzsche thinks that Kant's concerns with Leibniz's noumenal metaphysics are well founded, agreeing with some aspects of Kant's reasoning regarding the mind. In particular, Nietzsche contends that Leibniz's attempt to ground the physical world in the perceptions, whether continuous or not, of discrete monads perpetuates the Cartesian thesis that mind is ultimately indivisible and therefore immaterial. He argues, similarly to Kant, that it is our linguistically constrained thinking in terms of subjects and predicates that leads us to think of the mind as an immaterial or unextended substance (BGE, 54; WP, 765 KSA 13: 15 [30]) and to take this account of the mind as a model for reality. Nevertheless, despite his agreement with this aspect of Kant's critique of the substantial mind, Nietzsche is less sure about Kant's demotion of the principle of continuity as an appropriate way of understanding the relation between our mental states and the relation between mind and world. With regard to the latter, he argues that the continuity of the mind with nature follows directly from Kant's critique of Leibniz. This is because, according to Nietzsche, in the absence of a substantial immaterial self, Kant cannot intelligibly hold onto his mind-imposition thesis. As we have already witnessed in previous chapters, he contends, once we relinquish the idea of an immaterial substance-subject, we are forced to concede, contrary to Kant, that the human mind does not impose spatio-temporal or causal structures on knowable reality but rather that the human mind must be understood to be immanently situated within empirical reality, which now, however,

---

[31] Ibid., A264/B320, A267/B232, A268/B323, A270/B326, A43/B60.   [32] Ibid., A276/B332.
[33] Ibid., A265-261/B321-322.   [34] Ibid., A668/B696.   [35] Ibid.

must be understood in terms of the interaction of non-substantial forces or powers rather than discrete substance-atoms. Nietzsche writes:

> If we give up the effective subject, we also give up the object upon which effects are produced. Duration, identity with itself, being are inherent neither in that which is called subject nor in that which is called object: they are complexes of events apparently durable in comparison with other complexes – opposites that do not exist in themselves and that actually express only variations in degree that from a certain perspective appear to be opposites. (WP, 552 KSA 12: 9 [91])

Moreover, it follows from Nietzsche's rejection of Kant's mind-imposition thesis and the naturalistic conclusions that he draws from his critical interpretation of Kant that our conscious mental states must be continuous with unconscious mental states. Thus, contrary to Leibniz and through critical engagement with Kant's arguments, Nietzsche upholds his thesis about the continuity of our mental states with one another but concludes that the continuity of unconscious and conscious mental states cannot entail their grounding in discrete unextended substances. And, following from this, he claims that the continuity of the mind with the rest of nature must mean its continuity with spatio-temporal nature and not the supervenience or dependence of the latter on the former.

Although the continuity of the mind with nature, for Leibniz, follows from his claim about the continuity of our mental states with each other, Nietzsche sometimes alters this order of emphasis. Depending on where he puts the emphasis, we end up with two different accounts of the status of conscious mental states. When he takes the continuity of the mind with nature as his point of departure, we get the 'containment thesis', whereas when he emphasizes the continuity of mental states with one another, we get an account of the conscious mind that is closer to what goes by the name of higher-order theories of consciousness in contemporary discussions. Although both accounts presuppose that the mind is part of nature, they nonetheless provide different and opposing views of how we should understand the status and role of conscious mental states, which, in turn, has implications for Nietzsche's views regarding the possibility of human autonomy and freedom. The containment thesis secures the causal efficacy of consciousness but at the expense of making consciousness, contrary to Nietzsche's anti-Cartesianism, intrinsic to the mental. Although this conclusion does not have supernaturalist implications for the status of the mind in the wake of Nietzsche's critical engagement with Kant's arguments witnessed previously, it does make him guilty of inconsistency on the issue of the extrinsicality of consciousness to the mind. The second, higher-order account of consciousness, on the other hand, secures the anti-Cartesian thesis of the extrinsicality of consciousness but at the expense of rendering consciousness causally impotent. I will examine each of these arguments with a view to combining aspects of both in order to offer a reconstruction of Nietzsche's position that facilitates the extrinsicality and causal efficacy of conscious thought. I begin with the containment thesis.

According to the containment thesis, two things are continuous if they share a boundary in the specific sense of one thing being contained in the other. The containment thesis emphasizes the continuity of the mental with spatio-temporal reality by expanding the scope of the physical to include the intentional. He writes:

> Assuming that nothing real is 'given' to us apart from our world of desires and passions, assuming that we cannot ascend or descend to any 'reality' other than the reality of our instincts – may we not be allowed to perform an experiment and ask whether this 'given' also provides a *sufficient* explanation of the so-called mechanistic (or 'material') world? (BGE, 36)

That mental states, such as desires, instincts, passions and emotions, are intentionally directed, for Nietzsche, is evident in his description of these mental states as involving the activity of willing. He expands the physical to include the intentional by describing the material world in similar intentional terms. Thus, in opposition to the idealist reduction of the material to the mental which he detects in different ways in both Leibniz and Kant, Nietzsche describes the 'material world' not as a 'delusion', 'appearance' or 'representation' but rather 'as a world with the same level of reality that our emotion has' (BGE, 36). In addition to redefining the physical to accommodate the intentional such that intentionality is now considered to be all pervasive and the mental and physical non-opposed, Nietzsche also claims that consciousness must be continuous with non-conscious instinctual mental states. He writes that 'the largest part of conscious thinking has to be considered an instinctual activity – "consciousnesss" is scarcely *opposite* to the instincts in any decisive sense' (BGE, 3). Here Nietzsche argues that to the extent that we can intelligibly speak of a difference between conscious and unconscious thought, the difference is a first-order difference in degree rather than a difference in kind. According to Nietzsche, consciousness is not divorced from the instincts but rather is a refined instinct continuous with the intentionally directed character of nature.

However, there are reasons to be cautious about Nietzsche's appeal to physical intentionality here. These reservations are both metaphysical and methodological. First, if consciousness is to be understood as continuous in the non-radically emergent sense outlined previously, then it might be claimed that the physical must contain conscious experience. Since he has appealed to physical intentionality in order to redefine both the physical and the mental non-oppositionally, this would have the consequence of also rendering consciousness, contrary to his aims, an intrinsic property of the mental. Second, he must worry that his conclusions are vulnerable to the charge of anthropomorphizing nature (BGE, 3; TI, 'Errors', 3; GS, 374). He argues that consciousness is intimately connected to our awareness of both ourselves and the world (GM, II; WP, 524 KSA 13: 11 [145]). Therefore, to understand physical intentionality in terms of consciousness is to understand the world in anthropomorphic terms. However, I don't think that this is ultimately Nietzsche's position. Appealing to and developing our understanding of continuity from the previous chapter's discussion of the role of phenomenal feeling in relation to value, we can say that continuity does not entail identity. This allows Nietzsche to avoid concluding that consciousness is all pervasive. That is, he can hold that intentionality is the mark of the physical rather than the mental *per se* and that mind can be demarcated from such intentionality by the capacity for conscious thought.[36] This would entail acknowledging that human animals share a boundary with non-human animals such that whilst human animals are arguably demarcated from their non-human counterparts by their capacity for reflective thought and language, both animal forms are phenomenally conscious to the extent that they have the capacity to feel. Their shared capacity for phenomenal consciousness and intentional behaviour is contained in the boundary between them. In turn, non-human animals and inorganic nature are differentiated by the former's capacity for phenomenal consciousness and the latter's incapacity in this regard. But they share the capacity for intentional behaviour. Intentional behaviour goes all the way down, therefore, and is not indexed to the capacity for either phenomenal or reflective consciousness. All of this of course presupposes the intelligibility of such a highly contentious decoupling of the intentional and the conscious. Moreover, since intentional behaviour goes all the way down and permeates physical causal nature, it must be the case that conscious thought, by virtue of it being intentional, is causally efficacious. However, whilst allowing him to demarcate mind from nature and thus avoid the charge of anthropomorphism, this argument

---

[36] George Molnar, *Powers: A Study in Metaphysics* (Oxford: Oxford University Press, 2003), p. 71, makes a similar suggestion.

still has the consequence of making consciousness an intrinsic property of mind, which is incompatible with Nietzsche's anti-Cartesianism. And, in so doing, he presupposes the transparency of consciousness to itself. This presupposition is problematic, though, given his denial that our mental states can be immediately known with transparency and certainty (BGE, 16) and in light of the fact that he can be saved from this inconsistency by interpreting his reference to the givenness of the drives in BGE, 36, as we witnessed Clark and Dudrick suggest in Chapter 3, as entailing that the drives and passions are 'given' non-observationally and are subject to correction in light of observation rather than being transparent to consciousness and indubitably known.[37] Nevertheless, Nietzsche puts forward an alternative account of continuity, this time beginning with and highlighting the continuity of our mental states with each other. This second account, whilst presupposing that the mind is immersed in nature, does not, at least on the surface, presuppose the view of nature modelled on intentionality, and it is fully committed to the Leibnizean denial that consciousness is intrinsic to the mental. Describing consciousness as arising from an 'idea of an idea' (WP, 476 KSA 11: 26 [49]) and adopting something akin to what contemporary theorists of mind call a higher-order theory of consciousness, Nietzsche upholds his claim that consciousness of our own mental states is an extrinsic rather than intrinsic property of human minds. Unfortunately, however, whilst upholding Nietzsche's anti-Cartesian account of mind, this account, unless subject to considerable qualification, precludes the causal efficacy of consciousness.

Higher-order theories of consciousness contend that we become conscious of a mental state if it is accompanied by a suitable higher-order or monitoring thought.[38] We become conscious of our unconscious mental states when we have higher-order thoughts about them. According to this anti-Cartesian account, consciousness is an extrinsic and relational property of the mental. As David Rosenthal explains:

> . . . conscious states are simply mental states we are conscious of being in. So when we are aware that somebody thinks or feels something that that person is initially unaware of thinking or feeling, those thoughts and feelings are at first mental states that are not also conscious states. These considerations suggest a way of looking at things on which we have no more reason to identify being a mental state with being a conscious state than we have to identify physical objects with physical objects that somebody sees.

---

[37] Maudemarie Clark and David Dudrick, *The Soul of Nietzsche's Beyond Good and Evil* (Cambridge: Cambridge University Press, 2012), p. 231.

[38] David M. Rosenthal, *Consciousness and Mind* (Oxford: Oxford University Press, 2005), p. 27.

Consciousness is a feature of many mental states but, on this picture, it is not necessary or even central to a state's being a mental state.[39]

Nietzsche agrees with this contemporary theory that a higher-order thought is a transitive state (it is about something) whose object is an unconscious mental state. According to higher-order theory, the target state becomes conscious in the sense that we become conscious of being in it when it is accompanied by a higher-order thought. The object of the higher-order thought is precisely a first-order thought or feeling which does not change when it becomes conscious but rather enters into a relation with the, itself unconscious, higher-order mental state. Nietzsche differs from the contemporary theory in identifying consciousness, not with the – relational and extrinsic – quality of the mental state that we become conscious of being in, but rather with the – relational and extrinsic – quality of the monitoring activity of the higher-order thought that makes us aware *of* those unconscious mental states.[40] Nevertheless, a comparison of Nietzsche's account of consciousness with higher-order theory is instructive to the extent that both accounts appeal to the relational and extrinsic character of conscious thought. Thus, similarly to the contemporary theory, in GS Nietzsche appeals to higher-order thoughts as mirrors, which have as their object our unconscious thinking and feeling mental states and which allow me to communicate or report these mental states. He writes that consciousness emerges because in order to communicate his mental states to his peers, the human animal 'needed to "know" himself what distressed him, he needed to "know" how he felt, he needed to "know" what he thought' (GS, 354). Adopting a higher-order theory, then, Nietzsche rejects the idea that mental states are intrinsically conscious, arguing that most of our mental life is unconscious (GS, 333). Consciousness, he contends, 'merely accompanies events; it can also be absent' (TI, 'Errors', 3).

---

[39] Ibid., p. 21.

[40] For Rosenthal, conscious states are intransitively conscious, whereas for Nietzsche they are transitively conscious. According to Rosenthal, to identify consciousness with a quality of the higher-order monitoring thought is to succumb to an infinite regress of existential dependency between conscious thoughts and the higher-order thoughts that accompany them (ibid., p. 31). On Rosenthal's account, a thought becomes conscious only by being accompanied by a higher-order thought. For a second-order monitoring thought to be conscious, therefore, it would have to be accompanied by a third-order thought, which, he claims, is what happens in introspection. Nietzsche, however, has not worked out his account in this amount of detail and is therefore unsurprisingly silent on the matter, failing to distinguish between cases of lower-order thoughts being accompanied by higher-order ones and cases of introspection.

The instructive similarities between Nietzsche's account of consciousness and that of higher-order theory are further evident in his view that rational thinking is not necessarily conscious.[41] He writes:

> Man, like every living being, thinks continually without knowing it; the thinking that rises to *consciousness* is only the smallest part of all this – the most superficial and worst part – for only this conscious thinking *takes the form of words*, which is to say signs of *communication*, and this fact uncovers the origin of consciousness. (GS, 354)

According to Nietzsche here, human animals differ from their non-human counterparts not in terms of their capacity for rational thought or feeling but to the extent that they are capable, due to their capacity for language, of adopting propositional attitudes towards their unconscious thoughts and feelings, thus becoming conscious of these intentional mental states. Nietzsche describes unconscious thoughts and feelings as intentional because, in his view, these mental states are always already interpretations and hence aspectual independently of our conscious awareness of them (GS, 127).[42] And, because he thinks that thought and feeling are not different in kind[43] and that both human and non-human animal minds think and feel beneath the level of conscious awareness (GS, 354), he identifies our specifically human capacity of becoming conscious of these mental states with propositional awareness of them rather than with non-reflective phenomenal consciousness, which presumably both human and non-human animal minds experience. Unfortunately, Nietzsche is rather hazy about the character of phenomenal consciousness. To the extent that he defines consciousness in terms of propositional awareness *that* one is in those states, he arguably conflates phenomenally conscious mental states with mental states that are unconscious. Human and non-human animal minds have feeling-thinking mental states, for Nietzsche, regardless of whether we describe them as phenomenally conscious or as unconscious, by virtue of being sensate creatures. However, he might avoid conflating phenomenally conscious mental states with unconscious states by accounting for the possibility of the former along the lines of the higher-order theory of consciousness by claiming that non-reflective phenomenal awareness, perhaps in both human and non-human animal cases, arises when

---

[41] Recent experimental findings support Nietzsche's claim in this regard. See David M. Rosenthal, 'Consciousness and Its Function', *Neuropsychologia*, 46, 2008, pp. 829–840, p. 832.

[42] At GS, 127, Nietzsche denies that non-human animals interpret but he has clearly changed his mind by GS, 354.

[43] Thinking, for Nietzsche, is a composite of feeling and willing. See GS, 354; BGE, 36.

unconscious mental states are accompanied by non-linguistic higher-order thoughts, which makes them phenomenally but non-reflectively conscious.[44] Still, when adopting a higher-order view, Nietzsche's concern is with accounting for the character of reflective human conscious thought specifically. Thus, it is such propositionally structured conscious awareness that he has in mind when he writes:

> Consciousness is really only a net of communication between human beings; it is only as such that it had to develop; a solitary human being who lived like a beast of prey would not have needed it. (GS, 354)

Nietzsche's adherence to a higher-order theory of consciousness provides the solution to his claim that commitment to the principle of continuity is compatible with the extrinsicality of consciousness. It allows him to argue, with support from recent neurological findings,[45] that we become conscious of mental states when unconscious states, themselves physiological or special cases of the physical, are accompanied by higher-order, linguistically articulated, thoughts about them.[46] Nietzsche suggests that the accompaniment is brought about in the context of an asymmetric causal relation where unconscious thoughts give rise to their attendant higher-order thoughts. For example, at BGE, 17, he contends that a thought comes to consciousness when it wants to and not when 'I' want it to. And, in BGE, 20, he claims that language, which gives higher-order thoughts their propositional character, has an unconscious root and is grounded physiologically in the drives, although it also has a social dimension.[47] Consciousness, then, according to Nietzsche's version of the higher-order view of consciousness and in contrast to the containment thesis, arises as a result of the relations between mental states rather than from being contained within any mental state itself. Consciousness is

---

[44] Since Nietzsche's concern when adopting something like the higher-order view is to distinguish human from non-human mentality (GS, 354), he is unclear about the character of non-reflective phenomenal consciousness. According to Rosenthal, however, the higher-order thoughts that make non-human animal states phenomenally consciousness need not be linguistic (*Consciousness and Mind*, p. 40).

[45] David Rosenthal points to 'evidence that states are conscious when, but only when, a distinct neural state occurs in mid-dorsolateral pre-frontal cortex' (Rosenthal, 'Consciousness and Its Function', p. 835). See also Antonio Damasio, *The Feeling of What Happens* (London: Vintage, 2000).

[46] Writing that 'Intensity of consciousness stands in inverse ratio to ease and speed of cerebral transmission', Nietzsche describes unconscious mental states physiologically (Nietzsche, WP, 229 KSA 13: 14 [179]; GM, III 15, 17).

[47] Nietzsche seems to have held this view throughout his writings. In TL, for example, he refers to a drive to metaphor formation. For an examination of Eduard von Hartmann's influence on Nietzsche's thinking on the unconscious origins of language, see Claudia Crawford, *The Beginnings of Nietzsche's Theory of Language* (Berlin: de Gruyter, 1988), pp. 128–138.

nonetheless metaphysically continuous with unconscious mental states by virtue of the fact that conscious thoughts or feelings are not different in kind from their unconscious counterparts but, rather, have a physiological root and simply mirror unconscious mental states despite their linguistic mode of articulation in the higher-order thought. Moreover, despite the Leibnizean point of departure and despite upholding Leibniz's view that consciousness is extrinsic to the mental, Nietzsche's higher-order view proposes the proper continuity of consciousness with the physical contrary to Leibniz's reduction of the physical to the mental. That is, according to Nietzsche's higher-order view, and once again in contrast to the containment thesis, intentionality is a characteristic of the mental, but conscious mental states are continuous with unconscious mental states, which are, in turn, physical states.

Nietzsche's preference for one form of continuity over the other is not without implications, however, and his oscillation on the matter accounts for his inconsistency on the issues of self-knowledge and the causal efficacy of conscious mental states. If, as in the containment thesis, he opts for the ubiquity of the intentional and takes the intentional to be the marker of the physical and, by implication and despite his claims to the contrary, takes consciousness to be the mark of the mental, then he has no problem catering for the possibility of self-knowledge and the causal efficacy of consciousness. He can cater for self-knowledge because, on this formulation of the argument, he must presuppose the in-principle availability of mental contents to consciousness despite his denial of the transparency of consciousness to itself. Furthermore, by taking the intentional to be the marker of the physical and the causal-dispositional and by claiming that human reflectively conscious minds partake in the intentional, he can secure the causal efficacy of conscious thought. This fits with his presupposition throughout his writings that conscious thoughts can influence our actions. Still, he saves the possibility of self-knowledge and the causal efficacy of consciousness at the expense of renouncing his initial denial that consciousness is an intrinsic property of mind.

Conversely, if he rejects the containment thesis in favour of a higher-order account of consciousness, then he denies the possibility of meaningful self-knowledge in addition to characterizing conscious thought as epiphenomenal. Thus, unlike Leibniz who thinks that our petit perceptions or unconscious thoughts are in principle available to us whenever we choose to attend to them, Nietzsche's view that consciousness is an extrinsic property of the mental holds that we are in many instances strangers to ourselves and motivated by feelings, thoughts and desires that we do not have ready access to. In GM, he writes that '[w]e remain of necessity strangers to ourselves – with respect to ourselves we are not "knowers"' (GM, Preface, 1; GS, 354). Contrary to Leibniz, then, Nietzsche's account allows for a distinction between appearance and reality within the mental, thus accommodating his view that one can be radically mistaken and deceived about one's motivations.

A further related consequence of Nietzsche's argument that consciousness entails the accompaniment of an unconscious thought with a suitable higher-order one is that he attributes no discernible 'executive function'[48] to consciousness. The asymmetric causal relation between unconscious and conscious thought means that consciousness simply allows me to report on my unconscious patterns of reasoning, which operate independently of whether they are accompanied by thoughts of a higher-order. As a result, he writes of the 'ridiculous overestimation and misunderstanding of consciousness' (GS, 11) and argues that 'everything of which we become conscious is a terminal phenomenon, an end – and causes nothing' (WP, 478 KSA 13: 14 [152]). In passages such as these, Nietzsche contends that consciousness as an extrinsic feature of mental states is causally impotent. If Nietzsche persists in this claim he disallows, much to the consternation of many of his commentators, the possibility of substantive freedom. Whilst his suggestion that unconscious mental states can be understood in physiological terms facilitates real mental causation it,[49] at least on the surface, disallows the causal efficacy of consciousness, a necessary condition for free and autonomous human action. However, although Nietzsche sometimes adopts this surface conclusion and claims quite explicitly, as we have just seen, that consciousness 'causes nothing', his position on the matter in other places is a little more ambiguous. GS, 354, where Nietzsche adopts something very close to the higher-order view of consciousness, is a case in point. Whilst he holds in this passage that consciousness is 'superfluous' and thus a weakness generally (GS, 354), closer examination of his position here indicates that although he claims that the capacity for conscious thought is 'proportionate to the *need for communication*' and, hence, that it stresses what human beings have in common with one another rather than what individualizes them, he nonetheless argues that over generations we accumulate an 'excess' of our capacity for conscious communication allowing for the possibility that it might be 'squandered' in the production

---

[48] Rosenthal, 'Consciousness and its Function', pp. 834–837.
[49] In BGE, Nietzsche describes thinking as a relation of drives to each other (BGE, 36). In the same passage, he describes the drives as causal.

of art and, presumably, the realization of new values (GS, 354). When he suggests that an excess of our capacity for conscious thought can be creative rather than just monitor our unconscious mental states, he presupposes that consciousness can also be causally efficacious. Accordingly, he argues that what emerges initially out of a utilitarian need ultimately becomes a 'strength' or power (GS, 354). Consciousness is still superfluous in the sense that he claims that we can act and think in the absence of being consciously aware of our doing so, but when the latter capacity becomes excessive and creative, it becomes powerful. This power is evident in the fact that our capacity for conscious thought is no longer used up in merely protecting the human animal from the environment and can be redirected to creative ends. However, despite this claim, Nietzsche does not make it abundantly clear how he can combine the causal efficacy of consciousness with its monitoring role. A reconstruction of Nietzsche's argument is, accordingly, required.

A reconstruction of the argument indicates that Nietzsche has within his grasp the requisite conceptual and metaphysical resources to overcome the difficulties with regard to the possibility of self-knowledge and the causal efficacy of monitoring consciousness. In the next section, I undertake this reconstruction, which draws on elements from both Nietzsche's higher-order account of consciousness and his containment thesis and, in so doing, carries implications to be discussed in the final section for how we should ultimately understand his view of the relation between mind and world.

Reconstruction of Nietzsche's Argument

Informing the difficulty surrounding self-knowledge in Nietzsche's adumbration of something akin to contemporary higher-order theories of consciousness is his contention that the extrinsicality of consciousness precludes first-person incorrigible access to our own mental states (WP, 475 KSA 12: 2 [204]; GS, 354). However, this is a problem only if we accept that a first-person perspective is the sole way of coming to know about ourselves. On occasion Nietzsche recognizes that despite his denial of incorrigible and transparent facts of consciousness, self-knowledge is in principle attainable not directly but as the result of an interpretive process and by engaging in an inference to the best explanation. Thus he suggests that good philological practice can potentially heal the rift between appearance and reality with regard to the mental (WP, 479 KSA 13: 15 [90]). Similarly to his argument that sense-evidence must be interpreted if it is to mean anything (BGE, 12; WP, 481 KSA 12: 7 [60]), Nietzsche holds that our actions and behaviour are most fruitfully interpreted as manifestations of underlying psychological dispositions and motivations. This is not quite a behaviourist position because although Nietzsche clearly recognizes the formative role of external criteria, such as patterns of reward and punishment, particularly the latter (GM, II), he nonetheless denies that the mind is constituted solely by the influence of such criteria. Instead, as his denial that individuals can be identified exclusively by their actions attests (BGE, 287), he holds that human mentality is constituted by the twin influences of internal dispositions or natural physiological inclinations, which he describes in terms of type-facts characteristic of certain types of human beings, and social constraints that either facilitate or hinder the external manifestation of these internal dispositions and inclinations. Nietzsche contends that consciousness emerges from the hindering of the outward expression of internal dispositions and drives such that they turn inwards and give rise to higher-order monitoring thoughts (GM, II). This approach fits entirely with Nietzsche's naturalistic account of the mind in that it infers, on the grounds of best interpretive practice, 'external' and 'internal' causes of our monitoring conscious mental states, both of which, however, must be understood in terms of their continuity with the causal continuum that, in Nietzsche's view, constitutes nature as a whole and grounds the fundamental metaphysical unity rather than dualistic separation of mind and world. He writes that '[m]orality and religion belong entirely under the *psychology of error*: in every single case cause and effect are confused; or truth is confused with the effect of what is *believed* to be true; or a state of consciousness is confused with the causality of this state' (TI, 'Errors', 6). The key to unlocking the secrets of our mental life thus requires third- rather than first-person knowledge of cause and effect. According to Nietzsche, if we are to understand the mental, we must understand its causal connections in a causal and spatio-temporal world of nature. Moreover, knowledge of natural causality provides the basis upon which he can overcome the problem surrounding the causal efficacy of consciousness.

This problem faces two issues: First, Nietzsche's anti-Cartesian account of the mind commits him to the extrinsicality of consciousness. When adopting the higher-order view, Nietzsche thinks that the extrinsicality of consciousness can be secured by understanding consciousness in terms of a monitoring relation between higher-order and first-order mental states. Second, he sometimes maintains that this monitoring role precludes the causal efficacy of consciousness. However, this conclusion strictly follows only if we accept a model of causality that Nietzsche himself does not, at least for the most part, endorse. The model in question is the event model of causality, which holds that causes and effects are separable, atomistic and non-reciprocal events. But Nietzsche's commitment to the Leibnizean principle of continuity in its strictest terms commits him to a rejection of causality as a relation between events. This is implied in his account of the will to power, which informs his argument for the containment thesis. Despite the problems with that thesis regarding the intrinsicality of consciousness to the mental, Nietzsche's endorsement of the principle of continuity means that although we may abandon some of the particulars of the argument, we cannot abandon all of its particulars. This is especially the case with the account of causality that it presupposes even if Nietzsche ultimately wants to endorse the higher-order view of consciousness over that of the containment thesis. That is, if he is serious about the principle of continuity, Nietzsche must accept that natural causation operates in terms of reciprocal actions of forces or fundamental causal powers. His reluctance to explicitly countenance reciprocity at times (BGE, 21) can perhaps be explained if we take Schopenhauer's influence on Nietzsche's thought into consideration. Although Nietzsche is far from being an uncritical disciple of Schopenhauer (BGE, 16), he nonetheless seems to be swayed by Schopenhauer's criticism of Kant's appeal to reciprocal causality. Schopenhauer reasons that if causes are events and reciprocal causality entails a mutual relation between events, then we commit ourselves to the incoherent idea that event B is simultaneously the cause and effect of event A.[50] This objection clearly holds no water once we give up on understanding causality in terms of relations between events, something that Nietzsche does independently of endorsing the containment thesis and as a result of his endorsement of the principle of continuity more generally (GS, 112). His account of causality in terms of the interaction of forces necessitates a rejection of the event model. Unlike Leibniz, however, Nietzsche argues that forces are physical and metaphysically real, obtaining at the level of empirical relations.[51] This means, again contrary to Leibniz, that forces physically influence one another; they really interact. Accordingly, if monitoring consciousness of the higher-order view is to

---

[50] Arthur Schopenhauer, *Die Welt als Wille und Vorstellung*, 2nd ed. (Leipzig: Brockhaus, 1844), Erster Band, Anfang. Kritik der Kantischen Philosophie. See Arthur Schopenhauer, *The World as Will and Representation*, Volume I, trans. E. F. J. Payne (New York: Dover, 1969, p. 460).

[51] Leibniz argues that the physical cannot be metaphysically real on account of being relational and infinitely divisible. We recall from Chapter 3, however, that, for Nietzsche, metaphysical reality can be brought to bear at the level of empirical relations as the inner nature of force and as empirically instantiated by virtue of having an extrinsic spatial address. Accordingly, metaphysically real force is not constituted by spatial relations, although it is never without a spatial address.

be understood as causally efficacious, then it must be understood in terms of this power model of causality. This is because the power model allows for reciprocal causality and therefore makes possible a symmetrical causal relation between unconscious and conscious thoughts. Consequently, Nietzsche must be able to show that consciousness, which plays a monitoring role, is also a causal power. That is, we need to see Nietzsche as providing an argument in favour of emergent properties or the acquisition of powers. We can succeed in this by extending the scope of the power-thesis further than Nietzsche explicitly does.

At its most basic level, Nietzsche's understanding of causality in terms of reciprocally acting powers is a form of causal essentialism. He is a causal essentialist with regard not just to his appeal to psycho-physiological type-facts about human persons[52] but also about the constitution of the non-human natural world (BGE, 36). This essentialist position holds that the causal powers of an object must be intrinsic. Nietzsche understands the psycho-physical constitution of human persons similarly. However, if he is to be able to cater for the causal efficacy of consciousness as an extrinsic property of human minds, he must allow for the acquisition of non-essential and extrinsic causal capacities in addition to fundamental psycho-physical facts. That such acquisition is an intelligible possibility is evident in the non-human natural world. Consideration of such phenomena reveals that it is consistent with Nietzsche's power-thesis to hold that although some features of an object are essential, when it comes to more complicated things causal powers can be gained or lost according to the variability of external circumstances. Brian Ellis, a proponent of the 'new essentialism', calls these 'variable natural kinds', pointing out that a piece of iron, as a member of a natural kind, can become fatigued and hence brittle or may become magnetized and acquire the ability to attract other pieces of iron. He also remarks on the evident capacity of some things to change the dispositional properties of other things. A piece of iron, for example, can become magnetized by the capacity of a bar magnet. It is reasonable to suppose in the context of a naturalist account of the mind, that counterparts to these variable natural kinds are possible at the level of human minds and that consciousness can be understood as extrinsic but causally efficacious in terms of this possibility. Ellis argues that it is intelligible to hold that humans have acquired through the process of

---

[52] Brian Leiter also uses the term causal essentialism but denies that Nietzsche's will to power is intended to be anything other than a psychological thesis (Leiter, *Nietzsche on Morality*, pp. 138–144).

evolution, what he calls 'meta-powers', which include 'powers – for self-direction'.[53] Human deliberation is, he suggests, a manifestation of such meta-powers, which in turn presupposes the ability to monitor or scan first-order mental processes. Such monitoring, unlike Nietzsche's particular version of a higher-order account of consciousness, allows for the downward causal influence of our conscious mental states. Now, for Nietzsche, consciousness arises as the result of the causal influence of external circumstances in conjunction with the causal role of unconscious internal dispositions or drives. His appeal to external circumstances comes in the form of social conditions and he allows that humans can acquire, through the exercise of internal and external causal constraints combined, new powers (meta-powers) that can exert downward causal constraints on individual behaviour (BGE, 61–62; GM, II, D, 109). The breeding of an animal that is permitted to make promises, he argues, takes place through a process of social conditioning of our natural drives (GM, II, 2). Through the process of socialization the human animal becomes capable of conscious thought and awareness of their own mental states. Self-awareness, he contends, entails the acquisition of a counter-force, memory, to the natural 'force' (*Kraft*) of forgetfulness (GM, II, 1), and although initially acquired through the exercise of social constraints on the outward expression of our unconscious drives, this acquired force eventually becomes instinctual (GM, II, 2). The reciprocity of the downward causation of conscious thought is secured by the fact that consciousness arises not just through the exertion of external causes or constraints but also through the internal causal role of the unconscious drives and dispositions in striving to express themselves in the context of these external social constraints. Our unconscious drives and dispositions, then, play a role in giving rise to conscious thought, which then has the capacity to reciprocally influence or direct the unconscious drives in turn.

It has been suggested, however, that Nietzsche can accommodate the causal efficacy of consciousness if we view him as advocating a revised version of the higher-order theory of consciousness to that of Rosenthal proffered by Rocco J. Gennaro. If Gennaro's alternative is a successful fit with Nietzsche, then, it could be contended that my reconstruction of Nietzsche's argument, employing aspects of both his higher-order view and the containment thesis outlined earlier, to secure the extrinsicality and causal efficacy of conscious thought, is unnecessary. Gennaro responds to the potential epiphenomenality of consciousness in Rosenthal's higher-order

---

[53] Brian Ellis, *The Philosophy of Nature* (Chesham: Acumen, 2002), pp. 142–143.

model by focussing on the fact that the epiphenomenality of consciousness arises because the higher-order thought is extrinsic to the target mental state that becomes conscious. Gennaro writes:

> Rosenthal's HOT theory seems to threaten to make consciousness merely epiphenomenal (i.e., without any causal efficacy) because it construed the HOT as a distinct extrinsic state to its target state.[54]

Gennaro offers an alternative view that avoids this problem. According to him, the higher-order thought, what he dubs a meta-psychological thought (MET), is amalgamated into the target state such that the target state is altered and becomes a more complex composite state than it was originally. He writes that the MET 'actually changes the nature of the conscious state, so that, unlike HOT theory, the object of a MET is not merely passively there unaltered by the MET – it is not just the same state with consciousness added'.[55] The original unconscious target state is altered by becoming conceptualized and conscious as a result of its amalgamation with a MET/ HOT. Now, Paul Katsafanas has argued that Gennaro's view is a better fit with Nietzsche's view than that of Rosenthal's.[56] If Katsafanas is correct, then interpreting Nietzsche along the lines of Gennaro would solve the problem of the causal efficacy of consciousness. But whatever the philosophical merits of Gennaro's position, I don't think that it fits with Nietzsche's as easily as Katsafanas suggests. First, Gennaro's version makes consciousness an intrinsic rather than relational property of the transformed mental state. According to Gennaro's Wide Intrinsicality View (WIV), the MET becomes intrinsic to the target state. This runs counter to Nietzsche's description of consciousness as extrinsic to our mental states and as playing a monitoring role in relation to our other mental states. Described in terms of its monitoring role and identifying consciousness with an extrinsic and relational property of the higher-order monitoring thought, contrary to the strict terms and conditions of the contemporary higher-order theory of consciousness, Nietzsche understands consciousness, as consciousness of our mental states, in terms of a relation between mental states rather than the subsumption of one of them into the other. Yet it is clear that something needs to be done if Nietzsche is to allow for the causal efficacy of conscious mental states that are causally efficacious in virtue of their being conscious. It

---

[54] Rocco J. Gennaro, *The Consciousness Paradox: Consciousness, Concepts, and Higher-Order Thoughts* (Cambridge, MA: Massachusetts Institute of Technology Press, 2012), p. 93.

[55] Ibid., p. 92.

[56] Paul Katsafanas, *The Nietzschean Self: Moral Psychology, Agency and the Unconscious* (Oxford: Oxford University Press, 2016), pp. 41–44.

is also clear that any such remedial action, whilst drawing on the conceptual resources made available to us by Nietzsche, nonetheless has to develop these resources in a way that he himself does not do explicitly. Taking into consideration Nietzsche's identification of consciousness with an extrinsic and relational property of the higher-order monitoring thought, I have argued that his power model of causality provides the necessary conceptual resources to allow that monitoring thoughts can be causally powerful.

Consequently, Nietzsche's appeal to causal powers is, with some appropriate modification, best suited, and therefore necessary, to accommodating his anti-Cartesian account of the mind and his need to cater for the causal efficacy of consciousness and the possibility of self-knowledge. By combining his account of causal powers and the role of the internal causal efficacy of our unconscious mental states with due consideration of the role of external criteria such as social constraints, Nietzsche can allow that monitoring consciousness is an acquired power. Its role as such is not restricted to passive monitoring but rather can symmetrically causally influence or direct the manner in which our first order mental states manifest themselves. It might do this, for example, by facilitating a more 'healthy' expression of the drives than the turning inward that contributed to the emergence of conscious thought in the first place.[57] Since Nietzsche allows for such directive causality in the natural world (GS, 360), there is every reason, given his naturalization of the mind, to think that it can be intelligibly extended to consciousness. Indeed Nietzsche's description of how we teach or discipline the drives (D, 109; GM, II; BGE, 61–62) presupposes such an extension and it fits with his description of linguistically articulated conscious thoughts in terms of strength (*dieser Kraft und Kunst der Mittheilung*) (GS, 354). As an acquired property, the power or capacity that is consciousness is an extrinsic property of the mental but causally efficacious. As an extrinsic property, consciousness is not essential to mentality as such nor does it permeate all of nature, thus allowing Nietzsche to avoid anthropomorphizing nature. Still, consciousness, as an acquired causal power, is continuous with unconscious mental states because as a monitoring power it is contemporaneous with the states it monitors rather than successive and as causally potent it is not merely spatially contiguous with those states. Moreover, by virtue of being causally powerful, however extrinsically acquired, it is not metaphysically different in kind from our unconscious mental states. This is a suitable basis upon which to accommodate the

---

[57]   To the extent that Nietzsche allows that consciousness exerts a downward causal influence, it does so not by changing one's dispositional properties but by re-organizing the hierarchical relations of the drives as opposed to extirpating them (D, 109).

competing demands of an anti-Cartesian account of mind with a meaningful explanation of the possibility of human autonomy. Although speculative and metaphysically laden, this reconstruction of Nietzsche's dual and incompatible arguments for how the mind fits into nature facilitates such a satisfactory accommodation. Nevertheless, it brings a compromise in its wake. The compromise is that whilst the reconstruction of the higher-order theory of consciousness allows for the extrinsicality of consciousness, contrary to the containment thesis, it cannot secure the intentional as a characteristic of the mental only in the manner of the unreconstructed theory. In the next section, I explain why.

The Ubiquity of the Intentional

The preceding reconstruction allows Nietzsche to uphold the extrinsicality and causal efficacy of consciousness by appealing to the role of naturalistic causal powers. Although the reconstructed argument deals only with mental causality, it is nonetheless formulated against the backdrop of Nietzsche's power model of causality as constitutive of the natural world in the will to power thesis and with which, he argues, the human mind is continuous. However, the will to power thesis, as we have discovered in previous chapters, is far from being uncontroversial. Despite having addressed many of these controversies already as they arose in previous chapters, there is one final controversy, which has been lurking in the background throughout but which, in the context of our reconstructed argument, demands explicit treatment. The controversy is that of the ubiquity of the intentional in Nietzsche and the consequent issue of panpsychism, which arise from his view that the natural world is constitutively causal and powerful.

According to Nietzsche, a causal power is an ability or capacity to do something in particular, which is consonant with its nature and renders powers intentionally directed. Intentionality, for him, is thus characteristic of the causal and the dispositional in general. Now, to characterize the causality of reflective consciousness as intentional is hardly controversial. But it is arguably more so when intentionality is taken to be the marker of the causal-dispositional, more generally, and where reality itself is described in constitutively causal and, hence, intentional terms. There doesn't seem to be any way to avoid the ubiquity of the intentional in Nietzsche, whether we opt for our particular interpretation of the containment thesis or our reconstructed account of his argument for the extrinsicality of consciousness to the mental.[58] But its ubiquity in the context of the latter argument where intentionality, rather than consciousness, is the marker of the mental and where the intentional also characterizes the physical leaves Nietzsche vulnerable to the charge of panpsychism. This vulnerability is not evident in the containment thesis because there consciousness ultimately turns out to be the marker of the mental whilst intentionality is the marker of the physical.

The issue of whether Nietzsche should be interpreted as a panpsychist is a matter of much interpretive debate amongst Nietzsche commentators. However, Paul Loeb is one recent commentator who denies, contrary to some interpretations, that Nietzsche should be interpreted thus.[59] What is interesting about Loeb's argument for our purposes is that he reaches his conclusion despite taking the will to power seriously as a cosmological thesis. According to Loeb, Nietzsche is committed to panpsychism only if he is committed to drive physics. However, he argues that whilst Nietzsche is committed to drive and power psychology, he is not ultimately committed to drive physics, despite expounding a drive physics in BGE, 36. That Nietzsche is not ultimately committed to drive physics, however, can be discerned, initially, according to Loeb, from the fact that he offers independent support for his power physics in passages other than BGE, 36. Loeb is correct, I think, in this latter assertion. Nietzsche argues for power physics predominantly by juxtaposing it to the account offered by mechanical science. For example, in BGE, 22, he argues, contrary to the idea of 'laws of nature' understood in terms of observed correlations of events, in favour of understanding the operations of nature as an unrelenting assertion of power claims. In BGE, 186 he describes will to power as the essence of the world and in GM, II, 12, he describes the will to power not only as the essence of all organic life but also proposes it contrary to what he calls the 'mechanistic senselessness' of the supposedly 'objective sciences' (GM, II, 12). Power physics, according to Loeb, entails the view that '[t]he physical world is constituted of hierarchical power relations and power

---

[58] That is, unless we adopt a non-essentialist interpretation along the lines of Christian J. Emden's *Nietzsche's Naturalism: Philosophy and the Life Sciences in the Nineteenth Century* (Cambridge: Cambridge University Press, 2014). For my response to Emden, see my discussion in the notes in Chapter 3.

[59] Paul S. Loeb, 'Will to Power and Panpsychism: A New Exegesis of *Beyond Good and Evil*, 36' in Manuel Dries and P. J. E. Kail (eds.), *Nietzsche on Mind and Nature* (Oxford: Oxford University Press, 2015), pp. 57–88. Poellner and Hill interpret Nietzsche as a panpsychist. See Peter Poellner, 'Nietzsche's Metaphysical Sketches' in Gemes and Richardson (eds.), *The Oxford Handbook of Nietzsche*, pp. 675–700; R. Kevin Hill, *Nietzsche's Critiques: The Kantian Foundations of His Thought* (Oxford: Clarendon Press, 2003), p. 138.

struggles. This is because every aspect of the physical world is ultimately disposed toward controlling, commanding, mastering, and dominating every other aspect.'[60] Drive physics, in contrast, entails the view that '[t]he physical world is constituted of drives and their generated desires, passions, and affects.'[61] Loeb understands Nietzschean drives as dispositions that 'manifest themselves in a person by generating conscious desires (*Begierden*), passions (*Leidenschaften*) and affects (*Affekte*)'.[62] In so doing, whilst not defining the mental explicitly in terms of consciousness, Loeb nonetheless interprets it in terms of dispositions that manifest themselves in consciousness. Since physical powers do not manifest themselves in this way, he concludes that Nietzsche is not ultimately committed to drive physics.

Nevertheless, Loeb argues that if we take the content of BGE, 36, to constitute an argument based on premises that Nietzsche is actually committed to, then it appears as if Nietzsche is committed to drive physics after all. The structure of the 'argument' of BGE, 36, according to Loeb is as follows:

1. Solipsistic introspection shows us that drive psychology is true.
2. Methodological parsimony entails that drive physics must also be true.
3. Nietzsche himself discovered in addition that power psychology is true.
4. Hence power physics is true.[63]

However, Loeb argues that Nietzsche is not ultimately committed to the principle of parsimony on the basis that, for him, it amounts to a simplification that falsifies. As a result, Loeb contends that Nietzsche does not put forward the content of BGE, 36, either as a logical argument or as an inference to the best explanation. Rather, he argues that Nietzsche presents the content of this passage as a counterfactual imaginative experiment that asks us to appeal to our psychological experience of ourselves as will to power to arrive at a contentful imaginative idea of what a de-anthropomorphized world of power physics would be like. According to Loeb, Nietzsche uses analogy in BGE, 36, to afford us such imaginative acquaintance. Loeb writes:

> According to my interpretation, BGE 36 is not 'booby-trapped' and does not make implausible and self-contradictory appeal to panpsychism or anthropomorphism. Nor does it require some kind of unfalsifiable speculation about Nietzsche's esoteric, hidden, or subconscious motives. Instead, I

[60] Loeb, 'Will to Power and Panpsychism', pp. 57–88.   [61] Ibid., p. 61.   [62] Ibid.
[63] Ibid., p. 62.

have argued, the final result of Nietzsche's naturalistic methodology is an understanding of the true nature of the world as will to power. Human beings, he elaborates, also consist of will to power, but in drastically weakened form compared to cosmological will to power. So in BGE 36 Nietzsche proposes an imaginative strategy wherein human beings can gain a partial vision of will to power in its full strength. The key, he writes, is to adopt an introspective and solipsistic standpoint on the power relations as projected into the inorganic world. In this way, BGE 36 does indeed outline a panpsychist conception of the will to power, but only as a counterfactual thought-experiment that grants us a purely explanatory and analogical perspective on the radically de-anthropomorphic features of the will to power.[64]

Although I agree with Loeb that Nietzsche provides independent support for his power physics, I find his claim that BGE, 36, is an experiment rather than an argument less convincing. This is because Nietzsche makes it clear that experiment does not preclude argument or the giving of reasons. Rather, he writes that philosophy entails an experiment that incorporates the 'certainty of standards, the conscious use of a unified method' (BGE, 210). Nietzsche's statement here also indicates that he is not wholly critical of attempts to simplify or unify for explanatory purposes. That he is not is further indicated in his demand that we employ explanatory principles frugally (BGE, 13). Nonetheless, Nietzsche can hold to these principles of argument and frugality and still present the appeal to power physics in BGE, 36, analogously to human psychology. However, as we argued in Chapter 4, an argument from analogy is not tantamount to an argument to identity. Since it is not, we can agree with Loeb that Nietzsche offers independent philosophical support for his power physics, that he understands or imaginatively conceives this power physics analogously to human drives and yet that he does not identify or reduce one with or to the other. Loeb will surely contest my view arguing that if we take the will to power as it is articulated in BGE, 36, as an argument, then we commit Nietzsche to the Schopenhauerian attempt to capture the inner nature of things. As I have argued in Chapter 3 and elsewhere, I think Nietzsche is committed to capturing the intelligible character of things but that his attempt to do so is not Schopenhauerian in flavour.[65] Rather, Nietzsche rejects the Schopenhauerian appeal to the non-empirical thing-in-itself and, through his critical engagement with Kant, identifies the intrinsic character of

---

[64] Ibid., p. 84.
[65] See my 'The Kantian Background to Nietzsche's Views on Causality', *Journal of Nietzsche Studies*, 43, 1, 2012, pp. 44–56.

things with their ultimate mind-independent but empirically instantiated reality.

Yet, even if we find common ground between my interpretation and that of Loeb's or even if we accept his over mine or vice versa, I am not sure that the worry about panpsychism can be easily circumvented. This is because I don't think we can escape the conclusion that Nietzsche takes the intentional to be the marker of the dispositional. Loeb contends that if we were to take the content of BGE, 36, as an argument then methodological parsimony would entail that drive physics is true. Nietzsche's actual way of putting it, though, is to say that the principle of explanatory parsimony entails that we should test 'experimentally' to see if the causality of the will applies to the material world. Now, Loeb contends that Nietzsche ultimately denies that we are justified in believing in the causality of the will and directs us to passages such as GS, 127, and TI, 'Errors', 3, in support of this denial. However, it is not clear that Nietzsche is rejecting the causality of the will in these passages but more that he rejects a particular – simplistic – account of the will that presupposes that willing necessarily and directly brings about the willed effect.[66] As we saw in our discussion of BGE, 19, in the previous chapter, moreover, the causality of the will is dispositional, for Nietzsche, on account of fitting with the particular modality of dispositions. Being dispositional, the will does not necessitate its effects, and its causal influence, involving a relation between wills, is complicated rather than simple. The dispositional character of the causality of the will counts against the sharp demarcation that Loeb wants to draw between psychology and physics in Nietzsche because, as was argued in previous chapters, physical forces or causes, for him, are dispositional. That is, the notion of willing and the intentional is implied in the dispositional-causal, for Nietzsche. This is very evident in his description of fundamental physical forces as wills to power. Nonetheless, it is clear that Nietzsche distinguishes human minds from the rest of nature. The fact that they share some features in common does not entail their identity *in toto*. Rather, according to Nietzsche, human intentional activity can manifest itself in linguistically articulated conscious thought that is not shared by all of nature. This is not to say that such consciousness is intrinsic to the intentional or the mental as in the containment thesis discussed earlier but that it serves to highlight the irreducibility of human mentality to the rest of nature. Now, Nietzsche allows that human

---

[66] It might be argued that Nietzsche restricts willing to human animals in GS, 127. However, he holds that only humans consciously will, which does not rule out non-conscious willing beyond the human.

minds are continuous with non-human animal minds by virtue of having a sensory nature and by virtue of sharing a capacity for thought and feeling that is not shared by the rest of the natural world. However, although he allows that non-human animals think and feel, they do so without knowing it (GS, 354). But, as we suggested earlier, they are arguably capable of non-linguistically articulated experiences, which we might describe as non-reflective phenomenal awareness, a capacity that human minds may share with their non-human counterparts. Still, the capacity for propositional conscious thought is, for Nietzsche, exclusive to human minds. Since human propositionally conscious states, however, are physical states and causally efficacious, according to the reconstructed higher-order account, they are part of but irreducible to the rest of the natural world. This view fits with Loeb's claim that, for Nietzsche, both the world and the human self are will to power but that its human manifestation entails consciousness.[67] Specifically, it involves reflective – linguistically articulated – awareness. Loeb thinks this claim does not amount to panpsychism, but one wonders whether he would still hold this view were he to explicitly acknowledge that, for Nietzsche, power physics is intentionally structured. Nietzsche's reasons for taking the intentional to be the marker of the causal-dispositional arguably lie in his practice of arguing for the will to power on the basis of an analogy with human experience and his reasons for doing that seem to be that in the absence of the possibility of taking an extra-perspectival God's Eye View as our investigative starting point, we have to begin with the perspectival point of view that is most familiar to us. However, even if one doesn't accept this explanation, the very fact that Nietzsche describes both human and non-human nature as *will to* power indicates that there is no getting away from the fact that causal powers, for him, are intentionally structured. Loeb certainly describes power physics in intentional terms when he describes it in terms of controlling, commanding, mastering and dominating.[68] Perhaps

---

[67] Loeb, 'Will to Power and Panpsychism', p. 61. Loeb's reference to Nietzsche's discussion of internalized drives in GM, II, 16–19 (ibid., p. 77n32) indicates that he holds that Nietzsche thinks that worldly power is stronger than human will to power on account of the fact that the latter manifests itself in consciousness. Whilst it is true that Nietzsche sometimes describes conscious thought as superfluous, this is not always the case. As we have already argued in relation to GS, 354, he thinks that although consciousness emerges out of a need for communication, over time it can become an excessive strength that can give rise to artistic production rather than just serve to protect the human being from his vulnerability in the natural environment. Although, as I argued in Chapter 4, our power should not be understood in terms of power over nature, we can enhance (WP, 715 KSA 13: 11 [73]) our power through co-operation with the causal character of reality itself.

[68] Loeb, 'Will to Power and Panpsychism', pp. 61, 68. Loeb clearly takes Nietzsche's power physics to be a de-anthropomorphized view of the world (ibid., pp. 67–69). However, more is needed in the way of explanation of how Loeb's description of power physics as entailing the mastering of the less

Loeb takes panpsychism to entail the ascription of conscious mental activity to power physics. It is clear that Nietzsche does not make such an ascription and, accordingly, the identification of panpsychism with it would alleviate him of the charge.

Still, it will be objected that even if Nietzsche is not guilty of panpsychism, he is nonetheless guilty of re-enchanting nature, something which seems to worry him in passages such as GS, 109, for example. As a corollary to my argument in Chapter 2 that Nietzsche is really concerned with the problem of illegitimately anthropomorphizing nature in this passage and that this concern does not rule out offering a revisionary account of the natural world *per se*, it seems to me that Nietzsche shouldn't be so concerned with re-enchanting nature or indeed with the problem of panpsychism. Such issues are a problem if one is committed to the views of the Enlightenment and its mechanistic conceptions of matter. But it is clear that Nietzsche is critical of the Enlightenment in all its aspects, political, evaluative and scientific. Accordingly, Nietzsche's criticisms of the Enlightenment should include his criticism of mechanistic natural science, the logic of which points to the rejection of inert matter in favour of understanding the empirical world as causally powerful. Independently of this, if panpsychism's or its weaker cousin's appeal to the all pervasively intentional pays philosophical dividends, then we should not allow unreflective acceptance of Enlightenment values to dictate against it. Moreover, as I have already argued, even if Nietzsche holds that intentionality goes all the way down, this does not reduce human minds to nature. Rather, we have seen that human minds have capacities that are not possessed by non-human nature and that these capacities, however acquired and extrinsic, are nonetheless metaphysically continuous with the causal-dispositional character of reality. Nietzsche's appeal to the intentional as the marker of the dispositional – whether we label it panpsychism or not – entails the continuity of the mind with rather than its reducibility to nature. Moreover, the appeal to the all-pervasive intentional allows us to accept my reconstructed – and causally efficacious – version of Nietzsche's higher-order account of the extrinsicality of consciousness, thus making possible meaningful and autonomous human action.

---

powerful and the imposition of the meaning of a function onto the less powerful relata is non-anthropomorphic (ibid., pp. 68–69). The only option I can see is to say that the natural world is intentional but not conscious. Whether that can ultimately satisfy Loeb's view that 'Nietzsche thinks that the inorganic world is *not* in any way psychological' (ibid., p. 81) depends on whether we interpret intentionality or just consciousness as constituting the psychological.

Conclusion

We have seen that although the will to power thesis may not necessarily be, as Heidegger claims, Nietzsche's principal philosophical thought and although many of his arguments do not obviously appeal to the will to power, its particular metaphysics can still be made to do some very heavy lifting in terms of joining the dots in Nietzsche's thinking and making for a coherent philosophical whole of his arguments in relation to metaphysics and value. Clearly, joining the dots has involved some elements of reconstruction, but it seems to me this is what Nietzsche expects of his philosophical readers. Attention to the texts is of course important, and I don't think the analysis in the book has fallen short in this regard. But, for Nietzsche, genuine philosophy gets done not through textual exegesis alone but through interpretive and critical construction.[1] It has been my aim to offer such a construction with a view to highlighting the historical context and logic of Nietzsche's arguments in relation to metaphysics and value.

Although the metaphysics of the will to power is not mentioned explicitly throughout his writings, the logic that informs this metaphysics, particularly in relation to causality and Nietzsche's criticisms of mechanical science is implied in many of his arguments in relation to the character of the world and the human valuer's place in it. For Nietzsche, our engagement with the world is informed by our perspectival and evaluative interests. Our values reflect these interests but are not reducibly ideal or dualistically separate from the world by virtue of their metaphysical continuity with the powerful constitution of reality. Consequently, our evaluative immersion in and engagement with the world is subject to constraint by the world, precluding the possibility that all values are made equal. The degree to which our particular values are veridical is determined by their particular degree of

---

[1] Nietzsche writes: 'One repays a teacher badly if one always remains only a pupil. And, why, then, should you not pluck at my laurels?' (Z, Part One, 'Of the Bestowing Virtue').

power and their ability to cooperate with what the dispositional character of reality affords. In arguing in this way, Nietzsche's account of value sees the human mind as metaphysically continuous with the world rather than reducing either one to the other. Nietzsche's account of value is neither reductively realist nor idealist but manages to find a middle way between the two. Following the logic of Nietzsche's argument with regard to the metaphysics of the will to power and his account of value as will to power, we can avoid reducing our values to mind-dependent fictions or mere non-cognitive attitudes divorced from and unanswerable to the character of the world.

Moreover, the character of the world and our capacity to engage and interact with it informs, for Nietzsche, how we should distinguish between good reasons and flawed reasons for acting. What makes our reasons good or flawed, according to the interpretation of Nietzsche that I have offered, is their power, or lack thereof, to effect change in cooperation with the character of the world. Our values do not give us power over nature but rather our power is rooted in and 'enhanced' (WP, 715 KSA 13: 11 [73]) by cooperation with the powerful character of reality itself. Understood thus, Nietzsche's metaphysically laden account of values, which returns the human being to nature, has practical implications for how we should treat ourselves and nature.

However, a potential problem will raise its head if we attempt to take Nietzsche's account of values as a guide for practical policy with regard to issues of evaluative import. This is the problem of evaluative disagreement in Nietzsche's account of value. According to Nietzsche, as we saw in Chapter 4, values are normatively binding for those particular types that espouse them, but they are not generally applicable. Although he makes it clear that his is a form of value pluralism that denies that '[w]hat's good for the goose is good for the gander' (BGE, 221) and although he is equally clear that value pluralism does not entail relativism because, in his view, some values are better and more objective than others, he remains unconcerned about how we might convince those who disagree with us about the superiority of our values. Nietzsche's response to the problem of those with whom he disagrees and those who disagree with him, namely espousers of Christian thought or the democratic politics of the Enlightenment, is to say that he is not addressing them and that his concern is to disabuse potential nobles of the future of the notion that the one-size-fits-all approach of universal Christian philosophy or democracy applies to them and the particularity of their psychological type.[2] Nevertheless,

---

[2] Note that Nietzsche does not attempt to convince his opponents of the errors of their ways, believing such efforts to be futile. In Z, he explains to his 'brothers' that it is impossible to communicate with

Nietzsche has at his disposal some conceptual armour to assist him if he were interested in deploying it to the end of debating with his opponents. This conceptual armour comes in the form of conscious thought. Conscious thought, he argues, despite its superficiality, facilitates communication between individual human beings and their particular differences (GS, 354). It allows us to consider multiple perspectives in relation to one another rather than in isolation. Accordingly, it is entirely feasible that he could use this communicative and linguistic mechanism to show his opponents that although they do not see the world in the way that he does, their view of the world, when subject to critical constraint by other perspectives, is flawed. Their views are flawed because their values are a negative reaction to the world rather than positive cooperation with it. Despite Nietzsche's view that our values and perspectives are plural, there is just one world, however internally differentiated and plural the world itself happens to be. Yet he must still face a difficulty here in any attempt to convince those with whom he disagrees. The difficulty is that, for Nietzsche, our values, including non-objective ones, reflect an agent's particular and normatively structured way of acting in and interacting with the world. It is not the case, then, that non-objective value norms were ever cut off from the world. Consequently, showing the slave how things look from the noble's perspective will not do anything to alter the slave's perspective unless the slave consciously decides to deploy the mechanism of disciplining their dominant drives along the lines outlined in D, 109, to bring their dominant perspective into line with how things look from the noble's perspective. This is because although Nietzsche's appeal to the metaphysical continuity of mind and nature allows that reasons are grounded in causes and so can, accordingly, be causally efficacious, reasons for acting cannot, by virtue of the terms and conditions of his appeal to metaphysical continuity, be divorced from human psychology and the dispositionality of the human will. That is, although we can be brought to recognize the existence of alternative evaluative points of view, this in itself, without conscious intervention and discipline, does nothing to alter which of those perspectives is the dominant and more powerful in the hierarchical bundle of drives that Nietzsche calls the self. That he allows for the possibility of consciously disciplining our drives is evident from the fact that, for example, in BGE he is self-consciously addressing the potential

---

the 'mob' of the market-place. He writes: 'With the new morning, however, came to me a new truth: then I learned to say: "What are the market-place and the mob and the mob's confusion and the mob's long ears to me"' (Z, Part Four, 'Of the Higher Man', 1).

nobles of the future regarding their mistake of accepting that there is such a thing as a universally applicable morality.[3] But, since our values reflect our essential and particular physio-psychological type and since values and the desire to change them depends on variabilities in physio-psychological make-up, regardless of the fact that these types are defined in the context of their immersion in the world and by interacting with it, success in altering the values of his opponents, however non-veridical their values are, is rendered problematic from the beginning.[4] Their values reflect their particular natures and their specific degree of power in the world. One needs to be disposed and sufficiently powerful to effect a change in these values.[5] But, in line with his typology of weak and strong types, Nietzsche does not allow that all valuers are equally powerful. In Z, he warns against willing beyond one's powers, claiming that 'there is an evil falsity about those who will beyond their powers' (Z, Part Four, 'Of The Higher Man', 8). Nietzsche writes that it is the slave's weakness that leads them to adopt a narrow perspective, the perspective of the 'injured one', to the exclusion of other perspectives in the first place (GM, II, 11). Psychological particularity (albeit particularized to physio-psychological types) and variability precludes Nietzsche from appealing to the notion of intersubjective constraint as a suitable mechanism for subjecting our values to change. This is because he resists the idea that all human minds are constituted in the same way. For him, the thesis that all human minds are constituted alike is a symptom of the principle of equality that informs the democratic principles of the Enlightenment and which is, he argues, merely a secularized version of the Christian, anti-naturalistic principle that all men are

---

[3] The issue of whether Nietzsche is addressing nobles of the present or nobles of the future is much debated in the secondary literature (see Paul Loeb, 'Zarathustra's Laughing Lions' in Christa Davis Acampora and Ralph R. Acampora (eds.), *A Nietzschean Bestiary: Becoming Animal Beyond Docile and Brutal* (Oxford: Rowman and Littlefield Publishers, 2004), pp. 121–139, pp. 127–130, for discussion of this issue). I take it that Nietzsche is addressing the nobles of the present, who are a mixed race (BGE, 268), with a view to bringing about a noble race of the future that has surpassed the influence of the old tables and laws. Note, in this regard, that he addresses himself to the 'higher men' in Z whilst envisaging the arrival of the Übermensch (Z, Part Four, 'Of the Higher Man', 2).

[4] Nietzsche writes: 'But at the bottom of everyone, of course, way "down there", there is something obstinately unteachable, a granite-like spiritual *Fatum*, predetermined decisions and answers to selected, predetermined questions' (BGE, 231).

[5] It is to be noted that Nietzsche is not guilty of the genetic fallacy here, however. He is not claiming that all values are justified by virtue of being normatively binding on the psychological types that espouse them. Indeed, he criticizes certain psychological types for their lack of interest in justifying their values and subjecting them to adequate criticism (GS, 2, 319). But, even if they do subject their values to criticism, he claims, weak psychological types are insufficiently powerful to effect a change in their values.

made equal in the eyes of God.[6] Since all human beings are not made equal, in his view, the possibility of persuading those who disagree with us of our evaluative point of view is ruled out. We recall that in Chapter 4 we compared Nietzsche's view to the non-dualist argument of Joseph Rouse. However, there are some significant differences between the two thinkers. Whereas Rouse sees his non-dualism as supporting a politics of diversity rather than one of difference on the basis of the 'politics of the common' that emerges from his appeal to the notion of intra-action with a shared world, the more psychological and essentialist dimensions to Nietzsche's argument, which gives rise to his distinction between the normativity and objectivity of a value, prevent him from reaching a similar conclusion to Rouse.[7] However, in response to the failure of intersubjectively agreed upon reasons independent of the particularities of human psychology to effect a change in the values of those who do not share ours, we might adopt a more realist account of values by making values dispositional and powerful properties in the world itself such that their motivational efficacy does not depend completely on psychological variability. Although dispositions in the world would not be entirely mind-independent but rather would have the character of relational properties with subjective and objective aspects, Nietzsche's acceptance of the nihilistic conclusion that values cannot be instantiated in the world precludes the possibility of him adopting this more realist account of the status of our values.[8] His appeal to values as psychological dispositions, regardless of their metaphysical

---

[6] Nietzsche writes that 'the *democratic* movement is Christianity's heir' (BGE, 202).

[7] Joseph Rouse, *How Scientific Practices Matter: Reclaiming Philosophical Naturalism* (Chicago, IL: University of Chicago Press, 2002), p. 254.

[8] These dispositional relational properties are sometimes referred to as response-dependent properties in the literature. Michael Devitt, in his discussion of such properties, denies that they can be described realistically as a result of their having subjective aspects (Michael Devitt, *Putting Metaphysics First: Essays on Metaphysics and Epistemology* (Oxford: Oxford University Press, 2010), pp. 121–136). However, as James Gibson argues, relational properties should be understood as 'affordances' that mark the complementarity between an organism and its environment. Moreover, he contends that their subjective aspects do not diminish their mind-independency on the grounds that an object possesses these affordances by virtue of its objective properties. For example, an object is grasp-able because the width of the object is not greater than the span of the human hand. According to Gibson, 'An affordance cuts across the dichotomy of subjective-objective and helps us to understand its inadequacy' (James. J. Gibson, *The Ecological Approach to Visual Perception* (New York, NY: Psychology Press, 2014), p. 129). Yet some commentators contend that relational properties are subjective on the grounds that the property is constituted by our response. But, this view is founded on a misinterpretation of the relation between the property and the response in the biconditional 'X is good (that is, valuable) iff X is disposed to elicit emotions of commendation in appropriately receptive perceivers in suitable circumstances (with "appropriate perceiver" and "suitable conditions" to be specified)'. As Philip Pettit has argued, our responses denote the property, but they do not make or constitute the property (Philip Pettit, *Rules, Reasons, and Norms* (Oxford: Clarendon Press, 2002), pp. 12–13).

continuity with reality, is unable to satisfactorily address the problem of evaluative disagreement. Nietzsche is unmoved by this, however, on the grounds that he envisages a new world of higher-types[9] where the weak have been allowed and even perhaps assisted to perish (AC, 2).[10] Despite the unsavoury character of Nietzsche's suggestions here and despite the fact that it makes his value pluralism a mere transition from his current culture to one where the higher-types have won out over their weaker counterparts, it is clear that for anyone interested in the problem of conflicting values, without re-instantiating values mind-independently in the world, Nietzsche must leave the problem of evaluative disagreement unaddressed and unresolved. Nietzsche's protestations to the contrary notwithstanding, this is hardly a demonstration of genuine power in the sense of the ability to consider multiple perspectives (GM, III, 12) and to form a unified culture founded on hierarchical co-operation (WP, 561 KSA 12: 2 [87]) and must be considered a weakness to be ultimately overcome.

[9] See Nietzsche, Z, Part Four 'Of the Higher Man'.
[10] Nietzsche reaches this conclusion as a direct consequence of his alignment of value with the will to power in AC, 2. See also GS, 73, where he recommends infanticide in some cases of weakness. Note further his praise for the Indian law of Manu and the hierarchical caste system (TI, 'Improvers', 3). For a critical discussion of the unsavoury implications of Nietzsche's views on the higher and weak types, see Paul Loeb, 'Zarathustra's Laughing Lions', pp. 133–134.

Bibliography

Allison, David B., *The New Nietzsche: Contemporary Styles of Interpretation* (Cambridge. MA: Massachusetts Institute of Technology Press, 1985).
Reading the New Nietzsche (Lanham, MD: Rowman and Littlefield, 2000).
Anjum, Rani Lill, Svein Anders Noer Lie and Stephen Mumford, 'Dispositions and Ethics' in Ruth Groff and John Greco (eds.), *Powers and Capacities in Philosophy: The New Aristotelianism* (London: Routledge, 2013), pp. 231–247.
Ayer, A. J., *Language, Truth and Logic* (New York, NY: Dover, 1952).
Bailey, Tom, 'Nietzsche the Kantian' in Ken Gemes and John Richardson (eds.), *The Oxford Handbook of Nietzsche* (Oxford: Oxford University Press, 2013), pp. 134–159.
Barad, Karen, *Meeting the Universe Halfway: Quantum Physics and the Entanglement of Matter and Meaning* (Durham, NC: Duke University Press, 2007).
Blackburn, Simon, *Essays in Quasi-Realism* (Oxford: Oxford University Press, 1993).
'Perspectives, Fictions, Errors, Play' in Brian Leiter and Neil Sinhababu (eds.), *Nietzsche and Morality* (Oxford: Oxford University Press, 2007), pp. 281–296.
Brady, Michael, 'The Irrationality of Recalcitrant Emotions', *Philosophical Studies*, 145.3, 2009, pp. 413–430.
Brandom, Robert B. (ed.), *Rorty and His Critics* (Oxford: Blackwell, 2000).
Brobjer, Thomas, *Nietzsche's Philosophical Context: An Intellectual Biography* (Urbana, IL: University of Illinois Press, 2008).
Campioni, Giuliano, Paolo D'Iorio, Maria Cristina Fornari, Francesco Fronterotta, Andrea Orsucci and Renate Müller-Buck, *Nietzsches persönliche Bibliothek* (Berlin: De Gruyter, 2003).
Clark, Maudemarie and David Dudrick, 'The Naturalisms of *Beyond Good and Evil*' in Keith Ansell Pearson (ed.), *A Companion to Nietzsche* (Oxford: Blackwell, 2006), pp. 148–168.
'Nietzsche and Moral Objectivity: The Development of Nietzsche's Metaethics' in Brian Leiter and Neil Sinhababu (eds.), *Nietzsche and Morality* (Oxford: Oxford University Press, 2007), pp. 192–226.
The Soul of Nietzsche's Beyond Good and Evil (Cambridge: Cambridge University Press, 2012).

Clark, Maudemarie, *Nietzsche on Truth and Philosophy* (Cambridge: Cambridge University Press, 1990).

'On Knowledge, Truth and Value: Nietzsche's Debt to Schopenhauer and the Development of His Empiricism' in Christopher Janaway (ed.), *Willing and Nothingness: Schopenhauer as Nietzsche's Educator* (Oxford: Clarendon Press, 1998), pp. 37–78.

Cox, Christoph, *Nietzsche: Naturalism and Interpretation* (Berkeley, CA: University of California Press, 1999).

Crawford, Claudia, *The Beginnings of Nietzsche's Theory of Language* (Berlin: de Gruyter, 1988).

Crockett, Timothy, 'Continuity in Leibniz's Mature Metaphysics', *Philosophical Studies: An International Journal for Philosophy in the Analytic Tradition*, 94.1/2, 1999, pp. 119–138.

Crowther, Paul, *Defining Art, Creating the Canon: Artistic Value in an Era of Doubt* (Oxford: Clarendon Press, 2011).

Damasio, Antonio, *The Feeling of What Happens* (London: Vintage, 2000).

Deleuze, Gilles, *Nietzsche and Philosophy*, trans. Hugh Tomlinson (London: Athlone Press, 1992).

Devitt, Michael, *Putting Metaphysics First: Essays on Metaphysics and Epistemology* (Oxford: Oxford University Press, 2010).

Doyle, Tsarina, *Nietzsche on Epistemology and Metaphysics: The World in View* (Edinburgh: Edinburgh University Press, 2009).

'The Kantian Background to Nietzsche's Views on Causality', *Journal of Nietzsche Studies*, 43.1, 2012, pp. 44–56.

Ellis, Brian, *The Philosophy of Nature* (Chesham: Acumen, 2002).

Emden, Christian J., *Nietzsche's Naturalism: Philosophy and the Life Sciences in the Nineteenth Century* (Cambridge: Cambridge University Press, 2014).

'Nietzsche's Will to Power: Biology, Naturalism and Normativity', *Journal of Nietzsche Studies*, 47.1, 2016, pp. 30–60.

Findlay, J. N., *Values and Intentions* (London: George Allen and Unwin Ltd. and New York: The Macmillan Company), 1961.

Fink, Eugene, *Nietzsche's Philosophy*, trans. Goetz Richter (London: Continuum, 2003).

Fischer, Kuno, *Immanuel Kant und seine Lehre (geschichte der neuern Philosophie iv-v)*, 1st ed., 2 vols. (Heidelberg: C. Winter, 1898).

Foster, John, *The Case for Idealism* (London: Routledge and Kegan Paul, 1982).

Gemes, Ken, 'Nietzsche and the Affirmation of Life: A Review and Dialogue with Bernard Reginster', *European Journal of Philosophy*, 16.3, December 2008, pp. 459–466.

'Nietzsche on Free Will, Autonomy and the Sovereign Individual' in Ken Gemes and Simon May (eds.), *Nietzsche on Freedom and Autonomy* (Oxford: Oxford University Press, 2009), pp. 33–50.

'Life's Perspectives' in Ken Gemes and John Richardson (eds.), *The Oxford Handbook of Nietzsche* (Oxford: Oxford University Press, 2013), pp. 553–575.

Gennaro, Rocco J., *The Consciousness Paradox: Consciousness, Concepts and Higher-Order Thoughts* (Boston, MA: Massachusetts Institute of Technology Press, 2012).

Gibson, James J., *The Ecological Approach to Visual Perception* (New York, NY: Psychology Press, 2014).

Green, Michael Steven, *Nietzsche and the Transcendental Tradition* (Urbana, IL: University of Illinois Press, 2002).

Hales, Steven D. and Rex Welshon, *Nietzsche's Perspectivism* (Urbana, IL: University of Illinois Press, 2000).

Han-Pile, Béatrice, 'Transcendental Aspects, Ontological Commitments and Naturalistic Elements in Nietzsche's Thought', *Inquiry* 52.2, 2009, pp. 179–214.

Harré, Rom and E. H. Madden, *Causal Powers: A Theory of Natural Necessity* (Oxford: Basil Blackwell, 1975).

Heidegger, Martin, *Nietzsche*, Volume 3, trans. Joan Stambaugh, David F. Krell and Frank A. Capuzzi (New York: HarperCollins, 1991).

Hill, R. Kevin, *Nietzsche's Critiques: The Kantian Foundations of His Thought* (Oxford: Clarendon Press, 2003).

Nietzsche: A Guide for the Perplexed (London: Continuum, 2007).

Hume, David, *Enquiries Concerning Human Understanding and Concerning the Principles of Morals*, L. A. Selby-Bigge and P. H. Nidditch (eds.) (Oxford: Clarendon Press, 1987).

Essays: Moral, Political and Literary, Eugene F. Miller (ed.) (Indianapolis, IN: Liberty Fund, 1987).

A Treatise of Human Nature, L. A. Selby-Bigge and P. H. Nidditch (eds.) (Oxford: Clarendon Press, 1989).

Hussain, Nadeem J. Z., 'The Return of Moral Fictionalism', *Philosophical Perspectives*, 18, 2004, pp. 149–187.

'Honest Illusion: Valuing for Nietzsche's Free Spirits' in Brian Leiter and Neil Sinhababu (eds.), *Nietzsche and Morality* (Oxford: Oxford University Press, 2007), pp. 157–191.

'Metaethics and Nihilism' in Reginster's *The Affirmation of Life, The Journal of Nietzsche Studies*, 43.1, Spring 2012, pp. 99–117.

'Nietzsche and Non-Cognitivism' in Christopher Janaway and Simon Robertson (eds.), *Nietzsche, Naturalism and Normativity* (Oxford: Oxford University Press, 2012), pp. 111–132.

Jaspers, Karl, *Nietzsche: An Introduction to the Understanding of His Philosophical Activity*, trans. F. J. Schmitz (London: Johns Hopkins University Press, 1977).

Johnson, Dirk R., *Nietzsche's Anti-Darwinism* (Cambridge: Cambridge University Press, 2010).

Jorgensen, Larry M., 'The Principle of Continuity and Leibniz's Theory of Consciousness', *Journal of the History of Philosophy*, 47.2, 2009, pp. 223–248.

Joyce, Richard, *The Myth of Morality* (Cambridge: Cambridge University Press, 2001).

Kail, Peter, *Projection and Realism in Hume's Philosophy* (Oxford: Oxford University Press, 2007).

'Nietzsche and Hume: Naturalism and Explanation', *Journal of Nietzsche Studies*, 37, 2009, pp. 5–22.

Kalderon, Mark Eli (ed.), *Fictionalism in Metaphysics* (Oxford: Clarendon Press, 2005).

Moral Fictionalism (Oxford: Oxford University Press, 2005).

Kant, Immanuel, *Gesammelte Schriften* (Berlin: Reimer, later de Gruyter, 1910).

Critique of Pure Reason, trans. Norman Kemp Smith (London: Macmillan, 1929).

Kant's Inaugural Dissertation and Early Writings on Space, trans. John Handyside (Westport, CT: Hyperion Press, 1929).

Metaphysical Foundations of Natural Science, trans. James Ellington (Indianapolis, IN: Bobbs-Merril, 1970).

Universal Natural History and Theory of the Heavens, trans. Stanley L. Jaki (Edinburgh: Scottish Academic Press, 1981).

Critique of Judgment, trans. Werner S. Pluhar (Indianapolis, IN: Hackett Publishing, 1987).

Critique of Practical Reason, trans. Werner S. Pluhar (Indianapolis, IN: Hackett Publishing Company, 2002).

Katsafanas, Paul, 'Nietzsche on Agency and Self-Ignorance', *Journal of Nietzsche Studies*, 43.1, 2012, pp. 5–17.

Agency and the Foundations of Ethics: Nietzschean Constitutivism (Oxford: Oxford University Press, 2013).

'Nietzsche's Philosophical Psychology' in Ken Gemes and John Richardson (eds.), *The Oxford Handbook of Nietzsche* (Oxford: Oxford University Press, 2013), pp. 727–755.

The Nietzschean Self: Moral Psychology, Agency and the Unconscious (Oxford: Oxford University Press, 2016).

Kulstadt, Mark A., *Leibniz on Apperception, Consciousness and Reflection* (Munich: Philosophia Verlag, 1991).

Lange, Friedrich, *Geschichte des Materialismus und Kritik seiner Bedeutung in der Gegenwart* (Iserlohn: Baedeker, 1886/1882/1887).

Langer, Susanne K., *Feeling and Form* (New York, NY: Routledge and Kegan Paul, 1979).

Leibniz, G. W., *Sämtliche Schriften und Briefe, Philosophische Schriften* (Berlin: Akademie-Verlag, 1923).

Leibniz, Philosophical Essays, trans. Roger Ariew and Daniel Garber (eds.) (Indianapolis, IN: Hackett, 1989).

New Essays on Human Understanding, Peter Remnant and Jonathan Bennett (eds.) (Cambridge: Cambridge University Press, 1996).

G. W. Leibniz Philosophical Texts, R. S. Woolhouse and Richard Francks (eds.) (Oxford: Oxford University Press, 1998).

Leiter, Brian, *Nietzsche on Morality* (London: Routledge, 2002).

'Nietzsche's Theory of the Will' in Ken Gemes and Simon May (eds.), *Nietzsche on Freedom and Autonomy* (Oxford: Oxford University Press, 2009), pp. 107–126.

'Nietzsche's Naturalism Reconsidered' in Ken Gemes and John Richardson (eds.), *The Oxford Handbook of Nietzsche* (Oxford: Oxford University Press, 2013), pp. 576–598.

Lewis, David, 'Quasi-Realism Is Fictionalism' in Mark Eli Kalderon (ed.), *Fictionalism in Metaphysics* (Oxford: Oxford University Press, 2005), pp. 314–321.

'Quasi-Realism No Fictionalism' in Mark Eli Kalderon (ed.), *Fictionalism in Metaphysics* (Oxford: Oxford University Press, 2005), pp. 322–338.

Liebmann, Otto, *Zur Analysis der Wirklichkeit. Eine Erörterung der Grundprobleme der Philosophie*, 2nd edition (Straßburg: Trübner, 1880).

Gedanken und Thatsachen. Philosophische Abhandlungen, Aphorismen und Studien, pt. 1, *Die Arten der Nothwendigkeit – Die mechanische Naturerklärung – Idee und Entelechie* (Straßburg: Trübner, 1882).

Locke, John, *An Essay Concerning Human Understanding*, P. H. Nidditch (ed.) (Oxford: Oxford University Press, 1975).

Loeb, Paul, 'Zarathustra's Laughing Lions' in Christa Davis Acampora and Ralph R. Acampora (eds.), *Nietzschean Bestiary: Becoming Animal Beyond Docile and Brutal* (Oxford: Rowman and Littlefield, 2004), pp. 121–139.

'Will to Power and Panpsychism: A New Exegesis of *Beyond Good and Evil, 36*' in Manuel Dries and P. J. E. Kail (eds.), *Nietzsche on Mind and Nature* (Oxford: Oxford University Press, 2015), pp. 57–88.

Mackie, J. L., *Ethics: Inventing Right and Wrong* (Harmondsworth: Penguin, 1978).

Martin, C. B., 'Dispositionals and Conditionals', *The Philosophical Quarterly* 44.174, 1994, pp. 1–8.

The Mind in Nature (Oxford: Oxford University Press, 2007).

May, Simon, *Nietzsche's Ethics and His War on Morality* (Oxford: Oxford University Press, 1999).

'Nietzsche and the Free Self' in Ken Gemes and Simon May (eds.), *Nietzsche on Freedom and Autonomy* (Oxford: Oxford University Press, 2009), pp. 89–106.

McDowell, John, *Mind and World* (Cambridge, MA: Harvard University Press, 1996).

McRae, Robert, *Leibniz: Perception, Apperception, and Thought* (Toronto: University of Toronto Press, 1976).

Metzger, Jeffrey (ed.), *Nietzsche, Nihilism and the Philosophy of the Future* (London: Bloomsbury, 2013).

Molnar, George, *Powers: A Study in Metaphysics* (Oxford: Oxford University Press, 2003).

Moore, Gregory, *Nietzsche, Biology and Metaphor* (Cambridge: Cambridge University Press, 2002).

'Nietzsche and Evolutionary Theory' in Keith Ansell Pearson (ed.), *A Companion to Nietzsche* (Oxford: Blackwell, 2006), pp. 517–531.

Morgan, Diane, 'Nietzsche and National Identity' in Keith Ansell Pearson (ed.), *A Companion to Nietzsche* (Oxford: Blackwell, 2006), pp. 455–474.

Müller-Lauter, Wolfgang, *Nietzsche: His Philosophy of Contradictions and the Contradictions of His Philosophy*, trans. D. J. Parent (Urbana, IL: University of Illinois Press, 1999).

Nehamas, Alexander, *Nietzsche: Life as Literature* (Cambridge, MA: Harvard University Press, 1990).

Nussbaum, Martha, *Upheavals of Thought: The Intelligence of Emotions* (Cambridge: Cambridge University Press, 2003).

Owen, David, *Nietzsche, Politics and Modernity* (London: Sage Publications, 1995).

Parkinson, G. H. R., 'The Intellectualization of Appearances: Aspects of Leibniz's Theory of Sensation and Thought' in Michael Hooker (ed.), *Leibniz: Critical and Interpretive Essays* (Minneapolis, MN: University of Minnesota Press, 1982), pp. 3–20.

Pettit, Philip, *Rules, Reasons, and Norms* (Oxford: Clarendon Press, 2002).

Pitkin, Hanna F., *Wittgenstein and Justice: On the Significance of Wittgenstein's Social and Political Thought* (Berkeley, CA: University of California Press, 1972).

Place, U. T., 'Dispositions as Intentional States' in Tim Crane (ed.), *Dispositions: A Debate* (London: Routledge, 2002), pp. 19–32.

Poellner, Peter, *Nietzsche and Metaphysics* (Oxford: Oxford University Press, 1995).

'Perspectival Truth' in John Richardson and Brian Leiter (eds.), *Nietzsche* (Oxford: Oxford University Press, 2001), pp. 85–117.

'Nietzschean Freedom' in Ken Gemes and Simon May (eds.), *Nietzsche on Freedom and Autonomy* (Oxford: Oxford University Press, 2009), pp. 151–180.

'Affect, Value and Objectivity' in Brian Leiter and Neil Sinhababu (eds.), *Nietzsche and Morality* (Oxford: Oxford University Press, 2007), pp. 227–261.

'Nietzsche's Metaphysical Sketches' in Ken Gemes and John Richardson (eds.), *The Oxford Handbook of Nietzsche* (Oxford : Oxford University Press, 2013), pp. 675–700.

Putnam, Hilary, *Realism with a Human Face* (Cambridge, MA: Harvard University Press, 1990).

Rampley, Matthew, *Nietzsche, Aesthetics and Modernity* (Cambridge: Cambridge University Press, 2000).

Reginster, Bernard, *The Affirmation of Life: Nietzsche on Overcoming Nihilism* (Cambridge, MA: Harvard University Press, 2006).

'The Will to Power and the Ethics of Creativity' in Brian Leiter and Neil Sinhababu (eds.), *Nietzsche and Morality* (Oxford: Oxford University Press, 2007), pp. 32–57.

Rethy, Robert, '*Schein* in Nietzsche's Philosophy' in Keith Ansell Pearson (ed.), *Nietzsche and Modern German Thought* (London : Routledge, 1991), pp. 59–87.

Riccardi, Mattia, 'Nietzsche's Critique of Kant's Thing in Itself', *Nietzsche-Studien*, 39, 2010, pp. 333–351.

'Inner Opacity. Nietzsche on Introspection and Agency', *Inquiry*, 58.3, 2015, pp. 221–243.

Richardson, John, *Nietzsche's System* (Oxford: Oxford University Press, 1996).

Nietzsche's New Darwinism (Oxford: Oxford University Press, 2004).

'Nietzsche's Freedoms' in Ken Gemes and Simon May (eds.), *Nietzsche on Freedom and Autonomy* (Oxford: Oxford University Press, 2009), pp. 217–250.

Ridley, Aaron, 'Perishing of the Truth: Nietzsche's Aesthetic Prophylactics', *British Journal of Aesthetics*, 50.1, 2010, pp. 427–437.

Rorty, Richard, *Philosophy and the Mirror of Nature* (Oxford: Blackwell, 1996).

Truth and Progress: Philosophical Papers, Volume 3 (Cambridge: Cambridge University Press, 1998).

Rosenthal, David M., *Consciousness and Mind* (Oxford: Oxford University Press, 2005).

'Consciousness and Its Function', *Neuropsychologia*, 46, 2008, pp. 829–840.

Rouse, Joseph, *How Scientific Practices Matter: Reclaiming Philosophical Naturalism* (Chicago, IL: University of Chicago Press, 2002).

Russell, Bertrand, *The Philosophy of Leibniz* (London: Routledge, 1992).

Rutherford, Donald, *Leibniz and the Rational Order of Nature* (Cambridge: Cambridge University Press, 1998).

Schacht, Richard, *Nietzsche* (London: Routledge, 1983).

Schiller, Friedrich, *On the Aesthetic Education of Man*, trans. Reginald Snell (New York, NY: Dover Books, 2004).

Schopenhauer, Arthur, *Die Welt als Wille und Vorstellung*, 2nd ed., 2 vols. (Leipzig: Brockhaus, 1844).

The World as Will and Representation, trans. E. F. J. Payne (New York, NY: Dover Books, 1969).

Sellars, Wilfrid, 'Empiricism and the Philosophy of Mind' in Herbert Feigl and Michael Scriven (eds.), *Minnesota Studies in the Philosophy of Science* (Minneapolis, MN: University of Minnesota Press, 1956), pp. 253–329.

Shapiro, Gary, 'This Is Not a Christ: Nietzsche, Foucault and the Genealogy of Vision' in Alan D. Schrift (ed.), *Why Nietzsche Still? Reflections on Drama, Culture and Politics* (Berkeley, CA: University of California Press, 2000), pp. 79–98.

Smith, Michael, David Lewis and Mark Johnston, 'Dispositional Theories of Value', *Proceedings of the Aristotelian Society*, 63, Supplementary Volumes, 1989, pp. 89–111, 113–137, 139–174.

Spir, Afrikan, *Forschung nach der Gewissheit in der Erkenntniss der Wirklichkeit* (Leipzig: Förster und Findel, 1869).

Denken und Wirklichkeit. Versuch einer Erneuerung der kritischen Philosophie, 1st ed./2nd ed., 2 vols. (Leipzig: Findel, 1873/1877).

Stack, George J., *Lange and Nietzsche* (New York, NY: de Gruyter, 1983).

Stevenson, C. L., *Facts and Values* (New Haven, CT: Yale University Press, 1963).

Sturgeon, Nicholas L., 'Hume's Metaethics: Is Hume a Moral Noncognitivist?' in Elizabeth S. Radcliffe (ed.), *A Companion to Hume* (Oxford: Blackwell, 2008), pp. 513–528.

Swift, Paul A., *Becoming Nietzsche: Early Reflections on Democritus, Schopenhauer and Kant* (Lanham, MD: Lexington Books, 2008).

Thiele, Leslie Paul, *Friedrich Nietzsche and the Politics of the Soul* (Princeton, NJ: Princeton University Press, 1990).

Thomas, Alan, 'Nietzsche and Moral Fictionalism' in Christopher Janaway and Simon Robertson (eds.), *Nietzsche, Naturalism and Normativity* (Oxford: Oxford University Press, 2012), pp. 133–159.

Überweg, Friedrich, *Grundriß der Geschichte der Philosophie von Thales bis auf die Gegenwart*, 3 vols. (Berlin: Mittler & Sohn, 1866–1867).

Wiggins, David, *Needs, Values, Truth* (Oxford: Clarendon Press, 1998).

Williams, Garrath, 'Nietzsche's Response to Kant's Morality', *The Philosophical Forum*, 30.3 1999, pp. 201–216.

Wilson, Margaret, 'Confused Ideas', *Rice University Studies*, 63.4 1977, pp. 123–137.

Wolff, Robert Paul, *Kant's Theory of Mental Activity* (Gloucester, MA: Peter Smith, 1973).

Index

For EU product safety concerns, contact us at Calle de José Abascal, 56–1°, 28003 Madrid, Spain or eugpsr@cambridge.org.

www.ingramcontent.com/pod-product-compliance
Ingram Content Group UK Ltd.
Pitfield, Milton Keynes, MK11 3LW, UK
UKHW020354140625
459647UK00020B/2459